NO FUTURE
WITHOUT
FORGIVENESS

Desmond Tutu

RIDER

LONDON • SYDNEY • AUCKLAND • JOHANNESBURG

First published in 1999 by Rider,
an imprint of Ebury Press, Random House,
20 Vauxhall Bridge Road, London SW1V 2SA.
This paperback edition published in 2000
www.randomhouse.co.uk

Random House Australia (Pty) Limited
20 Alfred Street, Milsons Point, Sydney,
New South Wales 2061, Australia

Random House New Zealand Limited
18 Poland Road, Glenfield,
Auckland 10, New Zealand

Random House South Africa (Pty) Limited
Endulini, 5A Jubilee Road,
Parktown 2193, South Africa

The Random House Group Limited Reg. No. 954009

Grateful acknowledgement is given to Arthur James, Ltd. for permission to reprint
a selection from *Unrequited Being* by Mary MacAleese (copyright © 1997); to
HarperCollins, for permission to reprint a selection from *The Divine Milieu* by
Teilhard de Chardin (copyright © 1960), and to the South African Broadcasting
Corporation for the ability to print a selection from their transcripts of the Truth
and Reconciliation Commission. 'The Suffering God' by G.A. Stoddert Kennedy
is reprinted from *The Sorrows of God* (copyright © 1924 by George H. Doran
Company) by permission of Hodder & Stoughton Ltd.

Papers used by Rider are natural, recyclable products made from
wood grown in sustainable forests

Typeset by SX Composing DTP, Rayleigh, Essex
Printed and bound in Great Britain by Cox & Wyman Ltd, Reading, Berkshire

A CIP catalogue record for this book
is available from the British Library

ISBN 0 7126 0485 5

ABOUT THE AUTHOR

Desmond Tutu has played a leading part in the struggle to end apartheid in South Africa, recently as Archbishop of Cape Town, a post from which he retired in 1996. He was awarded the Nobel Peace Prize in 1984 and, in 1995, was appointed Chair of the Truth and Reconciliation Commission by President Nelson Mandela. He has recently been lecturing on theology at Emory University in Atlanta, and is regularly invited to travel and speak to political and spiritual organizations worldwide.

To the women and the 'little people'
of South Africa

Acknowledgements

I thank God for my fellow Commissioners, Committee members and the staff at the Truth and Reconciliation Commission for their incredible commitment to healing in our land.

This book was written during a visiting professorship at the Candler School of Theology at Emory University, where Dean Kevin LaGree and his colleagues provided me with a place to retreat from the pressures of recent years in order to reflect and write. My personal assistant, Lavinia Browne, deciphered my handwriting to produce the manuscript. The Carnegie Corporation of New York generously helped Candler to bring John Allen, who was quite invaluable in refining the manuscript, from South Africa to act as my research assistant. The script produced by the Truth and Reconciliation Commission radio reporting team from the South African Broadcasting Corporation for their set of CDs on the Truth and Reconciliation process helped us trace key pieces of evidence quickly. I am very grateful to them all.

The book would not have been possible without the assistance of a host of others, headed by Lynn Franklin, my literary agent, her colleague in London, Mary Clemmey, Trace Murphy and Eric Major at Doubleday, Judith Kendra at Rider/Random House, and Jacqueline Smith and Sandra Bryan at Candler.

I am not sure whether I would have coped with the Truth and Reconciliation Commission without my wife Leah, and I am deeply grateful to her for her loving support through the hearings and other processes of the Commission.

Contents

'Those who cannot remember the past are condemned to repeat it'

George Santayana

CHAPTER ONE

The turning point

27 April 1994 was the day for which we had waited many long years, the day for which the struggle against apartheid had been waged, for which so many of our people had been tear-gassed, bitten by police dogs, struck with quirts and batons, tortured, banned, imprisoned, sentenced to death and driven into exile. The day had finally dawned when we would vote, when we could vote for the first time in a democratic election in the land of our birth. I had had to wait until I was sixty-two years old before I could vote, Nelson Mandela until he was seventy-six.

The air was electric with excitement, anticipation and anxiety, and with fear that those on the right wing who had promised to disrupt this day of days might succeed in their nefarious schemes. Bombs had been going off right, left and centre. There had been explosions at the International Airport in Johannesburg. Anything could happen.

As always I had got up early for my quiet time and walk before morning prayers and the Eucharist in the Archbishop's Chapel in Bishopscourt. We wanted things to be as normal as possible on this extraordinary day in the history of our beloved, but oh so sad land whose soil was soaked with the blood of so many of her children. In the lead-up to this epoch-making event, a watershed in the history of South Africa, violence had become endemic. Up to the proverbial eleventh hour a major role-player, Chief Mangosuthu Buthelezi's Inkatha Freedom Party (IFP), had threatened to stay out of the election, and we were all bracing ourselves for the most awful bloodletting, especially in the IFP stronghold of KwaZulu/Natal, where the rivalry between the IFP and Nelson Mandela's African National Congress (ANC) was a gory affair – the shockingly high level of political intolerance there had already cost innumerable lives. It had been brinkmanship of an appalling nature. We had held our breaths and wondered what the body count would be. Mercifully, through the mediation of a somewhat mysterious Kenyan, Chief Buthelezi was persuaded to abandon his boycott, chilling in its prospect of a likely bloodbath. The country breathed an enormous sigh of relief.

So here we were, about to carry out what was a routine political and civic act in normal countries where the concern was usually about voter apathy, not about the risk of violence and mayhem at the polls. I was excited and apprehensive. There was a tight knot of anxiety in the pit of my stomach. I prayed earnestly that morning that God would bless our land and confound the machinations of the children of darkness. There had been so many moments in the past, during the dark days of apartheid's vicious awfulness, when I had preached, 'This is God's world and God is in charge!' Sometimes, when evil seemed to be about to overwhelm goodness, I had only just been able to hold on to this article of faith. It was a kind of theological whistling in the dark and I was frequently tempted to whisper in God's ear, 'For goodness sake, why don't You make it more obvious that *You are* in charge?'

After breakfast, we drove out of Bishopscourt, the official residence of the Archbishop of Cape Town (where Nelson Mandela had spent his first night of freedom after his release on 11 February 1990), and away from the leafy up-market suburb surrounding it. I had decided that I would cast my vote in a ghetto township. I wanted to demonstrate my solidarity with those who for so long had been disenfranchised, those living daily in the deprivation and squalor of apartheid's racially segregated ghettos. After all, I was one of them. When I became Archbishop in 1986 the Group Areas Act, which segregated residential areas racially, was still in force. It was a criminal offence for me, a Nobel laureate and now Archbishop and Metropolitan of the Anglican Church in southern Africa, to occupy Bishopscourt with my family unless I had first obtained a special permit exempting me from the provisions of the Group Areas Act. I had, however, announced after my election as Archbishop that I would not be applying for such a permit. I said I was Archbishop, would be occupying the Archbishop's official residence and that the apartheid government could act as it saw fit. No charges were ever preferred against me for contravening this obnoxious law.

I went to vote in Gugulethu, a black township with typical matchbox houses in row after monotonous row. There was a long queue already waiting. People were in good spirits, and they were going to need a great deal of patience and good humour because they were in for a long wait. My first democratic vote was a media event and many of our friends from overseas were present, acting as monitors to check whether the elections were fair and free. But they were doing a great deal more than that. They were really like midwives helping to birth this new, delicate infant – the free, democratic, non-racial, non-sexist South Africa.

The moment for which I had waited for so long came and I folded my ballot paper and cast my vote. Wow! I shouted, 'Yippee!' It was giddy stuff, like falling in love. The sky looked more blue and beautiful. I saw the people in a new light. They were beautiful, they were transfigured. I too was transfigured. It was dream-like. We were scared someone would rouse us and we would wake up back in the nightmare that was apartheid's harsh reality.

After voting, I went outside and the people cheered and sang and danced. It was like a festival. The atmosphere was wonderful and such a vindication for all those who had borne the burden of repression, the little people whom apartheid had turned into the anonymous ones – faceless, voiceless, counting for nothing in their motherland – whose noses had been rubbed daily in the dust. They had been created in the image of God but their dignity had been callously trodden underfoot every day by apartheid's minions, and by those others who perhaps said they were opposed to apartheid but had nonetheless gone on enjoying the privileges and huge benefits that apartheid brought them – just because of an accident of birth, a biological irrelevance: the colour of their skin.

I decided to drive around a bit to see what was happening. I was appalled by what I saw. The people who had come out in droves, standing in those long lines which have now become world-famous, were so vulnerable. The police and the security forces were probably stretched, but they were hardly a conspicuous presence. It would have taken just a few crazy extremists with AK-47 rifles to create havoc. It did not happen. And virtually everywhere there was a hitch of one sort or the other. Here there were insufficient ballot papers, there not enough ink pads, elsewhere the officials had not yet turned up hours after the polls were due to have opened. And the people were quite amazing in their patience. It was a comprehensive disaster waiting to happen. And it did not happen.

It was also an amazing spectacle. People of all races were standing in the same queues, perhaps for the very first time in their lives. Professionals, domestic workers, cleaners and their madams – all were standing in those lines that were snaking their way slowly to the polling booth. And what should have been a disaster turned out to be a blessing in disguise. Those lines produced a new and peculiarly South African status symbol. Afterwards people boasted, 'I stood for two hours to vote' – 'No, I waited for four hours!'

Those long hours helped us South Africans to find one another. People shared newspapers, sandwiches, umbrellas, and the scales began to fall from their eyes. South Africans found fellow South Africans – they realised what we had been at such pains to tell them, that they shared a common humanity; that race, ethnicity, skin colour were really irrelevancies. They discovered not a Coloured, a black, an Indian, a white. No, they found a fellow human being. What a profound scientific discovery for the whites, that blacks, Coloureds (usually people of mixed race), and Indians were in fact human beings, who had the same concerns and anxieties and aspirations as they did. They wanted a decent home, a good job, a safe environment for their families, good schools for their children. Hardly any of them wanted to drive the whites into the sea. They just wanted their place in the sun.

Everywhere else elections are secular political events. Ours was more than this, much, much more. It was a veritable spiritual experience, a mountain-top experience. The black person entered the booth one person and emerged on the other side a new, transfigured one. She entered weighed down by the anguish and burden of oppression, with the memory of being treated like rubbish gnawing away at her like some corrosive acid. She reappeared knowing she was free, walking away with her head held high, shoulders set straighter and an elastic spring in her step. How do you convey that sense of freedom which tastes like sweet nectar the first time you experience it? How do you describe it to someone who was born into freedom? It is impossible, like trying to describe the colour red to a person born blind. It is a feeling that makes you want to laugh and cry, to dance with joy and yet at the same time you fear that it is too good to be true and that it just might all evaporate. Perhaps that is how the victors felt on VE and VJ Days when the Allies roundly defeated the Nazis and the Japanese after the Second World War – people poured out on to the streets of their villages, towns and cities, hugging and kissing perfect strangers. That's how we felt.

The white person entered the voting booth burdened by the load of guilt at having enjoyed the fruits of oppression and injustice. He too emerged as somebody new, somebody transfigured, from whom a burden had been lifted, and who was now free. White people experienced that freedom was indeed indivisible. I had kept saying in the dark days of apartheid's oppression that white South Africans would never be truly free until we blacks were free as well. Many thought it was just another Tutu slogan, irresponsible as all his others had been. They were experiencing it as a reality today. I used to refer to an intriguing old film starring Sidney Poitier, *The Defiant Ones*. Two convicts, one white, the other black, escape from a chain gang manacled together. They fall into a ditch with slippery sides. One convict claws his way nearly to the top and out of the ditch but cannot make it because he is bound to his mate who has been left at the bottom in the ditch. The only way they can make it is together, clawing their way out, up and up and up and eventually over the side wall and out.

So too I would say we South Africans will survive and prevail only together, black and white bound together by circumstance and history as we strive to claw our way out of the abyss of apartheid racism, up and out, black and white together. Neither group on its own could make it. God had bound us together. In a way we are living out what Martin Luther King Jr said – 'Unless we learn to live together as brothers, we will die together as fools.'

How amazing that 27 April, that extraordinary day, ended with hardly any of the untoward things we had feared or which others had predicted. The election was declared to be free and fair. God be praised. We were delirious with joy. We had done it. We had amazed even ourselves. On 9 May Nelson Mandela was duly elected president by the first democratically elected national assembly of the new South Africa. Afterwards we went to the Grand Parade outside Cape Town City Hall which was a sea of humanity, a crowd as big as the one that had gathered there when Nelson Mandela was released from prison.

I had the very great honour of introducing the brand-new President and his two deputies, Thabo Mbeki and F. W. de Klerk, to the waiting and impatient throng and to the world. When I led Nelson Mandela to the podium and gave him to his people the cheers were deafening.

After the election we South Africans found that the coming of democracy and freedom to our land served to open doors that had previously been slammed shut. Now the international community that had treated us as a pariah state threw open its arms to us. We were welcomed back into the Commonwealth in a deeply moving ceremony and church service in Westminster Abbey in London, when the new South African flag was carried into the sanctuary to join those of other Commonwealth lands. The sporting world, which had in most cases boycotted us, put out the red carpet of welcome. South Africans had a new kind of experience to deal with. Our country was now the flavour of the month. Whereas previously South Africans travelled abroad furtively, hiding their national identity for fear of being rebuffed, now they walked tall wearing their country's flag on their lapels and stuck prominently on their luggage, blazoning abroad for all and sundry to know they were from South Africa, that land that had confounded all the prophets of doom by making a remarkably peaceful transition from repression and injustice to democracy and freedom.

The world probably came to a standstill on 10 May when Nelson Mandela was inaugurated as South Africa's first democratically elected President. If it did not stand still then it ought to have, because nearly all the world's leaders were milling around in Pretoria. Anyone who was anyone was there. One of the most unforgettable moments on that historic inauguration day was when South African Air Force jets flew overhead in salute to the new President, trailing smoke in the colours of the new national flag. Tears were streaming down my face. Almost as if from one throat, an ear-piercing roar broke forth from the South Africans who were there, and I think especially the black South Africans. It was as if it occurred to all of us simultaneously that these war machines that had for so long been ranged against us were now *ours* – no longer just *theirs* – that this was indeed now *our* country in the profoundest possible way.

It was a poignant moment when Nelson Mandela arrived accompanied by his elder daughter, and the various heads of the security forces, the police and the correctional services strode to his car, saluted him and then escorted him as the Head of State. Only a few years previously he had been their prisoner, and if free would have been a terrorist they would have hunted down. What a metamorphosis, what an extraordinary turnaround. He invited his white gaoler to attend his inauguration as an honoured guest, the first of many spectacular gestures he made that showed his breathtaking magnanimity and willingness to forgive. He has been a potent agent for the reconciliation he urged his compatriots to work for and which was central to the purpose of the Truth and Reconciliation Commission he appointed to deal with our country's past. This man, who had been vilified and hunted down as a dangerous fugitive and incarcerated for nearly three decades, was transformed into the embodiment of forgiveness and reconciliation, and had most of those who had hated him eating out of his hand. The prisoner become

President, and someone who was admired by the whole world in an extraordinary outpouring of adulation and hero-worship – internationally the most admired and revered head of state. South Africa has never had as many state visits as there have been since April 1994. Virtually every head of state has wanted his or her picture taken with our president.

And yet at the time we kept wondering whether it was not all going to blow up in our faces. We were scared that somewhere in another part of our country some madmen would go on the rampage and subvert the entire negotiated settlement. It did not happen. Many things went wrong. In some places this was clearly the result of a deliberate intention to sabotage the whole exercise, and yet the country managed to take everything in its stride.

The outside world saw a miracle unfolding before their eyes. They witnessed the almost-unbelievable. Instead of the horrendous bloodbath that so many had feared and predicted, here were these amazing South Africans, black and white together, crafting a relatively peaceful changeover and transfer of power.

We won a spectacular victory over injustice, oppression and evil and it is wonderful to be able to say to the international community that that spectacular victory would have been totally impossible without your help, your prayers, your commitment to our cause. On behalf of millions of my compatriots it is a great privilege to say, 'Thank you, thank you, thank you. Our victory in a real sense is your victory. Thank you.' I spoke once at Cambridge University in England and amongst other things I said, 'Now the boycott of South African goods is lifted.' After my address a middle-aged woman accosted me and said, 'Archbishop, I hear you and cerebrally I agree with you. But my parents brought me up to boycott South African goods and I have brought up my children to boycott South African goods too. So even now, when I buy South African goods I am furtive because all of me says I am doing something wrong.' I doubt that any other cause has evoked the same passion and dedication as the anti-apartheid cause and I doubt that any other country has been prayed for by so many people so intensely and for so long as has my motherland. In a sense if a miracle was to happen anywhere then South Africa must have been the obvious candidate.

When I became Archbishop I set myself three goals for my term of office. Two had to do with the inner workings of our Anglican (Episcopalian) Church – the ordination of women to the priesthood, which our church approved in 1992 and through which our church has been wonderfully enriched and blessed; and the division of the large and sprawling Diocese of Cape Town into smaller episcopal pastoral units (in which I failed to get the Church's backing). The third goal was the liberation of all our people, black and white, and that we achieved in 1994.

So my wife Leah and I could look forward happily to my retirement in 1996. We had been wonderfully blessed in that we had seen what we could only have hoped would happen one day in our lives, to see our land and its people emancipated from the shackles of bondage to racism.

I had been involved in the struggle in a public and high-profile way from 1975 when I became Dean of Johannesburg. In 1976 I wrote a letter to the Prime Minister of the day, Mr B. J. Vorster, warning him of the growing anger of the black community. He treated my letter with disdain. A few weeks later Soweto exploded and South Africa was never to be the same again. I had been in the public arena for twenty years and now with the political processes being normalised it was time to move off centre stage. I had not reckoned with the Synod of Bishops of our Church or with our President and the Truth and Reconciliation Commission.

CHAPTER TWO

Nuremberg or national amnesia? A third way

Under apartheid, a small white minority had monopolised political power, which gave it access to all other kinds of power and privilege. It had maintained its tight control by vicious and immoral means. This white minority used a system of 'pigmentocracy' to claim that what invested human beings with worth was a particular skin colour, ethnicity and race. Since these attributes were enjoyed by only a few, the pigmentocracy was exclusive to a limited number of all human beings.

In Ancient Greece the otherwise wise and astute philosopher Aristotle was guilty of a similar delusion. He claimed that human personality was not a universal possession enjoyed by all human beings, since slaves were devoid of it. It is odd that Aristotle should have failed to note the utter absurdity of his position, which must have given great comfort to slave owners who thus could ill-treat their chattels with impunity, knowing that they were not really being cruel since their slaves were not quite as human as themselves. (Presumably freed slaves suddenly acquired humanity!) The ancients can to some extent be forgiven for believing such irrational and immoral ideas. The perpetrators of apartheid were not benighted pagans, however, and so could not plead ignorance. They were as civilised as the Westerners they claimed to be and, what is more, they were Christians. That is what they asserted vehemently when they sought to oppose sanctions being imposed on them. They were able to convince a too readily gullible West that they were in fact the last bastion of Western Christian civilisation against the depredations of Soviet Communist expansionism. They read the Bible, they went to church – how they went to church! I recall on one occasion driving with my mother-in-law, who was a domestic worker with no more than elementary school education, past a white Dutch Reformed church. There were scores of cars outside in its parking lot. I pointed to those cars and remarked that the Afrikaners were clearly a God-fearing and certainly a churchgoing lot. My mother-in-law replied quietly, with a chuckle, 'My child, if God treated me as He is treating them, I too would be a very regular churchgoer!'

Our people were often left perplexed by this remarkable fact, that those who treated them so abominably were not heathen but claimed to be fellow Christians who read the same Bible. Thus the proponents of apartheid really had no excuse for their peculiar doctrine. The Bible they and we both read is quite categorical – what endows human beings, every single human being without exception, with infinite worth is not this or that biological or any other external attribute. No, it is the fact that each one of us has been created in the image of God. This is something intrinsic. It comes as it were with the package. It means that each one of us is a God-carrier, God's viceroy, God's representative. This is why treating anybody as if they were less than this is veritably blasphemous. It is like spitting in the face of God. That is what filled some of us with such a passionate commitment to fight for justice and freedom. We were inspired not by political motives but by our biblical faith. The Bible turned out to be the most subversive book imaginable in a situation of injustice and oppression.

We frequently tried to point out the absurdity of racism in the hope that our white compatriots would be embarrassed into dropping something so ludicrous. For instance, I would suggest that instead of skin colour we should substitute a large nose, since I possessed one. Imagine a certain university is reserved not for whites, as happened under apartheid, but for large noses only – that is the chief require-ment, not academic ability. If you are afflicted with a small nose, you have to apply to the Minister of Small Nose Affairs for permission to attend the university reserved for large noses. Most audiences I told this story to would be rolling in the aisles at the stupidity and the absurdity of it all. If only the reality had been a laughing matter.

My father was headmaster of an elementary school. Although my mother, as a domestic servant, was hardly well educated, and the family income was nothing to write home about, we were shielded to some extent from the worst of the rigours of South Africa's racism in the years before apartheid as refined by the Nationalist Government. I was not particularly politically conscious and I even thought that the racist ordering of affairs was something divinely ordained. That is how things were and you had better accept it and not be too fussy. Actually, most people adjusted extraordinarily well even to the most awful circumstances. We lived in Ventersdorp, a small town to the west of Johannesburg which was later to gain notoriety as the head-quarters of the neo-Nazi Afrikaner Weerstandsbeweging (AWB, or Afrikaner Resistance Movement, which was formed in the late 1970s to fight against limited reforms to apartheid). I used to go from our ghetto into the white town to buy newspapers for my father. Quite frequently I would see black urchins scavenging in the dustbins of the white school and coming up with perfectly edible apples and sandwiches which the white pupils had thrown away. They preferred the picnic lunches their mothers had prepared for them to the free lunch the government gave to white pupils (and not to blacks). It was part of the perverse nature of racism that those who did not need it and could afford their own food were provided with free school meals. Those who were often desperately in need of good food and who could not afford it were not given free school meals. This was possible only because their parents had no clout. They were invisible in the land of their birth except when they were required to do work, usually as servants. I did notice this different treatment, but I can't pretend that I was aware it was going to make an indelible impression on me. It was only much later when Dr Verwoerd introduced the deliberately inferior education for blacks known as Bantu Education, and stopped the free school meals which had been introduced in some black schools that my boyhood memories were revived. When Dr Verwoerd was asked why he had ended this fairly cheap but effective way of combating malnutrition among the poorest sections of the population, his reply was quite mind-boggling, although it was consistent with the total irrationality of racism and apartheid. He said that if you could not feed all, then you should not feed any. That surely takes the cake. Why don't we try to cure those people suffering from TB? No, we won't do it because we really must not try to treat some TB patients unless we can treat them all. It was possible to spew forth such arrant nonsense because the victims had no political leverage. They could not vote you out.

Thousands of blacks were arrested daily under the iniquitous pass law system, which severely curtailed their freedom of movement. All black people aged sixteen and over had to carry a pass. It was an offence not to have it on your person when a police officer demanded to see it – it was no good saying you had left it in the office in your jacket pocket when you went out to buy a packet of cigarettes. The system conspired to undermine your sense of worth. Blacks did not have a right to be in the urban areas. They were there by the grace and favour of their white overlords. It is difficult to describe the daily public humiliation of having to produce your pass or else join the human crocodile of those who had fallen foul of the law and were now handcuffed together, a public spectacle, whilst the police waited to have a large enough quota to fill their troop carrier. This was called a pick-up van or a *kwela-kwela* (from the Xhosa for 'get on, get on', shouted by the police to their prey). Decent men were driven to prison with hardened criminals and then were bewildered in court the next day by the extraordinary rate at which the cases were processed: one person every two minutes, a kind of human-conveyor-belt justice. Before they could say 'Nelson Mandela' they would have been found guilty and sentenced to what for them was a very heavy fine or a prison term. This particular violation of human rights was something that nearly every black person had experienced at one time or another.

I remember so vividly accompanying my schoolteacher father to town and how sorry I felt for him when he would almost invariably be stopped. Now there was something funny. Because he was educated he qualified for what was called an 'exemption', in that the ordinary pass laws did not apply to him and he had the privilege, denied to other blacks, of being able to purchase the white man's liquor without running the risk of being arrested. But in order for the police to know that he was exempted he had to carry and produce his superior document, the exemption. Thus it did not spare him the humiliation of being stopped and asked peremptorily and rudely to produce his exemption in the street. It sickened me.

Many of our neighbours suffered the further indignity of pass raids on their homes. There was no such thing as a man's home being his castle. The police came at the most inconvenient times, in the small hours, making the most awful noise and getting people out of their beds with scant regard for modesty: *'Kom, kom – maak oop, julle verdomde kaffers'* ('Come on – open up, you damned kaffirs'). Scantily clad mothers would stand perplexed and hurt, children would be scared and yelling, and the man would be standing feeble, emasculated, humiliated in front of his children – treated as if he were just a nonentity. He *was* a nonentity in the eyes of the law, with the minimum rights of a third-class citizen.

It was not usually the big things, the awful atrocities, that got to you. No, it was the daily pinpricks, the little discourtesies, the minute humiliations: having one's dignity trodden underfoot, not always with jackboots – though that happened too. It was the occasions such as going into a shop with my father, this dignified, educated man, and a slip of a girl behind the counter, just because she was white, addressing him, *'Ja*, boy'. I died many deaths for my father, who would often then be ingratiating and obsequious to this badly brought-up child; I knew there was very little he could do about it. If he took his custom to another shop, he would inevitably be subjected to the same treatment there. There were exceptions, but they were as rare as snow in hell. This kind of treatment demeaned our people and had a deeply corrosive effect on their dignity.

When I came to Johannesburg as Dean of Johannesburg and later as Bishop, Leah and I had to be 'endorsed' into this urban area. We had to go to the Native Commissioner's offices to have our passes stamped with the correct stamp to say we were permitted to live in Johannesburg as long as I was employed by the Church. The many black men standing in long lines would have to wait whilst the white masters chatted among themselves, read their newspapers or drank their tea. When they deigned to attend to their charges they hardly ever addressed them courteously. They would almost always shout rudely and further confuse the already bewildered country people. The black officials were little better. Leah was permitted to be in Johannesburg as long as she was married to me. She was discriminated against at least twice over – as a black and as a woman. She had very few of even the minimal rights that black males had.

What was important in the eyes of the government was that you were black. That was the most significant fact about you, not that you were in fact a human being. Thus it was that even when I was Bishop of Johannesburg and a Nobel laureate, when we were stopped at roadblocks during states of emergency, my wife and daughters would face being body-searched by the roadside. This did not happen because I protested, so they would be marched to a nearby police station to be searched there instead. If that was the treatment they could routinely mete out to fairly prominent blacks, what were they not doing to less well-known black people, I wondered, knowing the awful answer.

In a submission quoted in the Truth and Reconciliation Commission's main report, Justice Pius Langa, later Deputy President of the Constitutional Court, told of his experiences as a black person:

My first real encounter with the legal system was as a young work-seeker in Durban . . . in 1956. It was during that period that I experienced the frustration, indignity and humiliation of being subject to certain of the provisions of the Population Registration Act, No. 30 of 1950, the Natives (Urban Areas) Consolidation Act, No. 25 of 1945 as well as other discriminatory legislation of that time . . . The immediate impact on me was severe disillusionment at the unfairness and injustice of it all. I could never understand why race should have been the determinant of where I should live and where I could work. I was never able to understand why, whilst still a teenager, I was expected to live at a men's hostel and needed a permit to stay with my parents in the township . . . In that first flush of youth, I had thought I could do anything, aspire to anything and that nothing could stop me. I was wrong. My dreams came up against the harsh apartheid realities. The insensitive, demeaning and often hostile environment it had created around me proved to have been crafted too well; it was designed to discourage those who, like me, sought to improve their circumstances and those of their communities . . .

The pass laws and influx control regulations were, for me, the focal point of the comprehensive network of laws and regulations which dominated my early working life . . . I was merely one of tens of thousands who peopled those seemingly interminable queues at the end of which, in general, bad-tempered clerks and officials might reward one with some endorsement or other in the 'dompas' [a colloquial reference to the 'pass']. The whole process of the influx control offices was painful and degrading and particular aspects of it inflicted deep humiliation on the tens of thousands who were on the receiving end of these regulations. As a seventeen-year-old, I remember having to avert my eyes from the nakedness of grown men in a futile attempt to salvage some dignity for them in those queues where we had to expose ourselves to facilitate the degrading examination. To anyone who failed to find work during the currency of their permits, loomed the very real threat of being declared 'an idle and undesirable Bantu' by the Commissioner's court and being subject to be sent to a farm colony. Scores of people were processed through those courts and sentenced on charges such as failing to produce a reference book on demand . . .

It was one thing, however, having the overtly discriminatory and repressive laws on the statute book. Their ugliness was exacerbated to a large degree by the crude, cruel and unfeeling way in which many of the officials, black and white, put them into operation. There was a culture of hostility and intimidation against those who came to be processed or for assistance. The face presented by authority, in general, was of a war against people who were unenfranchised, and human dignity was the main casualty.

The apartheid government began engaging in an orgy of racist legislation as soon as they came to power in 1948. They demolished many black townships and uprooted many settled communities, depositing God's children in poverty-stricken Bantustan homeland resettlement camps, really no better than dumping grounds. You don't dump people, you dump things. Yet that is what they did to those created in God's image whose crime was to be black. They treated us as if we were things. We had a struggle song, *'Senzenina? – Isono sethu bubumnyama'* ('What have we done? – Our sin is that we are black'). The Nationalists developed the separation of the races to a fine art – we were segregated residentially, at school, at play, at work. We were not allowed to marry across racial lines – sexual intercourse between the races was taboo. Mixed marriages were taboo. Job reservation prohibited blacks from doing certain jobs which were the preserve of whites – and today they cry 'foul' at affirmative action.

Three-and-a-half million people were forcibly removed in a heartless piece of social engineering that attempted to unscramble the racial omelette that was South Africa. Those are the bare statistics, but it was flesh-and-blood people who were the pawns in these forced removal schemes. Leah and I were married in a Roman Catholic church in Munsieville, a black township on the West Rand nineteen kilometres west of Johannesburg. That church was razed to the ground along with many residential buildings because Munsieville was doomed to be demolished. It was that aberration, a black spot in what should have been a lily-white area. Munsieville was reprieved only by the intervention of Leon Wessels, the Nationalist MP for Krugersdorp, who later apologised handsomely for apartheid. He was to become Deputy Chair of the Constituent Assembly that gave us our wonderful constitution. But other places were not so fortunate. I lived or studied in at least five places – Sophiatown, for instance – that were not spared. A certain man worked as a gardener in Johannesburg and had built himself a nice home in one of the villages. One day it was announced that his home village was to be demolished and the community moved elsewhere. The gardener asked for one favour, which was granted him. He wanted to demolish the house which he had built so painstakingly over the years himself. The following morning he was found hanging from a tree. He had committed suicide. He could not take it any longer.

In Cape Town there was a vibrant, cosmopolitan part of the city called District Six, which nestled at the foot of Table Mountain. It was a lively, multiracial community with a diversity of Christians, Muslims and Jews who lived with one another amicably with hardly any incidents of racism. Then the Nationalists came along and through the quaintly named Department of Community Development decreed in the name of racial harmony that District Six should die. And so the Coloureds and Africans were moved miles away from the city centre where they worked, from spacious homes to matchbox houses clustered together claustrophobically in yet another ghetto township. Soon after becoming Archbishop I visited Bonteheuwel, one of apartheid's spawns. Inside one of the minute dwellings of the township was one of our parishioners, an old man who had been moved from District Six in 1960. It was now 1986. He had not unpacked the cartons and boxes into which he had stuffed his possessions. The boxes littered the very modest accommodation. When I asked why the boxes were there, unopened, he replied that he was waiting to return home to District Six. The three-and-a-half million consisted of people such as these. He later died of a broken heart, his boxes still unopened.

Somebody produced a musical called *District Six*, which described the vibrancy of this suburb in Cape Town and how it finally succumbed to apartheid's madness. One of my staff, who had lived in District Six as a child, returned after attending a performance and told us that he had wept with nostalgia. His own mother in her old age used to say she wanted to go home, meaning to return to her house in District Six. Stephen Naidoo had come from Durban with his merchant father, his mother and sister. His father had prospered and built a nice house in Retreat, close to Cape Town. Stephen became my counterpart as Roman Catholic Archbishop of Cape Town. I told him what my staffer had said and he asked what I thought he had done when he went to see the same show – he too had broken down. Community Development had decreed that their section of Retreat was white so the Naidoos would have to move. His father had died and his widowed mother pleaded with the authorities to let them remain in their house, but to no avail. So they found a one-roomed apartment they shared with others. They were not allowed in it during the daytime, so Stephen and his sister would go and sit in the waiting room of a nearby railway station until they were allowed back in. After he had told me his story, it struck me that there were many people walking around who looked normal but who were in fact carrying a burden of anguish and grief statutorily inflicted on them for no other reason than that they were not white.

When as a family we returned from England where I had gone to study, we travelled home through France, Italy and the Holy Land. We were going to Alice in the Eastern Cape, where I would teach at the Federal Theological Seminary. Once back in South Africa, we went to East London to buy furniture for our new home. When lunchtime came we knew there would be no restaurant available for blacks to eat in so we bought fish and chips and sat in the car, which was parked in the street. A few weeks previously we had been able to eat in a posh restaurant in Paris and to enjoy the delicious French cuisine. Not in our motherland.

We would often go for picnics on the beach in East London. The portion of beach reserved for blacks was the least attractive, with quite a few rocks lying around. Not far away was a playground with a miniature train, and our youngest, who was born in England, would say, 'Daddy, I want to go on the swings,' and I would have to reply in a hollow voice, a dead weight in the pit of my stomach, 'No, darling, you can't go.' What was I to say when my baby insisted, 'But Daddy, there are other children playing there' – how could I tell her that she could not go because she was not the right kind of child. I died inside many times and was not able to look my child in the eyes because I felt so dehumanised, so humiliated, so diminished. Now I probably felt as my father must have felt when he was humiliated in the presence of his young son.

Apartheid systematically stripped Coloureds, Indians and especially blacks of their rights and denuded their humanity. It offered them a travesty for education; inadequate housing; insufficient health care, so that children suffered from easily preventable deficiency diseases; and it undermined black family life with the migrant labour system and its single-sex hostels. Apartheid was pervasive and inflicted unnecessary and untold suffering on all its victims. And you might say without exaggeration that every person who was not white to some extent was a victim of this horrendous policy. Black people should by rights have been filled with hatred and resentment and should have been baying for the blood of white people for all that apartheid had done to them. Our new Minister of Justice, Dullah Omar, called us 'a nation of victims' and that was an apt description up to a point. But we should also declare that ours was also wonderfully a nation of survivors, with some quite remarkable people who astounded the world with their capacity to forgive, their magnanimity and nobility of spirit.

Malusi Mpumlwana, now a priest working for the US Kellogg Foundation, was in the late 1970s and early 1980s a young, enthusiastic activist; a close associate of Steve Biko in the crucial black consciousness movement. He was involved with others in vital community development and health provision work with impoverished and often disillusioned and demoralised rural communities. As a result he and his wife were under strict surveillance by the ubiquitous security police and were constantly harassed. They were frequently held in detention without trial and it was while he was serving a five-year banning order that confined him to his Eastern Cape township that he somehow gave the security police the slip, came to Johannesburg, and met me in my office there (I was General Secretary of the South African Council of Churches at the time). He said that in his frequent stints in detention the security police had told him, 'We are running this country,' and when they routinely tortured him he used to think, 'These are God's children and yet they are behaving like animals. They need us to help them recover the humanity they have lost.' In the end our struggle *had* to be successful when it had such remarkable people involved in it.

Election day, 27 April 1994, was South Africa's turning point. It marked the beginning of the new South Africa, the democratic, non-racial, non-sexist South Africa of the election slogans. This was something completely new. The old system of apartheid, with its vicious repression and injustice was now discredited. In this new era almost nobody would admit to having supported it.

No longer would someone seriously injured be left by the roadside because the ambulance that had rushed to the scene of the accident was one reserved for another race group. Never again would people be uprooted from their homes to be dumped as if they were rubbish in poverty-stricken Bantustan homelands (areas designated for black people). Never again would God's children be humiliated by the crude methods employed by the Race Classification Boards as they sought to classify South Africa's inhabitants by race as if they had been so many cattle. (Often members of the same family were assigned to different race groups – the one whose skin was of a slightly darker hue would be penalised by being consigned to a lower and less privileged group. Some people had committed suicide rather than accept this bizarre and arbitrary classification.) Never again would any child receive the thin 'gruel' that purported to be an education but was in fact a travesty, designed to prepare black children for perpetual serf-dom as the servants of their high-and-mighty white bosses. Dr Hendrik Verwoerd, architect of this education system, high priest of apartheid and later Prime Minister, had not been abashed to state categorically:

> The school must equip the Bantu [Black South African] to meet the demands which the economic life will impose on him . . . What is the use of teaching a Bantu child mathematics when it cannot use it in practice? . . . Education must train and teach people in accordance with their opportunities in life . . .[1]

I say 'never again' because in the new South Africa it is true – never again can legislation be passed quite legally and in an orderly fashion to turn the lives of so many into a hell on earth because in the new South Africa it is not parliament that is sovereign. No, it is our new constitution, regarded by many as one of the most libertarian and human rights-oriented constitutions in the world. Legislation cannot now be passed as the fancy takes parliament. It must pass muster with our highest court, the Constitutional Court, which has already shown in its short life that it will strike down anything that runs counter to the spirit and the letter of the constitution. The constitution is not just a piece of paper. It is a solemn covenant entered into by all South Africans through their elected representatives.

But no one possesses a magic wand which the architects of the new dispensation could wave and, 'Hey presto!', South Africa would be transformed overnight into a promised land flowing with milk and honey. There are aspects of the old system that linger on, that hang over the bright new era as a dark and sombre pall. The pernicious and debilitating legacy of apartheid, firmly entrenched for a long half-century and enforced with ruthless efficiency, is going to be with us for many a long day yet.

Many South Africans had terrible memories of the apartheid years. They remembered the Sharpeville massacre on 21 March 1960: a peaceful crowd were demonstrating against the pass laws and then sixty-nine people were mown down when the police panicked and opened fire on the demonstrators, most of whom were shot in the back while fleeing; also the Soweto uprising of 16 June 1976: unarmed schoolchildren were shot and killed when they demonstrated against the use of Afrikaans as a medium of instruction (Afrikaans was regarded as the language of the oppressor, the enforcers of the apartheid policy, since it was the overwhelmingly Afrikaans-speaking Nationalist Party that had inflicted it on the nation from 1948.). Then there were the people who, over the years, had died mysteriously while they were in police detention. It was alleged by the authorities – who might perhaps have been believed by most of the white community (they were certainly not believed by most of the black community) – that they had committed suicide by hanging themselves with their belts, or slipped on soap while showering, or that they had a penchant for jumping out of the windows of the buildings where they were being detained and questioned. Others died, so we were told, from self-inflicted injuries. One such was Steve Biko, the young student-founder of the black consciousness movement who, it was said, had banged his head against the wall in an inexplicable and quite unreasonable altercation with his interrogators in September 1977. Steve had been driven naked on the back of a police truck over 1,500 km to Pretoria where it was reported he would have received medical treatment, except that he had died soon after he arrived there. No one ever explained why he could not have got the emergency treatment in Port Elizabeth where he had been detained, nor why, if he had had to be taken to Pretoria, he had had to be humiliated, comatose as he was, by being transported without any clothes on.

People remembered the bombing in Amanzimtoti, KwaZulu/ Natal, in 1985 when a limpet mine placed in a refuse bin outside a shopping centre exploded amongst holidaymakers doing last-minute Christmas shopping, killing five people and injuring over sixty. Then there was the Magoo's Bar bombing of June 1986 when three people were killed and sixty-nine injured by a car bomb planted by Robert McBride and his two accomplices, allegedly on the orders of a commander of the ANC's armed wing, Umkhonto weSizwe[2] (MK), based in neighbouring Botswana.

Many South Africans had been filled with revulsion when they saw how people were killed so gruesomely through the so-called 'necklace', a tyre that was placed round the victim's neck, filled with petrol and then set alight. This horrible execution was used by township ANC-supporting 'comrades', especially against 'sell-outs', those who were suspected of being collaborators with the State. It was also used in the internecine strife between warring liberation movements, for example the United Democratic Front (UDF), which largely comprised ANC sympathisers while that party remained banned, and the Azanian People's Organisation (Azapo), the party espousing the principles of black consciousness developed by Steve Biko and his colleagues. We were appalled that human beings, youngsters, could actually dance around the body of someone dying in such an excruciating fashion. Apartheid had succeeded only too well in dehumanising both those who implemented it and its victims.

People were appalled at the carnage in Church Street, Pretoria, in May 1983 when a massive bomb exploded outside the administrative headquarters of the South African Air Force. Twenty-one people died and over two hundred were injured. The ANC claimed responsibility for this outrage. Then there was the St James' Church massacre in Cape Town in July 1993. In that attack, two members of the armed wing of the Pan Africanist Congress (PAC) – the liberation movement which had broken away from the ANC in 1959 – burst into a Sunday church service and fired machine-guns, killing eleven worshippers and injuring fifty-six. Nothing, it seemed, was sacrosanct any more in this urban guerrilla warfare.

These and similar atrocities pockmarked our history and on all sides it was agreed that we had to take this history, this past, seriously into account. We could not pretend that it had not happened. Much of it was too fresh in the memories of many communities.

There was in fact hardly any controversy about whether we should deal effectively with our past if we were going to be making the transition to a new dispensation. No, the debate was not on *whether* but on *how* we might deal with this only-too-real past.

There were those who wanted to follow the Nuremberg trial paradigm, by bringing to book all perpetrators of gross violations of human rights and letting them run the gauntlet of the normal judicial process. It turned out that this was not really a viable option at all, perhaps mercifully for us. After the Second World War, the Allies defeated the Nazis and their allies comprehensively and were thus able to impose what has been described as 'victor's justice'. The accused had no say whatsoever in the matter and because some of those who sat in judgement on the accused, such as the Russians, were themselves guilty of similar gross violations (in the excesses perpetrated under Stalin), the whole process left a simmering resentment in many Germans – as I found out when I participated in a BBC-TV panel discussion in the very room in Nuremberg where the trial had taken place fifty years previously. The Germans had accepted Nuremberg because they were down and out and so the victors, as it were, could kick the vanquished even as they lay on the ground. In South Africa neither side could impose victor's justice because neither side won the decisive victory which would have enabled it to do so. Thus the Nuremberg option was rejected by those who were negotiating the delicate process of transition to democracy, the rule of law and respect for human rights.

It is as certain as anything that the security forces of the apartheid regime would not have supported the negotiated settlement which made possible the 'miracle' of our relatively peaceful transition from repression to democracy (when most people had been making dire predictions of a bloodbath, of a comprehensive disaster that would overwhelm us) had they known that at the end of the negotiations they would face the full wrath of the law as alleged perpetrators. They still controlled the guns and had the capacity to sabotage the whole process.

Looking back from where we are now, the beneficiaries of a peaceful transition, some South Africans – and others in the international community – enjoy the luxury of being able to complain that all the perpetrators ought to have been brought to justice. The fact of the matter is that we have remarkably short memories. We have forgotten that we were on tenterhooks until 1994, within a hair's-breadth of comprehensive disaster from which, in God's mercy, we were spared. Those who now enjoy the new dispensation have forgotten too soon just how vulnerable and indeed how unlikely it all was, and why the world still looks on in amazement at the unfolding of this miracle. The miracle was the result of the negotiated settlement. There would have been no negotiated settlement and so no new democratic South Africa had the negotiators on one side insisted that all perpetrators would be brought to trial. While the Allies could pack up and go home after Nuremberg, we in South Africa had to live with one another.

That is why our Chief Justice, Judge Ismail Mahomed, when he was deputy president of the Constitutional Court and considering a challenge to the constitutional validity of the amnesty provision in our law, could quote with such approval the words of Judge Marvin

Frankel in his book, *Out of the Shadows of Night: The Struggle for International Human Rights:*[3]

The call to punish human rights criminals can present complex and agonising problems that have no single or simple solution. While the debate over the Nuremberg trials still goes on, that episode – trials of war criminals of a defeated nation – was simplicity itself as compared to the subtle and dangerous issues that can divide a country when it undertakes to punish its own violators.

A nation divided during a repressive regime does not emerge suddenly united when the time of repression has passed. The human rights criminals are fellow citizens, living alongside everyone else, and they may be very powerful and dangerous. If the army and police have been the agencies of terror, the soldiers and the cops aren't going to turn overnight into paragons of respect for human rights. Their numbers and their expert management of deadly weapons remain significant facts of life . . . The soldiers and police may be biding their time, waiting and conspiring to return to power. They may be seeking to keep or win sympathisers in the population at large. If they are treated too harshly – or if the net of punishment is cast too widely – there may be a backlash that plays into their hands. But their victims cannot simply forgive and forget.

These problems are not abstract generalities. They describe tough realities in more than a dozen countries. If, as we hope, more nations are freed from regimes of terror, similar problems will continue to arise. Since the situations vary, the nature of the problems varies from place to place.

Judge Mahomed then commented on the situation in South Africa:

For a successfully negotiated transition, the terms of the transition required not only the agreement of those victimised by abuse but also those threatened by the transition to a 'democratic society based on freedom and equality' [from the Constitution]. If the Constitution kept alive the prospect of continuous retaliation and revenge, the agreement of those threatened by its implementation might never have been forthcoming . . .[4]

There were other very cogent and important reasons why the Nuremberg trial option found little favour with the negotiators in South Africa. It would have placed an intolerable burden on an already strained judicial system. We had some experience of cases of this nature because the State had prosecuted Colonel Eugene de Kock, former head of a police death squad, in two major trials in 1995 and 1996, and then also in 1996 General Magnus Malan, former Minister of Defence, and a number of generals and other military officers. It had taken a whole bevy of Department of Justice and Safety and Security (police) personnel eighteen months to make a case successfully against de Kock, and since he had been a former state employee, the state was obliged to foot his legal bill which came to R5 million (nearly US $1 million) – plus the cost of the prosecution and its bureaucracy, and an expensive witness protection programme. In the case of General Malan and his co-accused, the prosecution failed and the costs were astronomical, running to nearly R12 million (US $2 million) just for the defence, which again had to be borne by the state. In a country strapped for cash and with a whole range of pressing priorities in education, health, housing, and other fields, tough decisions had to be made about what the country could be expected to afford.

We also could not allow details from such cases of human rights abuse to be aired for an unconscionably long time since they would be distressing to many and too disruptive of our fragile peace and stability. We certainly could not have afforded the tenacity of the Nazi-hunters who are still at it more than fifty years later. We have had to balance the requirements of justice, accountability, stability, peace and reconciliation. We could very well have had retributive justice, and had a South Africa lying in ashes – a truly Pyrrhic victory if ever there was one.

Another important reason why the trial option was not a viable one was that a criminal court requires the evidence produced in a case to pass the most rigorous scrutiny and to prove the case beyond reasonable doubt. In many of the cases which came before the Truth and Reconciliation Commission, the only witnesses to events who were still alive were the perpetrators, and they had used the considerable resources of the state to destroy evidence and cover up their heinous deeds. We discovered in the course of the Commission's investigations that the supporters of apartheid were ready to lie at the drop of a hat. This applied to cabinet ministers and commissioners of police right down to rank-and-file supporters. They lied as if it were going out of fashion, brazenly and with very considerable conviction. In the courts it was the word of one bewildered victim against that of several perpetrators, usually officers in the police or armed forces who, as they later admitted in their applications for amnesty, perjured themselves. (The Commission proved to be a better way of getting at the truth than court cases: amnesty applicants had to demonstrate that they had made a full disclosure to qualify for amnesty, so the normal legal process was reversed as applicants sought to discharge the onus on them to reveal all.) It would have had to be a very brave judge or magistrate who would find in favour of the solitary witness, a black person facing a phalanx of white police officers.

No wonder the judicial system gained such a notorious reputation in the black community. It was taken for granted that the judges and magistrates colluded with the police to produce miscarriages of justice. Until fairly recently the magistrates and judges were all white, sharing the apprehensions and prejudices of their white compatriots, secure in enjoying the privileges that the injustices of apartheid provided them with so lavishly and therefore inclined to believe that all opposition to that status quo was Communist-inspired. They generally supported the executive and legislative branches of government against the black person, who was excluded by law from a share in the governance of his motherland. Many judges in the old dispensation were blatantly political appointments and they did nothing to redeem the reputation of the judiciary as a willing collaborator with an unjust system. Of course there were some exceptions but by and large the dice were heavily loaded against the black complainant or accused. It will take some time for black South Africans to have confidence in the police and the judicial system, which have been so badly discredited.

I cannot do better than to quote again from Judge Mahomed's elegant judgement:

> Every decent human being must feel grave discomfort in living with a consequence which might allow the perpetrators of evil acts to walk the streets of this land with impunity, protected in their freedom by an amnesty immune from constitutional attack, but the circumstances in support of this course require carefully to be appreciated. Most of the acts of brutality and torture which have taken place have occurred during an era in which neither the laws which permitted the incarceration of persons or the investigation of crimes, nor the methods and the culture which informed such investigations, were easily open to public investigation, verification and correction. Much of what transpired in this shameful period is shrouded in secrecy and not easily capable of objective demonstration and proof. Loved ones have disappeared, sometimes mysteriously, and most of them no longer survive to tell their tales. Others have had their freedom invaded, their dignity assaulted or their reputations tarnished by grossly unfair imputations hurled in the fire and the cross-fire of a deep and wounding conflict. The wicked and the innocent have often both been victims. Secrecy and authoritarianism have concealed the truth in little crevices of obscurity in our history. Records are not easily accessible, witnesses are often unknown, dead, unavailable or unwilling. All that often effectively remains is the truth of wounded memories of loved ones sharing instinctive suspicions, deep and traumatising to the survivors but otherwise incapable of translating themselves into objective and corroborative evidence which could survive the rigours of the law . . . [5]

Thus in many cases there was a lack of evidence, and others were affected by the statute of limitations, the crimes having taken place too long ago. The consequences of such judicial stalemates were pointed out by Judge Mahomed in another passage of his judgement:

> The alternative to the grant of immunity from criminal prosecution of offenders is to keep intact the abstract right to such a prosecution for particular persons without the evidence to sustain the prosecution

successfully, to continue to keep the dependants of such victims in many cases substantially ignorant about what precisely happened to their loved ones, to leave their yearning for the truth effectively unassuaged, to perpetuate their legitimate sense of resentment and grief and correspondingly to allow the culprits of such deeds to remain perhaps physically free but inhibited in their capacity to become active, full and creative members of the new order by a menacing combination of confused fear, guilt, uncertainty and sometimes even trepidation.[6]

Thus the option of trials, which represented one extreme of the possible ways of dealing with our past, was rejected.

Then there were those who opposed the trial option and suggested rather glibly that we let bygones be bygones. This was an option much sought after by the members of the previous government and those in the security forces who had carried out their demands. They clamoured for a blanket or general amnesty as had been granted in Chile, for instance, where General Augusto Pinochet and his cohorts gave themselves amnesty as a precondition to handing over from their military junta to a civilian government. Even though they agreed to the appointment of a Truth Commission, it was to deliberate only behind closed doors, and the record of General Pinochet and his government and the security forces would not be scrutinised by the commission, certainly not for the purpose of apportioning blame. General Pinochet and his officers and government forgave themselves: they alone knew what precisely they had done; they were the accused, the prosecution and the judges in their own case. In the absence of an amnesty designed, as it was in South Africa, to establish accountability, I am a strong supporter of the recent extradition proceedings against General Pinochet. It would be quite intolerable that the perpetrator should decide not only whether he should get amnesty but that no one else should have the right to question the grounds on which he had so granted himself amnesty and for what offence.

In the South African case there was to be no general amnesty. Each person who had been involved in the abuses had to make an individual application, and then appear before an independent panel which decided whether the applicant satisfied the stringent conditions for granting amnesty. Apart from the reasons given above, it was felt very strongly that general amnesty was really amnesia. It was pointed out that we, none of us, have the power to say, 'Let bygones be bygones' and, hey presto, they then become bygones. Our common experience in fact is the opposite – that the past, far from disappearing or lying down and being quiet, is embarrassingly persistent, and will return and haunt us unless it has been dealt with adequately. Unless we look the beast in the eye we will find that it returns to hold us hostage.

The history of the British and the Afrikaners (white settlers of Dutch, German or Huguenot origin) in South Africa is a perfect case in point. During the Anglo-Boer War at the turn of the century, the British incarcerated more than 200,000 people, including Boer women and children and black workers on Boer farms, in what was a new British invention at the time – concentration camps, which were to gain appropriately a foul reputation as a special feature of the Jewish Holocaust in Hitler's mad obsession with Aryan purity. Nearly 50,000 of the inmates are estimated to have died in unacceptable conditions. At the end of the war neither side ever sat down with the other to talk about this aspect of their war. It seemed that in time the wounds inflicted then had healed, and the British and Afrikaner settlers seemed to live happily together. Alas, however, underneath this superficial friendship, their relationship was unstable and uneasy. In 1998 I travelled by road from Zürich to attend the World Economic Forum in Davos. I was accompanied by a young Afrikaner who told me he remembered so clearly his grandmother telling him of the awful things that had happened to his people in the concentration camps. He said with some feeling that he was ready to fight the Anglo-Boer War over again whenever he remembered his grandmother's stories.

At Dachau, the former concentration camp near Nuremberg, they have a museum to commemorate what happened there – you can see the gas chambers and the ovens where the bodies of the Jews were incinerated. The gas chambers look so innocuous, like normal shower rooms, until you see the vents through which the lethal gas could be pumped into the chamber. In the museum there are pictures of prisoners marching behind brass bands as they carry some inmate to his execution – macabre humour indeed. The Germans were so methodical and systematic. They recorded everything, including the experiments they carried out to see what depths and altitudes human beings could tolerate – of course, the guinea pigs were the subhuman, non-Aryan, Jewish inmates. It is all there to see in photographs that show faces grimacing like hideous gargoyles.

Over the entrance to this museum are the philosopher George Santayana's haunting words, 'Those who cannot remember the past are condemned to repeat it.' Those who were negotiating our future in South Africa were aware that unless our past was acknowledged and dealt with adequately it could blight our future.

The notion of national amnesia was rejected for yet another telling reason. Accepting that option would have victimised the victims of apartheid a second time round. It would have meant denying their experience, a vital part of their identity. Ariel Dorfman, the Chilean playwright, has written a play entitled *Death and the Maiden*. The maiden's husband has just been appointed to his country's Truth Commission. While she is busy in the kitchen, someone whose car has broken down enters the house to ask for help. The woman does not see him but hears him speak and she recognises his voice as that of the man who had tortured and raped her when she was in detention several years before. The scene then changes to show the man completely at her mercy, tied up and helpless. She holds a gun to him and is ready to kill him because he denies strenuously that he could have done this and tries to produce an elaborate alibi. Much later, he eventually admits that he was the perpetrator and, very strangely, she lets him go. His denial hit at the core of her being, at her integrity, at her identity and these were all tied up intimately with her experiences, with her memory. Denial subverted her personhood. She was, in a real sense, her memory.

Our nation sought to rehabilitate and affirm the dignity and humanity of those who were cruelly silenced for so long, turned into anonymous, marginalised victims. Now, through the Truth and Reconciliation Commission, they would be empowered to tell their stories, allowed to remember and in this public recounting their individuality and inalienable humanity would be acknowledged.

When it came to hearing evidence from victims, because we were not a criminal court, we established facts on the basis of a balance of probability. Since we were exhorted by our enabling legislation to rehabilitate the human and civil dignity of victims, we allowed those who came to testify mainly to tell *their* stories in their own words. We did do all we could to corroborate these stories and we soon discovered that, as Judge Albie Sachs, a member of our Constitutional Court, has pointed out, there were in fact different orders of truth which did not necessarily mutually exclude one another. There was what could be termed forensic factual truth – verifiable and documentable – and there was 'social truth, the truth of experience that is established through interaction, discussion and debate'.[7] The personal truth – Judge Mahomed's 'truth of wounded memories' – was a healing truth and a court of law would have left many of those who came to testify, who were frequently uneducated and unsophisticated, bewildered and even more traumatised than before. Whereas many bore witness to the fact that coming to talk to the Commission had had a marked therapeutic effect on them. We learned this from an unsolicited comment by the brother of one of the Cradock Four, ANC-supporting activists who left their homes in Cradock to attend a political rally in Port Elizabeth and never made it back home, having been gruesomely murdered by the police. The brother said to me after one of his relatives had testified at the Commission's first hearing, and before the policemen responsible had confessed and applied for amnesty: 'Archbishop, we have told our story to many on several occasions, to newspapers and to the TV. This is the first time, though, that after telling it we feel as if a heavy load has been removed from our shoulders.'

Our country's negotiators opted for a 'third way' that avoided the two extremes of Nuremberg trials and blanket amnesty (or national amnesia). This third way was the granting of amnesty to individuals in exchange for a full disclosure relating to the crime for which amnesty was being sought. It was the carrot of possible freedom in exchange for truth, and the stick was the prospect of lengthy prison sentences for those already in gaol, and the probability of arrest, prosecution and imprisonment for those still free.

The main thrust of most of the work of the Commission concerned victims and survivors of gross violations of human rights – taking statements from them, investigating their accounts, giving a cross-section of them a chance to tell their stories publicly and drafting recommendations for reparations and rehabilitation to place before the government. However, the agreement on amnesty reached by the politicians made amnesty, and the work of the committee established to decide on amnesty applications, a crucial part of our operations.

There are still major issues which this third way raises such as, was this approach going to encourage people to think they could commit crimes, knowing that they would get amnesty? Is it ever enough for perpetrators merely to apologise and be humiliated through public exposure? What about justice? And since amnesty expunged the civil and criminal liability of the successful applicant, was it fair to deny victims their constitutional right to claim civil damages from the perpetrator and the state?

I will touch on these questions later but I want to conclude this chapter by pointing out that this third way of conditional amnesty was consistent with a central feature of the African *Weltanschauung* (or world-view) – what we know as *ubuntu* in the Nguni group of languages, or *botho* in the Sotho languages. What is it that con-strained so many to choose to forgive rather than to demand retribu-tion, to be so magnanimous rather than wreaking vengeance?

Ubuntu is very difficult to render into a Western language. It speaks of the very essence of being human. When we want to give high praise to someone we say, '*Yu, u nobuntu*'; 'Hey, he or she has *ubuntu*.' This means they are generous, hospitable, friendly, caring and compassionate. They share what they have. It also means my humanity is caught up, is inextricably bound up, in theirs. We belong in a bundle of life. We say, 'a person is a person through other people'. It is not 'I think therefore I am'. It says rather: 'I am human because I belong.' I participate, I share. A person with *ubuntu* is open and available to others, affirming of others, does not feel threatened that others are able and good; for he or she has a proper self-assurance that comes from knowing that he or she belongs in a greater whole and is diminished when others are humiliated or diminished, when others are tortured or oppressed, or treated as if they were less than who they are.

Harmony, friendliness, community are great goods. Social harmony is for us the *summum bonum* – the greatest good. Anything that subverts or undermines this sought-after good is to be avoided like the plague. Anger, resentment, lust for revenge, even success through aggressive competitiveness, are corrosive of this good. To forgive is not just to be altruistic. It is the best form of self-interest. What dehumanises you, inexorably dehumanises me. Forgiveness gives people resilience, enabling them to survive and emerge still human despite all efforts to dehumanise them.

Ubuntu means that in a real sense even the supporters of apartheid were victims of the vicious system which they implemented and which they supported so enthusiastically. Our humanity was intertwined. The humanity of the perpetrator of apartheid's atrocities was caught up and bound up in that of his victim whether he liked it or not. In the process of dehumanising another, in inflicting untold harm and suffering, the perpetrator was inexorably being dehumanised as well. I used to say that the oppressor was dehumanised as much as, if not more than, the oppressed and many in the white community believed that this was just another provocative hate-mongering slogan by that irresponsible ogre, Tutu, whom most whites at the time most loved to hate. And yet we had an extraordinary example of my contention in the chilling retort by Mr Jimmy Kruger when told of Steve Biko's death in detention. Mr Kruger was at the time Minister of Police. He joked at a party rally that Biko had died as a result of being on a protest fast, and declared that it showed that Steve

Biko had freedom in South Africa. He was free to starve himself to death if he so wished. He said Biko's death 'leaves me cold'. You had to ask what had happened to the humanity of anyone who could speak so callously about the death of a fellow human being.

When freedom and independence came to Kenya, many people expected the Mau Mau to embark on a campaign to turn Kenya into the white man's grave through an orgy of revenge and retribution. Instead President Jomo Kenyatta came to be so revered that there was much consternation at his death. There was anxiety about what Kenya would become after Kenyatta. *Ubuntu* was abroad in the post-independence Kenya. And in Zimbabwe, after one of the most bruising bush wars, Robert Mugabe, on the night of his election victory in 1980, amazed everyone by talking about reconciliation, rehabilitation and reconstruction. That was *ubuntu* at work. In Namibia, after SWAPO won the first democratic elections in 1989, President Sam Nujoma wowed everyone with his engaging smile. There were no reprisals against whites. That was *ubuntu* showing.

It doesn't always happen, of course. Where was *ubuntu* in the Belgian Congo in the early 1960s? Why did the Rwandans forget *ubuntu* in 1994 and instead destroy one another in that most awful genocide that overwhelmed their beautiful country? I don't really know except to say that honouring *ubuntu* is clearly not a mechanical, automatic and inevitable process and that we in South Africa have been blessed with some quite remarkable people of all races, not just black South Africans. Mr Johan Smit of Pretoria lost his young son in an ANC bomb blast. Mr Smit is an Afrikaner, and most people expected him to be bristling with anger and hostility against those the apartheid government's propaganda made out to be Communist-inspired terrorists. When Mr Smit spoke about his son's death what he said was quite breathtaking. He said he was not angry. If he was angry at all it was against the apartheid government. He believed that his son's death had contributed to the transition we were experiencing from repression and injustice to democracy and freedom. The time for change had come.

CHAPTER THREE

In the fullness of time

Why did the turning point happen in South Africa when it did? There is a lovely phrase which St Paul uses in his letter to the new Christian converts in Galatia: 'in the fullness of time'.[1] Paul speaks about how when Jesus was born it was at just the right time, all the pieces had fallen into place, the antecedents were just right and it all happened at exactly the right moment. A little earlier would have been too soon and a little later would have been too late. When it happened it could not have been at any other moment.

Freedom broke out in the 1990s in the most unlikely places – the Berlin Wall fell in 1989 and the Communist empire began to unravel as a result of Mikhail Gorbachev's *perestroika* and *glasnost*. It would have been impossible for all these changes to have happened as they did in the time of his more hard-line predecessors such as Leonid Brezhnev, and had the global geopolitical scene not changed as it did, much of what did take place subsequently would not have done so, or it would have occurred at much greater cost in human lives and resulted in very much more unrest and turmoil.

In South Africa, the disintegration of a robust and predatory Communist empire, President Reagan's 'evil empire', was one of the pieces that helped to bring about the changes in our troubled country. The apartheid regime had been able to hoodwink an easily gullible and willing West into believing that South Africa was indeed the last bastion against Communism in Africa. By 1990, however, it was no longer credible for the apartheid government to claim that it had to use repressive measures to stem the flow of

Communism, since Communism had been routed.

We were also richly blessed that at this crucial time in the history of the world and of South Africa, F. W. de Klerk replaced the stiff-necked and irascible P. W. Botha as President of South Africa. In 1985, Mr Botha had failed dismally to rise to the occasion when he produced a damp squib in place of what had been billed as a major speech in which he would 'cross the Rubicon' and announce reforms. It is inconceivable that the granite-like Botha would have announced the kind of bold initiatives that F. W. de Klerk proclaimed to a startled and scarcely believing world in a speech to parliament on 2 February 1990: that the political process in South Africa was to be normalised through the unbanning of political organisations (which had been proscribed since the Sharpeville Massacre of 1960); that the ANC, PAC and the South African Communist Party (SACP) would be permitted to operate again as legal entities in a South Africa seeking to emerge from the claustrophobia of apartheid's injustice and oppression.

Nothing can ever take away from F. W. de Klerk the enormous credit that belongs to him for what he said and did then. He has carved out a niche for himself in the history of South Africa, and whatever his reasons for doing so and whatever our assessment of what he did subsequently, we should salute him for what he did in 1990.

I believe that had he not done what he did, we would have experienced the bloodbath and disaster that so many were predicting would be South Africa's lot. It required a considerable degree of courage to try to persuade the white community that their best interests would be served by negotiating themselves out of exclusive control of political power. Very few constituencies are likely to take too kindly to candidates for political office who say their platform is to hand over power to their traditional adversaries. Mr F. W. de Klerk did not of course say anything quite that categorical. He spoke about power-sharing and made what was unpalatable and even unthinkable a little less off-putting to his constituency. He put his political career on the line and we would be churlish in the extreme if we did not praise him for that. He may have hoped to be able to negotiate a position for the whites where he and his followers would be able to exercise a veto. He might have hoped to rule in a rotating presidential triumvirate. Be that as it may, we were blessed at that critical point in our history by having him there, ready to take risks and to lead.

Of course, all this would have been utterly pointless had his counterpart on the other side been someone who did not measure up to the challenges of the time. Had F. W. de Klerk encountered a man in gaol bristling with bitterness and a lust for retribution then it is highly unlikely that he would have gone ahead with announcing his initiatives. Mercifully he encountered a man who had developed into the prisoner of conscience par excellence. Nelson Mandela had developed such stature during his imprisonment that many were concerned that such a saint could only disillusion those who venerated him by turning out to have feet of clay once he emerged. In fact a rumour had been going round that some in his movement were planning his assassination because they were scared that the world would be so deeply disappointed that he did not measure up to its image of him. They feared that the ANC might lose the enormous international support it had received, largely because of the almost larger-than-life image the world had built of their leader in prison.

We need not have worried. Mr de Klerk had not met someone vindictive, hell-bent on paying back the whites with their own coin, seeking to give them liberal doses of their own medicine. He found a man regal in his dignity, overflowing with magnanimity and a desire to dedicate himself to the reconciliation of those whom apartheid and the injustice and pain of racism had alienated from one another. Nelson Mandela did not emerge from prison spewing words of hatred and revenge. He amazed us all by his heroic embodiment of reconciliation and forgiveness. No one could have accused him of speaking glibly and facilely about forgiveness and reconciliation. He had been harassed for a long time before his arrest, making a normal family life impossible, and had spent all of twenty-seven years in gaol by the time of his release on 11 February 1990. No one could say that he knew nothing about suffering.

A famous picture shows him on Robben Island with Walter Sisulu in the courtyard where they and others – who can be seen behind them in the photograph – sat in a row breaking rocks into small pieces. Such utterly futile drudgery could have destroyed lesser mortals with its pointlessness. And we know that his eyesight was ruined by the glare to which prisoners were exposed as they laboured in the lime quarry. Everything possible was done to break his spirit and to fill him with hate. In this the system failed dismally. He emerged a whole person.

It would be easy to say that those twenty-seven years were utter shameful waste: just think of all he could have contributed to the good of South Africa and the world. I don't think so. Those twenty-seven years and all the suffering they entailed were the fires of the furnace that tempered his steel, that removed the dross. Perhaps without that suffering he would have been less able to be as compassionate and as magnanimous as he turned out to be. And that suffering on behalf of others gave him an authority and credibility that can be provided by nothing else in quite the same way. The true leader must at some point or other convince her or his followers that she or he is in this whole business not for self-aggrandisement but for the sake of others. Nothing is able to prove this quite as convincingly as suffering.

It is easy for outsiders to think that Mr Mandela is such a colossus, such a moral giant standing head and shoulders above others, that he just has to say something for everyone to scramble to do his bidding. This is to misconstrue the nature of the ANC and his own remarkable loyalty as a party member. The ANC, like other political collectives of its kind, is really a huge coalition of different political philosophies, views and attitudes. Founded in 1912, it united a range of African leaders who combined in order to resist their exclusion from political power in the newly formed Union of South Africa and the extension of controls over Africans by the white government of the Union. During the course of the struggle there were, and to this day there are, all sorts of personalities and affiliations and organisations contained within that union, from hard-core Marxists to the most outright libertarians. There are young Turks who want to storm the Bastille at the drop of a hat and scholarly, urbane thinkers. When it was unbanned in 1990, its leader was Oliver Tambo, who had played an extraordinary role in holding together the movement in exile. He and his fellow leaders had to integrate an organisation comprising exiles, underground activists within South Africa, and those emerging from prison after many years. It is a considerable feat to hold together so disparate a party whose members also believe deeply in consensus, in what they call 'receiving the mandate'. It is wonderful to behold people so deeply serious about a participatory way of operating, which involves taking the views of the least of them seriously into account. But it can also debilitate initiative, forcing the entire organisation to move forward at the pace of the slowest. (I came to believe that whilst Mr Mandela's loyalty to the party was something to admire, it was excessive and turned out to be his chief weakness. He would usually not want to move ahead of the party consensus: that is how they had operated in gaol and that is how he would operate outside. It led him to keep people in his Cabinet who should have been jettisoned as dead wood. Perhaps he feared that being of royal blood he might be tempted to become high-handed and arrogant, so tried to ensure he did not appear dictatorial.)

In such a party it could not be taken for granted that all would acquiesce in a conciliatory approach. It was certainly not automatic – after all the suffering – that all members would agree that the perpetrators of human rights violations should not in fact face trial and be dealt with harshly. The ANC had to decide seriously whether even to negotiate. Many of the younger members were often hot-headed and they readily pandered to the angry emotions of their contemporaries. I recall that when the Truth and Reconciliation Commission charged Mr P. W. Botha with contempt for disregarding a subpoena to appear before it, a young black man, who was present in court every day during that trial, said to me during a lunch break one day: 'Archbishop, this old man [P. W. Botha] should be sent to gaol even just for a few days.' When I remonstrated with him that Botha was such an old man, he retorted, 'He should feel a little what

our leaders experienced. After all, they imprisoned Oscar Mpetha.'
(Mr Mpetha was a leader in the Western Cape who had been detained
even though he was in his eighties and suffering from diabetes.)

There were other political organisations that sought to portray
themselves as more radical than the ANC and which opposed any
suggestion of negotiating with the 'enemy' as a sign of weakness.
The PAC and its armed wing, the Azanian People's Liberation Army
(APLA), continued the armed struggle even at the time negotiations
were taking place. There were some in the ANC who were
sympathetic to this point of view. Mr Mandela had to contend with
all these people.

It required a great deal of political courage, skill and authority to
bring his organisation along with him. We were fortunate that he and
others in the leadership were convinced that this was the way to go.
Mr Mandela was aided and abetted by some of the more radical
among the party hierarchy, who carried a lot of clout with the
younger members. The much-admired General Secretary of the
Communist Party, Joe Slovo, for example, was committed to the
entire process of negotiation and of making concessions and accom-
modations. He was particularly responsible for persuading the
firebrands to accept what have been called the 'sunset clauses',
which ensured no government official or civil servant of the old
dispensation would stand to lose his or her job or pension when the
transition happened. Only someone with the credibility of Joe Slovo
could persuade those who might have wanted to penalise apartheid's
servants to accept this compromise. It was this kind of spirit that
permeated the negotiation process, certainly from the ANC side.

Chris Hani, who was later assassinated on the eve of our historic
elections, had established his unassailable place in the hearts of the
militant township youth. He had been a leader of the ANC's armed
wing, Umkhonto weSizwe, and had succeeded Joe Slovo as General
Secretary of the Communist Party. So he had impeccable credentials,
and had most of the young eating out of his hand. A military man
himself, he could have drawn a great many to his side had he declared
himself opposed to the negotiation process and aligned himself with

those who wanted to continue the armed struggle. Instead he took his reputation in his hands and went round the country urging young people to be henceforth 'soldiers of peace', a call to which they responded enthusiastically.

At this critical point in South Africa's history, we were blessed to have outstanding leadership on both sides of the racial divide, who were ready to take risks and put their political careers and their lives on the line to promote peace, forgiveness and reconciliation. When I visited countries in Africa and other parts of the world that were experiencing conflict or were dealing with the aftermath of conflict and repression, almost everywhere the lament was that they lacked leaders of the calibre, courage, stature and vision of Nelson Mandela, and also someone like de Klerk, who had the courage and common sense to make himself redundant.

While Nelson Mandela was the most spectacular embodiment of the ANC's commitment to peace and reconciliation, he was not the only one. There were others, younger and less well-known, who had had harrowing experiences under apartheid but had emerged from the ordeal unscathed, and seeking not revenge against the perpetrators but healing for their traumatised and divided nation. Patrick 'Terror' Lekota and Popo Molefe, for example, were up-and-coming stars in the political firmament. They had been among the accused in one of the longest trials, dubbed the Delmas Treason Trial after the small town on the East Rand where it was held. Both had spent a spell in gaol, where they met legends such as Nelson Mandela on Robben Island. Both were later elected premiers of provinces in the new South Africa, and Terror and another premier, Tokyo Sexwale, both spoke warmly and appreciatively to our synod of bishops about the work of the churches in South Africa, particularly their role in education. Nearly all the leaders in the black community had been educated in Church mission schools. They said their commitment to reconciliation was due to the influence and witness of the Christian Churches.

Popo Molefe became Premier of the North-West Province when democracy came. A while later, he organised a rally in the capital of his province to thank the Council of Churches and others for their support during the Delmas trial. Andrew Young, former US Ambassador to the UN, was present, and I sat next to him at the main table. He said he had asked Popo who the white man was who was sitting next to the Premier, and who was among those who had received gifts. Andy Young says he nearly broke down when Popo Molefe told him, 'This is the man who was the judge in our trial.'

Clearly the Church had made a contribution to what was happening in our land, even though its witness and ministry had been something of a mixed bag. Presumably without that influence things might have turned out a little differently. At a very difficult time in our struggle, when most of our leaders were in gaol, in exile, or proscribed in some way or other, some Church leaders were thrust into the forefront of the struggle and had thereby given the Church a particular kind of credibility – people like Allan Boesak, formerly leader of the Dutch Reformed Mission Church, Frank Chikane, former General Secretary of the South African Council of Churches (SACC), Peter Storey, former head of the Methodist Church, Beyers Naudé, the most prominent Afrikaner Church dissident and also a General Secretary of the SACC, Denis Hurley, formerly Roman Catholic Archbishop of Durban, and leaders of other faiths who were there where the people were hurting. Thus when they spoke about forgiveness and reconciliation they had won their spurs and were listened to with respect.

Dullah Omar, the new Minister of Justice, introduced the Act that brought the Truth and Reconciliation Commission into being. I recall how devastated he had been as a lawyer who had defended some of apartheid's opponents when, after obtaining a scholarship to study at the University of London, he had been denied a passport at the last moment before his departure. More than that, it was to be revealed much later that, at another time, he had been on a death list compiled by a South African government hit-squad. They had tried to swop the tablets he had to take for a heart condition so that he would take the wrong medication. The legislation he piloted through Parliament would enable the men who had tried to kill him to apply for amnesty.

It was a member of the ANC, Professor Kader Asmal, who suggested in his inaugural lecture as Professor of Human Rights Law at the University of the Western Cape, that South Africa should look not to have Nuremberg trials but a Truth and Reconciliation Commission. The ANC had paved the way for such a commission when, in order to deal with allegations that atrocities had taken place in its camps outside South Africa, it had done something almost unprecedented as a liberation movement. It had set up no less than three Commissions of Inquiry, and its leaders had accepted responsibility for the abuses that came to light and had publicly apologised.

Thus it was not surprising that after the long and exhausting negotiations which provided our land with the interim constitution which led us to democracy, this historic instrument should have contained a postscript that became the constitutional underpinning for the Truth and Reconciliation Commission:

<u>National Unity and Reconciliation</u>
This Constitution provides a historic bridge between the past of a deeply divided society characterised by strife, conflict, untold suffering and injustice, and a future founded on the recognition of human rights, democracy and peaceful co-existence and development opportunities for all South Africans, irrespective of colour, race, class, belief or sex. The pursuit of national unity, the well-being of all South African citizens and peace require reconciliation between the people of South Africa and the reconstruction of society.

The adoption of this Constitution lays the secure foundation for the people of South Africa to transcend the divisions and strife of the past, which generated gross violations of human rights, the transgression of humanitarian principles in violent conflicts and a legacy of hatred, fear, guilt and revenge. These can now be addressed on the basis that there is a need for understanding but not for vengeance, a need for reparation but not for retaliation, a need for ubuntu but not for victimisation.

In order to advance such reconciliation and reconstruction, amnesty shall be granted in respect of acts, omissions and offences associated with political objectives and committed in the course of the conflicts of the past. To this end, Parliament under this constitution shall adopt a law determining a firm cut-off date . . . and providing for the mechanisms, criteria and procedures, including tribunals, if any, through which such amnesty shall be dealt with at any time after the law has been passed.

CHAPTER FOUR

What about justice?

Can it ever be right for someone who has committed the most gruesome atrocities to be allowed to get off scot-free, simply by confessing what he or she has done? Are the critics right: was the Truth and Reconciliation process immoral? The Promotion of National Unity and Reconciliation Act, which established the Commission, did not even require an applicant to express any contrition or remorse. The only conditions for gaining amnesty were:

- The act for which amnesty was required should have happened between 1960, the year of the Sharpeville massacre, and 1994, when President Mandela was inaugurated as the first democratically elected South African Head of State.

- The act must have been politically motivated. Perpetrators did not qualify for amnesty if they killed because of personal greed, but they did qualify if they committed the act in response to an order by, or on behalf of, a political organisation such as the former apartheid state and its satellite Bantustan homelands, or a recognised liberation movement such as the ANC or PAC.

- The applicant had to make a full disclosure of all the relevant facts relating to the offence for which amnesty was being sought.

- The rubric of proportionality had to be observed – that the means were proportional to the objective.

If those conditions were met, the law said that amnesty 'shall' be granted. Victims had the right to oppose applications for amnesty by trying to demonstrate that these conditions had not been met, but they had no right of veto over amnesty.

Later we realised that the legislature had been a great deal wiser than we had at first thought in not making remorse a requirement for amnesty. If there had been such a requirement, an applicant who made a big fuss about being sorry and repentant would probably have been judged to be insincere, and someone whose manner was formal and abrupt would have been accused of being callous and uncaring and not really repentant. It would have been a no-win situation. In fact, most applicants have expressed remorse and asked for forgiveness from their victims. Whether their requests have stemmed from genuine contrition is obviously a moot point.

So is amnesty being given at the cost of justice being done? This is not a frivolous question, but a very serious issue, one which challenges the integrity of the entire Truth and Reconciliation process.

The Act required that where the offence is a gross violation of human rights – defined as an abduction, killing, torture or severe ill-treatment – the application should be dealt with in a public hearing unless such a hearing was likely to lead to a miscarriage of justice (for instance, where witnesses were too intimidated to testify in open session). In fact, virtually all the important applications to the Commission have been considered in public in the full glare of television lights. Thus there is the penalty of public exposure and humiliation for the perpetrator. Many of those in the security forces who have come forward had previously been regarded as respectable members of their communities. It was often the very first time that their communities and even sometimes their families heard that these people were, for instance, actually members of death squads or regular torturers of detainees in their custody. For some it has been so traumatic that marriages have broken up. That is quite a price to pay.

The South African Broadcasting Corporation's radio team covering the Truth and Reconciliation Commission received a letter from a woman calling herself Helena (she wanted to remain anonymous for fear of reprisals) who lived in the eastern province of Mpumalanga. They broadcast substantial extracts:

My story begins in my late teenage years as a farm girl in the Bethlehem district of the Eastern Free State. As an eighteen-year-old, I met a young man in his twenties. He was working in a top security structure. It was the beginning of a beautiful relationship. We even spoke about marriage. A bubbly, vivacious man who beamed out wild energy. Sharply intelligent. Even if he was an Englishman, he was popular with all the 'Boere' Afrikaners. And all my girlfriends envied me. Then one day he said he was going on a 'trip'. 'We won't see each other again . . . maybe never ever again.' I was torn to pieces. So was he. An extremely short marriage to someone else failed all because I married to forget. More than a year ago, I met my first love again through a good friend. I was to learn for the first time that he had been operating overseas and that he was going to ask for amnesty. I can't explain the pain and bitterness in me when I saw what was left of that beautiful, big, strong person. He had only one desire – that the truth must come out. Amnesty didn't matter. It was only a means to the truth.

After my unsuccessful marriage, I met another policeman. Not quite my first love, but an exceptional person. Very special. Once again a bubbly, charming personality. Humorous, grumpy, everything in its time and place. Then he says: He and three of our friends have been promoted. 'We're moving to a special unit. Now, now my darling. We are real policemen now.' We were ecstatic. We even celebrated. He and his friends would visit regularly. They even stayed over for long periods. Suddenly, at strange times, they would become restless. Abruptly mutter the feared word 'trip' and drive off. I . . . as a loved one . . . knew no other life than that of worry, sleeplessness, anxiety about his safety and where they could be. We simply had to be satisfied with: 'What you don't know, can't hurt you.' And all that we as loved ones knew . . . was what we saw with our own eyes. After about three years with the special forces, our hell began. He became very quiet. Withdrawn. Sometimes he would just press his face into his hands and shake uncontrollably. I realised he was drinking too much.

Instead of resting at night, he would wander from window to window. He tried to hide his wild, consuming fear, but I saw it. In the early hours of the morning between two and half-past-two, I jolt awake from his rushed breathing. Rolls this way, that side of the bed. He's pale. Ice cold in a sweltering night – sopping wet with sweat. Eyes bewildered, but dull like the dead. And the shakes. The terrible convulsions and blood-curdling shrieks of fear and pain from the bottom of his soul. Sometimes he sits motionless, just staring in front of him. I never understood. I never knew. Never realised what was being shoved down his throat during 'the trips'. I just went through hell. Praying, pleading: 'God, what's happening? What's wrong with him? Could he have changed so much? Is he going mad? I can't handle the man anymore! But, I can't get out. He's going to haunt me for the rest of my life if I leave him. Why, God?'

Today I know the answers to all my questions and heartache. I know where everything began, the background. The role of 'those at the top', the 'cliques' and 'our men' who simply had to carry out their bloody orders . . . like 'vultures'. And today they all wash their hands in innocence and resist the realities of the Truth Commission. Yes, I stand by my murderer who let me and the old White South Africa sleep peacefully. Warmly, while 'those at the top' were again targeting the next 'permanent removal from society' for the vultures.

I finally understand what the struggle was really about. I would have done the same had I been denied everything. If my life, that of my children and my parents was strangled with legislation. If I had to watch how white people became dissatisfied with the best and still wanted better and got it. I envy and respect the people of the struggle – at least their leaders have the guts to stand by their vultures, to recognise their sacrifices. What do we have? Our leaders are too holy and innocent. And faceless. I can understand if Mr (F. W.) de Klerk says he didn't know, but dammit, there must be a clique, there must be someone out there who is still alive and who can give a face to 'the orders from above' for all the operations. Dammit! What else can this abnormal life be other than a cruel human rights violation? Spiritual murder is more inhumane than a messy, physical murder. At least a murder victim rests. I wish I had the power to make these poor wasted people whole again. I wish I could wipe the old South Africa out of

everyone's past. I end with a few lines that my wasted vulture said to me one night: 'They can give me amnesty a thousand times. Even if God and everyone else forgives me a thousand times – I have to live with this hell. The problem is in my head, my conscience. There's only one way to be free of it. Blow my own brains out. Because that's where my hell is.'
Helena

It is also not true that the granting of amnesty encourages impunity in the sense that perpetrators can escape completely the consequences of their actions, because amnesty is granted only to those who plead guilty, who accept responsibility for what they have done. Amnesty is not given to innocent people or to those who claim to be innocent. It was on precisely this point that amnesty was refused to the police officers who applied for it for their part in the death of Steve Biko. They denied that they had committed a crime, claiming that they had assaulted him only in retaliation for his inexplicable conduct in attacking them.

Thus the process in fact encourages accountability rather than the opposite. It supports the new culture of respect for human rights and acknowledgment of responsibility and accountability by which the new democracy wishes to be characterised. It is important to note too that the amnesty provision is an ad hoc arrangement meant for this specific purpose. This is not how justice is to be administered in South Africa for ever. It is for a limited and definite period and purpose.

Further, retributive justice – in which an impersonal state hands down punishment with little consideration for victims and hardly any for the perpetrator – is not the only form of justice. I contend that there is another kind of justice, restorative justice, which was characteristic of traditional African jurisprudence. Here the central concern is not retribution or punishment but, in the spirit of *ubuntu,* the healing of breaches, the redressing of imbalances, the restoration of broken relationships. This kind of justice seeks to rehabilitate both the victim and the perpetrator, who should be given the opportunity to be reintegrated into the community he or she has injured by his or her offence. This is a far more personal approach, which sees the offence as something that has happened to people and whose consequence is a rupture in relationships. Thus we would claim that justice, restorative justice, is being served when efforts are being made to work for healing, for forgiveness and for reconciliation.

Once amnesty is granted, and this has to happen immediately all the conditions laid down in the Act have been met, the criminal and civil liability of the perpetrator, and of the state in the case of its servants, are expunged. The effect of amnesty is as if the offence had never happened, since the perpetrator's court record relating to that offence becomes a tabula rasa, a blank page. This means that the victim loses the right to sue for civil damages in compensation from the perpetrator. That is indeed a high price to ask the victims to pay, but it is the price those who negotiated our relatively peaceful transition from repression to democracy believed the nation had to ask of victims.

Our freedom has been bought at a very great price. But to compute the price properly, we should compare the high level of stability that we enjoy with the turmoil and upheaval that have so sadly character-ised similar radical change in the former Soviet Union, not to mention the awful carnage and instability in the former Yugoslavia, where some are being sought by the international community to answer charges of being responsible for horrendous war crimes. Most victims of apartheid violations of human rights were well represented by those who had their tacit mandate to speak on their behalf. They were generally ready to accept the decisions their representatives came to as the closest they could hope to get to fulfilling their aspirations, taking into account the prevailing circum-stances and the realities that had to be contended with.

In January 1999 I described the Truth and Reconciliation Com-mission process to a large gathering in a synagogue in Jerusalem. There, as in most other such meetings, I was accosted by someone who spoke very passionately about the moral requirement of justice which our process had seemed to undermine. He was strongly of the opinion (shared, I suspect, by many there and elsewhere) that morally speaking such an arrangement could really only be entered into by the victims themselves and not by others, however lofty their motives. I was, I hope, able to satisfy him on that point by my response. And it is this: those who negotiated our reasonably peaceful transition included in their delegations on the liberation movements' side those who were themselves victims of the viciousness of apartheid. Many had been detained, harassed, imprisoned, tortured and exiled, and before all this had happened to them had been victims in various ways of the injustice and oppression of apartheid. They could all speak of it from personal experience. Almost all of them, for instance, were disenfranchised until that memorable day in April 1994: they had never voted in the land of their birth until that day. They had suffered the humiliations of the iniquitous pass laws and had seen their people uprooted and dumped as if they were rubbish in the massive forced population removal schemes that had traumatised so many from that community. I was thus able to reassure my Jewish questioner that the negotiators had not acted presumptuously, for they were speaking about what they and their loved ones had lived through.

When the election results came in, far from these negotiators being repudiated for not reflecting the views and the attitudes of their constituencies, they were massively endorsed in a landslide election victory that brought the ANC to the helm of a government of National Unity. It was these selfsame, now elected, representatives who gave us our new constitution and who, in accordance with its provisions, passed the Act that brought the Truth and Reconciliation Commission into being. It was not the work of some idealistic upstarts but the product of hard-nosed politicians, who usually have an eye on the next election and would not normally be caught doing anything that was likely to alienate the voters who put them into office. These politicians have operated under the leadership of Nelson Mandela and his successor, Thabo Mbeki. Had what they did in the Act been at variance with the feelings of their constituency, that would have been reflected in their ratings in opinion polls. After three years of the Truth and Reconciliation process, and many controversial amnesty decisions, Nelson Mandela scored nearly eight out of ten, and Mr Mbeki nearly seven, in the popularity stakes as political leaders. (Their closest rival trailed at a disturbing three.) This seemed to indicate that, despite the electorate's natural disillusionment with the first post-oppression government, and its unfulfilled promises and deficits in fulfilling expectations, the ANC was still being endorsed. More recently, the political parties which supported the establishment of the Commission received the support of about 90 per cent of voters in the 1999 election. In a memorable turn of phrase used by one of my teachers at King's College, London, 'it would not be unreasonable to assert' that those who had negotiated and who produced the Truth and Reconciliation Commission did in fact have the credentials to speak on behalf of the victims, and have been heartily endorsed in so doing.

They could claim they were speaking as victims themselves when they accepted that part of the price for getting us to this point would be to expunge the right of the victim not only to press criminal charges but to claim civil damages in compensation for their loss. This is a position that was not arrived at lightly. It was something that caused a great deal of anguish, but it is clear even in the case of civil damages that had those applying for amnesty known that it might remove their criminal liability but not their civil liability, it is highly unlikely that they would have come forward at all. The carrot that drew them to the Truth and Reconciliation Commission would have been significantly diminished. We can conclude that many more would have taken the risk (as many in the former South African Defence Force did after the acquittal of General Malan and his co-accused) of possible prosecution in the knowledge that their complicity in awful atrocities had remained hidden because they were conspirators sworn to silence or had covenanted with their colleagues to perjure themselves. The solution arrived at was not perfect but it was the best that could be had in the circumstances – the truth in exchange for the freedom of the perpetrators.

The denial of the right of victims to claim compensation in the civil courts raises the whole matter of reparations, an aspect of the

Commission's work that often receives too little attention but is quite crucial to the process of establishing reconciliation. As we said in our Report:

> Without adequate reparation and rehabilitation measures, there can be no healing and reconciliation, either at an individual or a community level . . . In addition . . . reparation is essential to counterbalance amnesty. The granting of amnesty denies victims the right to institute civil claims against perpetrators. The government should thus accept responsibility for reparation.

In his Constitutional Court judgement, Judge Mahomed has lucidly and eloquently pointed out that 'nuanced and individualised reparations' could offer a more imaginative way of addressing the massive problems created by the legacy of apartheid than allowing the limited number of victims who might successfully sue the state to pursue their civil claims:

> The families of those whose fundamental human rights were invaded by torture and abuse are not the only victims who have endured 'untold suffering and injustice' in consequence of the crass inhumanity of apartheid which so many have had to endure for so long. Generations of children born and yet to be born will suffer the consequences of poverty, of malnutrition, of homelessness, of illiteracy and disempowerment generated and sustained by the institutions of apartheid and its manifest effects on life and living for so many. The country has neither the resources nor the skills to reverse fully these massive wrongs. It will take many years of strong commitment, sensitivity and labour to 'reconstruct our society' so as to fulfill the legitimate dreams of new generations exposed to real opportunities for advancement denied to preceding generations initially by the execution of apartheid itself and for a long time after its formal demise, by its relentless consequences. The resources of the state have to be deployed imaginatively, wisely, efficiently and equitably, to facilitate the reconstruction process in a manner which best brings relief and hope to the widest sections of the community, developing for the benefit of the entire nation the latent human potential and resources of every

person who has directly or indirectly been burdened with the heritage of the shame and the pain of our racist past.

Those negotiators of the constitution and leaders of the nation who were required to address themselves to these agonising problems must have been compelled to make hard choices. They could have chosen to direct that the limited resources of the state be spent by giving preference to the formidable delictual [civil] claims of those who had suffered from acts of murder, torture or assault perpetrated by servants of the state, diverting to that extent, desperately needed funds in the crucial areas of education, housing and primary health care. They were entitled to permit a different choice to be made between competing demands inherent in the problem. They could have chosen to direct that the potential liability of the state be limited in respect of any civil claims by differentiating between those . . . [whose claims related to events which occurred too long ago to be eligible for damages] and those whose claims were of such recent origin that a defence of prescription would have failed. They were entitled to reject such a choice on the grounds that it was irrational. They could have chosen to saddle the state with liability for claims made by insurance companies which had compensated institutions for delictual acts performed by the servants of the state and to that extent again divert funds otherwise desperately needed to provide food for the hungry, roofs for the homeless and blackboards and desks for those struggling to obtain admission to desperately overcrowded schools. They were entitled to permit the claims of such schoolchildren and the poor and the homeless to be preferred.

The election made by the makers of the constitution was to permit Parliament to favour 'the reconstruction of society' involving in the process a wider concept of 'reparation', which would allow the state to take into account the competing claims on its resources but, at the same time, to have regard to the 'untold suffering' of individuals and families whose fundamental human rights had been invaded during the conflict of the past. In some cases such a family may best be assisted by a reparation which allows the young in this family to maximise their potential through bursaries and scholarships; in other cases the most effective reparation might take the form of occupational training and rehabilitation; in still other cases complex surgical interventions and medical help may be facilitated; still others might need subsidies to prevent eviction from homes they can no longer maintain and in suitable cases the deep grief of the traumatised may most effectively be assuaged by facilitating the erection of a tombstone on the grave of a departed one with a public acknowledgement of his or her valour and nobility. There might have to be differentiation between the form and quality of the reparations made to two persons who have suffered exactly the same damage in consequence of the same unlawful act but where one person now enjoys lucrative employment from the state and the other lives in penury.[1]

The law, and the Commission's final recommendations to President Mandela, made provision for those who were designated victims under the Act to be eligible for reparation. The Commissioners deliberately tried to avoid using the word 'compensation'. We agreed that there was no way in which anyone could claim to compensate, for instance, a family for the brutal murder of their beloved husband, father and breadwinner. There is no way of computing the devastation of such a loss. Moreover, if we were to try to compensate them, would victims be eligible for the same compensation for the same kind of loss despite all kinds of difference in circumstances? Thus our recommendations to the President and parliament provided that a sum of money reasonably significant in amount would be paid to those designated as victims, but that it would be acknowledged that it was really meant to be symbolic rather than substantial. The nation said, in effect, to victims: 'We acknowledge that you suffered a gross violation of your rights. Nothing can ever replace your loved one. But as a nation we are saying, we are sorry, we have opened the wounds of your suffering and sought to cleanse them; this reparation is as balm, an ointment, being poured over the wounds to assist in their healing.'

The Act which established the Truth and Reconciliation Commission exhorted it to be 'victim friendly' in trying to restore the human and civil dignity of victims. But one of its major weaknesses is that perpetrators have been granted amnesty as soon as their applications have been successful, whereas in the case of the victims, the Commission could only make recommendations to the President some years into the process, when our Report was handed to him. In his turn, the President would take those recommendations he had accepted to parliament, which in its turn would function through a special committee. This committee's recommendations would then be approved finally by parliament, at which point reparations would hopefully be granted to the victims. It is, unfortunately, a convoluted process and as a consequence no final reparation had been approved three years after the Commission got under way, while all this time perpetrators had been granted amnesty. One can very well understand the frustration and anger of disgruntled victims who came before the Commission, as well as the cynicism of harsh critics who pooh-poohed the vaunted victim-friendliness of the Commission and claimed that the process was really perpetrator-friendly.

We at the Commission have expressed our own dissatisfaction with this aspect of the law. As a consequence, what was termed 'urgent interim relief' began to be paid to the 20,000 or so victims whom the Truth and Reconciliation Commission had designated at the stage when the Report was handed to the President on 29 October 1998. This urgent relief consisted of a uniform amount, usually no more than R2,000 (US$330) per victim.

In addition to the urgent relief, we recommended in our Report that the state should pay 'individual reparation grants'. Our hope is that nearly all the victims will qualify for final reparation grants of up to R23,000 (US $3,830) a year, payable for six years. We estimated the cost to the country at R2.9 billion (about US $477 million). At the time of writing, the government had budgeted a total of one-fifth of this, payable over three years.

Our recommendation for individual grants of money raises a number of questions. Can a monetary value be given to suffering? Can the country afford to pay even this amount, taking into account the various competing demands being placed on an exchequer strapped for cash? If apartheid itself was a gross abuse of human rights, as condemned by five senior judges, and a crime against humanity, then in a very real sense all who had suffered under this evil system should surely be designated victims? Where was the fairness in all this? What about those who had been forcibly moved, or those whose lives had been more or less permanently blighted because of the inferior education they had received, or who would have been affected by the preventable deficiency diseases they contracted because of an inequitable allocation of resources along racial lines? The list could indeed be almost endless.

None of us in the Commission doubted that there was a measure of arbitrariness in the way the law limited the meaning of human rights violations. But it was clear that the legislature felt the need to deal with something manageable in scope. Reparations *could* have been extended backwards a great deal further than 1960 – perhaps to 1948 when the National Party first came to power and embarked on their orgy of racist legislation designed to make the majority of South Africans second-class citizens in the land of their birth by systematic-ally abrogating their fundamental human rights. However, I feel parliament's decision was eminently sensible, giving us a reasonable chance of accomplishing our task. It also ensured that the nation would not be bogged down in dealing with the past for so long that we were held to ransom by it, effectively sabotaging the peaceful transition.

We used the same rationale in recommending to the government that only those victims who had approached the Commission should qualify for reparations, imposing what we called a 'closed list' of victims. We argued that people had been given the opportunity to testify through an extensive publicity campaign and only those who had taken the trouble to testify or to make a statement should benefit from reparations. It would have been unmanageable for the govern-ment to commit itself to paying reparations when we had no way of estimating how many victims there were.

Nobody was ever under any illusions about the significance of the reparations. The Minister of Justice, Mr Dullah Omar, under whose auspices the Truth and Reconciliation Commission operated, quite rightly said in the debate that followed the presentation of our Report that we were a nation of victims and, perhaps more importantly, of survivors. He also suggested that communal reparations would have to be considered as well, since often it had been communities that had been devastated more than individuals. Most sensible people would concur with that, though I would still want to maintain that everything should be done to ensure that those entitled to individual reparations were not cheated out of them. After all, they had given up their right to sue for damages, and they ought not to be made to sacrifice too excessively.

We in the Commission were often deeply humbled that those who came before us were frequently so modest in their expectations and requests. 'Can I have a tombstone erected for my child?' 'Could the Commission help to find the remains of my son, even just a bone, so that we could give him a decent burial?' 'Could I get assistance to educate my children?' It would be a very sad day if we were to disappoint those with such pathetic requests. We are aware of the enormous pressures on government resources, and distressingly hard choices will have to be made.

The Commission recommended too that streets and schools could be named after fallen heroes and communal facilities – such as clinics, community centres, recreational facilities – erected in their memory, and this has already begun to happen. We also thought there should be monuments and memorials to honour those to whom we owe our freedom. These should be as inclusive as possible, and designed to help us to remember in a positive, rather than a vindictive, way; memorials that would not alienate some but would have the capacity to contribute to the process of healing and reconciliation; that would give us memories that would bind us together after so long enduring things that were designed to tear us apart and instill hostility and disharmony. I hope we will learn to celebrate occasions and events which have brought us together, such as our historic election, the inauguration of Nelson Mandela as President, or our victories in the rugby World Cup or the African Nations Cup in soccer, when we discovered that we were indeed the rainbow nation.

CHAPTER FIVE

Up and running

I thought I was about to retire as Archbishop when in September 1995 my penultimate meeting of our synod of bishops unanimously nominated me to the President for membership of the Truth and Reconciliation Commission. I was one of about forty-five who made the shortlist from an original list of approximately 200 nominations. We were interviewed by a multi-party panel in public hearings held in several centres of South Africa. The panel sent twenty-five names to the President who, in consultation with the cabinet of his Government of National Unity, chose seventeen people to be the new Truth and Reconciliation Commission. I was appointed Chairperson, with Dr Alex Boraine as the Deputy Chair.

When the President requests, then lesser mortals have little option. Who could say no to Mr Mandela? My much-longed-for break went out of the window. For nearly three years we would be involved in the devastating but also exhilarating work of the Commission, listening to the harrowing tales of horrendous atrocities and being uplifted by the extraordinary generosity of spirit of so many of our compatriots. It was an incredible privilege.

The President established the Commission in the *Government Gazette* of 15 December 1995 and we held our first meeting on the next day, 16 December. For those looking for omens, it did seem auspicious that we should have gathered together on the public holiday that was now called the Day of Reconciliation. This particular holiday had undergone an interesting evolution. At one time it had been known as Dingaan's Day, not in honour of the Zulu king of that name but instead a jingoistic commemoration of the unlikely victory of a small group of Afrikaner *Voortrekkers*, those who had left the Cape in high dudgeon in the 1830s when they were incensed by British policies that appeared to want to treat the 'natives' as somehow equal to the whites. They undertook what came to be called the Great Trek, perceiving themselves as somehow re-enacting the Exodus of God's chosen people from their bondage in Egypt. They were the new elect, God's chosen, escaping from the bondage of British imperialism. In 1838 one of the Voortrekker bands, faced with a battle against *impis* (regiments of the Zulu army), had prayed fervently to God to bless them in the coming unequal struggle, promising in a covenant that should God grant them victory over these benighted native hordes they and their posterity would forever observe that day as a solemn commemoration. They adopted their new strategy of forming a circle with their wagons as a kind of mobile fortress – the *laager* – from whose safety they would hope to repulse their foes. A miracle happened. God answered their prayers and they inflicted a resounding defeat on an enemy that had vastly outnumbered them. From that time on Afrikaners celebrated their victory at the Battle of Blood River on 16 December, a victory which in their view clearly demonstrated their superiority over the black heathen natives. The public holiday became notorious: black South Africans dreaded the advent of Dingaan's Day. I recall as a small boy how we were warned that awful things would happen to you if you left the ghetto townships and went to the white man's town that day. Most blacks did in fact avoid the towns like the plague on that holiday. There were many hair-raising stories of what had happened to people foolhardy enough to ignore the advice, how they had been subjected to racist assaults, jeered at and taunted with humiliating remarks. There were stories of how black men with beards had had them virtually torn off their faces because the whites regarded beards as a distinctive feature of the Voortrekker and it was intolerable for a black to ape his master's forebears in this fashion.

It was bizarre in the extreme that such a sectional, chauvinistic holiday was known as Dingaan's Day, as if it was the Zulu king who was being honoured instead of his defeat that was being recalled. And so the National Party government changed the name to the Day of the Covenant. It was deemed inappropriate to open old wounds of a smarting defeat for the Zulus at a time when the government was trying to woo them to accept the policy of Bantustan homelands. Under this policy, blacks would enjoy autonomy in their own tribally-defined little states with a spurious independence recognised only by South Africa and its satellites and by no one else in the world; in this Alice-in-Wonderland scenario black South Africans would become aliens in the land of their birth, unable to claim political rights in South Africa itself. This policy was touted seriously by the Nationalists as South Africa participating in the new process of decolonisation and helping people evolve into new nations, when all it really was, was the old policy of divide and rule, of encouraging tribalism to counter the movement to unite black South Africans as Africans and not as members of different tribal entities. The upholders of white supremacy were ready to try anything however stupid and immoral.

The focus of the celebrations on the renamed holiday was to be more religious – it would be the promise, the covenant that those Voortrekkers had made with God on the eve of the battle that a God-given victory over their foe would be commemorated in perpetuity as a religious observance. From this new understanding it was a relatively small step to focus on promoting healing, reconciliation and the recognition that South Africa – in the words of the Freedom Charter, adopted by the liberation movement in 1955 – 'belonged to all who lived in it'.

The holiday had come to embody the philosophy of the Truth and Reconciliation Commission – that more and more South Africans would find commonalities, things that bound a diverse people together, those that were inclusive and not sectional; events and people and occasions that did not exalt one section by denigrating another. This was a tall order for a society where people had been alienated from one another for so long and where unjust and discriminatory laws had reinforced their mutual hostility. But if we were going to survive as a rainbow people then this was a process that just had to succeed.

So it was that the new Commission met on this Day of Reconciliation.

We met at Bishopscourt, the official residence of the Anglican Archbishop of Cape Town. There was also a piquancy to this, because it had at one time been Bosheuvel, the residence of Jan van Riebeeck, who in 1652 became the first white settler in South Africa. Sent from Holland to the Cape to establish a halfway station for sailors on their way to the East, one of the things he did was to plant a bitter almond hedge to keep the indigenous Khoikhoi people out of the area he settled. The remains of that hedge are still visible near Bishopscourt – a hedge that, as journalist Allister Sparks has pointed out,[1] symbolised so much about the South Africa that was to be. Van Riebeeck had brought Europe to Africa, and the natives became aliens to be kept out. The ultimate fruit of that symbolic hedge was the portion of South Africa's conflict-laden past, characterised by hostility between the white people and other races, that our Commission was created to deal with. Although we were asked to look at a period of thirty-four years, from 1960 to 1994, we were really talking about what had been happening in our beautiful land since 1652.

For me there was a special poignancy about meeting at Bishopscourt. Frequently in the late 1980s it had been the venue of meetings by leaders of the growing resistance to the increasingly repressive apartheid regime. It was one of these meetings which helped to organise the mammoth march of 13 September 1989, which set off the huge demonstrations that took place all over the country in succeeding weeks, helping to bring about the epoch-making changes that Mr de Klerk announced on 2 February 1990. The march arose out of calls to boycott the racist election of 6 September 1989. Around Cape Town, several people were killed by the security forces whilst demonstrating peacefully. Youngsters were some of the casualties – shot even when they were standing in the yards of their homes. I recall how, when my staff reported that about twenty people had already been killed, I went into the Bishopscourt chapel quite distraught, and tearfully remonstrated with God: 'How could you let all this happen? How could you let them do this to us?' I don't claim to have a hot-line to heaven, but I emerged from that wrestling with God knowing that God wanted us to march. I announced to my somewhat startled staff that we were going to march for peace, to demonstrate the sense of outrage that possessed most inhabitants of Cape Town, who needed to find a way of expressing their revulsion.

It was also at Bishopscourt that Nelson and Winnie Mandela spent his first night of freedom on 11 February 1990. After an evening of taking calls from presidents and kings, including one from the White House, it was here that he met with his closest colleagues to discuss their future strategy now he was free. I went into that meeting and started a hymn which is almost another national anthem, *'Lizalis' idinga lakho'* ('Let your will be done, O Lord God of truth') and that group belted it out as if their very lives depended on it. I said a prayer of thanksgiving for the wonders of God's ways, praying for His mercy for all gathered there and for our country. Then I left them to their deliberations. It was in the gardens at Bishopscourt on the following day that he conducted his first news conference after his release. It was also in Bishopscourt that church leaders later convened an important summit of black political leaders, when some of the most radical agreed for the first time to sit at the same table with leaders from the controversial Bantustan homelands, whom they had been castigating as untouchables for collaborating with the apartheid government.

The Commissioners meeting at Bishopscourt were as diverse a group of South Africans as you could ever hope to assemble. There were sixteen of us, as one Commissioner was unable to attend. There were ten blacks and six whites, including two Afrikaners. We were Coloured, Indian, African and white, the entire racial spectrum in our race-obsessed society. Politically we had everything from the left to the conservative white right-wing. There were a number of Christians, a Muslim, a Hindu, some lapsed believers and possibly an agnostic or two.

Dr Boraine, the Deputy Chair, had once served as an opposition member of parliament, where his views led to strong attacks on him by pro-apartheid MPs, but he had left in frustration in the 1980s to found and work in extra-parliamentary organisations working for democracy. Ms Mary Burton was known as one of the stalwarts of the Black Sash, a women's movement which worked for the rights of black South Africans. Chris de Jager, Senior Counsel, had been a member of far right-wing parties and an acting judge. The Right Revd Bongani Finca was a high-profile Eastern Cape church leader who had fought apartheid. Ms Sisi Khampepe was an attorney who had been deeply involved in the struggle for labour rights. Mr Richard Lyster was a human-rights lawyer who had worked in the strife-torn province of Natal. Mr Wynand Malan was a lawyer who had been a member of parliament for the ruling National Party, then had broken away to help form a new white opposition party. Dr Khoza Mgojo was a former president of the Methodist Church, and also president of the South African Council of Churches, and a prominent member of a group of Natal church leaders working for peace in that province. Ms Hlengiwe Mkhize was a psychologist who had worked as a mental health specialist in the civil service.

Mr Dumisa Ntsebeza, who was often to act in Alex Boraine's or my place, was a former political prisoner and leading human-rights lawyer in the Eastern Cape. Dr Wendy Orr had gained renown when she had secured a court interdict against police in the Eastern Cape after finding evidence of torture among detainees while working as a state doctor. Advocate Denzil Potgieter, Senior Counsel, was a Cape Town lawyer who had appeared for the defence in political trials. Dr Mapule Ramashala was a clinical psychologist and former exile who had a top position in the Medical Research Council. Dr Fazel Randera was a medical doctor who had long been active in the struggle against apartheid. Ms Yasmin Sooka was also a lawyer and was the South African leader of the multi-faith World Conference on Religion and Peace. Ms Glenda Wildschut was a psychiatric nurse and leader of the Trauma Centre for the Victims of Violence in Cape Town, and had considerable experience in dealing with victims of torture and conflict.

At our Bishopscourt meeting (we later moved into our own offices) we allocated Commissioners to the three constituent committees of the Commission. Fifteen of the seventeen Commissioners were split between the Committee on Human Rights Violations, which I also chaired, and the Committee on Reparation and Rehabilitation. The Commission had the power to appoint additional committee members, who were not full members of the Commission, to these two committees. In choosing these extra members, we took very seriously regional, gender, political and religious representivity into account, making good any gaps in the Commission's composition. For instance, we ensured that there was at least one Jew, as well as a leader of the white Dutch Reformed Church.

Two Commissioners who were lawyers were appointed to the Committee on Amnesty. Soon afterwards the President appointed three judges to make up the initial complement of five on that committee – which was increased subsequently to nineteen in an effort to speed up the process of handling over 7,000 amnesty applications. (The Amnesty Committee had a peculiar position in the Commission: it was headed by judges who were not Commissioners but were appointed directly by the President, and it was autonomous in its decision-making powers. Neither I nor any Commissioner outside the committee had any influence over its decisions to grant or refuse amnesty; the Commission was statutorily prohibited from reviewing its decisions.)

The Commission also decided at one of its early meetings to regionalise its operations. As a result we opened offices in Durban, East London, Johannesburg and Cape Town, the latter being also the Commission's headquarters. Very soon we had a staff of nearly 350 in place and we hit the ground running. A great deal of credit for this goes to Dr Boraine, who worked marvels in finding office accommodation and appointing staff.

I would not wish on my worst enemy the task of starting up from scratch a huge operation such as ours turned out to be. But we managed and ended up with an efficient outfit with a most outstanding, conscientious and dedicated team of Commissioners, committee members and staff. It was a great privilege to be captain of such a superb team. It is always easy to be captain of a winning side, which is what we became, and I want to pay a very warm tribute to them. Two of our fellow Commissioners resigned before we handed in our Report: Dr Ramashala was appointed Principal and Vice-Chancellor of the University of Durban-Westville, whilst Advocate de Jager, formerly a member of the Conservative Party, felt he could not continue with a Commission with which he was at odds. He has remained as an Amnesty Committee member. Thus we ended up with only one Afrikaner Commissioner.

I suggested at another early meeting that it might be a worthwhile gesture for us all to resign any membership of political parties or organisations we might have. Quite rightly it was pointed out that people had almost certainly been nominated for membership of the Truth and Reconciliation Commission at least in part because of their political affiliations. We were expected to bring all that we were, all our personal and corporate baggage, our political biases and perceptions, our insights and blind spots, all this to bear on the crucial work of this important Commission. Most Commissioners argued that we would be engaging in a misleading charade if those who were members of political parties resigned from them. They said it was being somewhat disingenuous and less than totally transparent to pretend that we would be apolitical. We would be even-handed but that did not mean that the jury was still out on issues such as whether apartheid was evil or only a good policy that had gone awry in its application. Most of us were on record as asserting quite categorically that apartheid was intrinsically in and of itself evil. It had in part been this condemnatory stance that had given us the credibility which had led to our appointment on the Commission.

So we were broadly representative, though we were criticised from day one by some of the Afrikaans media and political leadership as a flawed commission, packed with those who were dismissively described as 'struggle' types (referring to the anti-apartheid struggle) and so biased in favour of the ANC. They called for a commission in which those who had supported apartheid would equal in number those who had been on the other side. They hardly noticed the arrogance of their demand, so typical of how they had organised things when the vast majority of the land had had absolutely no say at all in how they were to be ruled. The supporters of the old and discredited apartheid dispensation still wanted things to be organised in the old, skewed way. They declared, without benefit of any evidence whatsoever (since we had not even begun working), that the Truth and Reconciliation Commission was intended to be a witch-hunt against the old order and specifically against the Afrikaners.

We sought to disabuse them of this notion by declaring that some of us had been committed passionately to reconciliation a very long time ago, long before there had been any thought of a Truth and Reconciliation Commission, and that we were dedicated to the healing of a traumatised and wounded people too fervently to want to jeopardise that enterprise by being anything but scrupulously fair. I told a group of white Dutch Reformed Church leaders who expressed similar concerns that they would have to look at my track record to depend on my own personal integrity. I reminded them that many of them had believed that I was opposed to apartheid only for political reasons, despite my protestations to the contrary, and that they had taken it for granted that I would be muted in my criticism of an ANC-led government – if I voiced any at all. They had been certain I would enter the public political arena by accepting a political post. I pointed out that, on the contrary, I had not sought or been offered any political position and that very soon after the ANC took office I criticised them for accepting unduly high salaries. I suggested they should wait and see what sort of report we would produce and judge us on that basis.

(I don't suppose in the event that they are likely to be too vocal about the fact that we were true to our promise to be even-handed, so much so that the ANC complained and wanted to block the publication of our report, claiming it was saying things which were not in fact the case – that we placed those who fought against apartheid on the same moral plane as those who had implemented apartheid.)

Sadly we were not ever able to win over some of the more vocal and indeed strident in the Afrikaner community, who held on to their jaundiced views whatever evidence we might put forward to demonstrate our commitment to being even-handed. We did our very best to paint as complete a picture of the gross violations of human rights that had occurred in our country as a result of the political conflict of the past. We apportioned blame in ways designed to help cultivate a culture of accountability and respect for human rights. We were determined to carry out this crucial function without fear or favour and it seems the world and most reasonable South Africans believe we did not do too bad a job.

We were, as I said, broadly representative of South African society. That representativeness was a vital attribute, but it caused us a major headache. We came from diverse backgrounds and we were to discover that apartheid had affected us all in different ways. We learned to our chagrin that we were a microcosm of South African society, more deeply wounded than we had at first imagined. We found that we were often very suspicious of one another and that it was not easy to develop real trust in one another. We realised only later that we were all victims of a potent conditioning which gave us ready-made judgments of those who belonged to other groupings, although we would, most of us, have protested vehemently that we were not using stereotypes.

Our meetings for the first year or so were hell. It was not easy to arrive at a common mind as each of us tried to stake our claim to the turf and to establish our particular space. You wondered as a black whether your white colleague would have reacted in that way to a fellow white, and vice versa. Some members were castigated for being liberal whites – 'liberal' being a swear word in South Africa – intent on manipulating things so that they would be top dogs. As it happened the first staff we appointed were all white, and all kinds of alarm bells started ringing, with some members immediately fearing that the Commission would be taken over by whites pushing a white agenda. I had not been prepared for this atmosphere because I had been spoiled by our church meetings, especially by our synod of bishops meetings, which we all looked forward to eagerly. They were so congenial, so affirming, so positive, with none of the barbs, innuendoes and slights, real and imagined, that characterised those first Truth and Reconciliation Commission meetings. We were certainly authentic in reflecting the alienations, chasms and suspicions that were part and parcel of our apartheid society. We were a useful paradigm for our nation, for if we could eventually be welded into a reasonably coherent, united and reconciled group then there was hope for South Africa.

It is interesting that the President appointed an Archbishop as chairperson of the Commission and not, for instance, a judge, since we were to some extent a quasi-judicial body. Seven of the Commissioners were lawyers, the legal profession thus possessing the largest representation. But there were three active ordained ministers, all of whom had been the national heads of their denominations. In addition, Dr Boraine had at one time been the youngest President of the Methodist Conference, before he had resigned as a minister to go into politics. So you could say that there were four ordained Commissioners and that was bound to have a marked influence on our deliberations and on how we carried out our work.

The President must have believed that our work would be profoundly spiritual. After all forgiveness, reconciliation and reparation were not the normal currency in political discourse. There it was more normal to demand satisfaction, to pay back in the same coin, to give as good as you got, to believe it's a dog-eat-dog world. Most politicians were not there to heal, to redress imbalances and to reduce differences. They were elected because they were different and they existed to accentuate differences. Forgiveness, confession and reconciliation were far more at home in the religious sphere.

Despite our diversity, the Commissioners agreed to my proposal at the first meeting that we should go on a retreat, where we sought to enhance our spiritual resources and to sharpen our sensitivities. We sat at the feet of Dr Francis Cull, my own spiritual counsellor, whilst we kept silence for a day, seeking to open ourselves to the movement and guidance of the transcendent Spirit, however conceived or named. Near the end of our term as a Commission we had another retreat, a deeply moving experience on Robben Island. Before it we went on a tour of the island and were steeped in all its history and anguish as we processed from one cell to another and realised the price that had been paid to bring us to the point we had reached in our country. By then we had grown a great deal closer to one another.

The Commission also accepted my call for prayer at the beginning and end of our meetings, and at midday when I asked for a pause for recollection and prayer. In the Human Rights Violations Committee, we agreed that when victims and survivors came to our victim-oriented hearings to testify about their often heart-rending experiences, we would have a solemn atmosphere with prayers, hymns and ritual candle-lighting to commemorate those who had died in the struggle. When I asked before our first hearings in the Eastern Cape whether I should preside over the proceedings in my purple Archbishop's cassock, part of my public *persona*, the Commission said I should, with my Hindu colleague insisting.

As soon as I was appointed to the Truth and Reconciliation Commission, I asked the secretariat of the world-wide Anglican Communion to alert the nuns and monks of the religious communities of our Church to our desperate need for regular intercession during the life of the Commission. Thus we knew that we were surrounded on a regular basis by the fervent prayers of at least this group of Christians. I know from other contacts that we were being sustained by the love and prayers of many round the world, and I want to say a very big thank you to them for this wonderful work. Whatever we may have achieved is due in large measure to this cloud of witnesses surrounding us and upholding us. Most of us felt that what we were being asked to undertake was profoundly religious and spiritual.

Very few people objected to the heavy spiritual, and indeed Christian, emphasis of the Commission. When I was challenged on it by journalists, I told them I was a religious leader and had been chosen as who I was. I could not pretend I was someone else. I operated as who I was and that was accepted by the Commission. It meant that theological and religious insights and perspectives would inform much of what we did and how we did it. We were only too happy to be guided where it was appropriate by the health-care providers on the Commission – the psychologists, medical doctors and a nurse, who made very significant contributions to the evolution of the policies on reparation and rehabilitation that we eventually presented as our recommendations to the President.

As I grow older I am pleasantly surprised at how relevant theology has become, as I see it, to the whole of life. In our particular work as the Commission it was a relief to discover that in fact we were all really children of Adam and Eve. When God accosted Adam and remonstrated with him about contravening the order He had given about not eating a certain fruit, Adam was less than forthcoming in accepting responsibility for that disobedience. He shifted the blame to Eve, and when God turned to her, she did the same and tried to pass the buck. (We are not told how the serpent responded to the blame pushed on to it.) So we should not have been surprised at how reluctant most people were to acknowledge their responsibility for the atrocities of apartheid. They were just being true descendants of Adam and Eve when they denied what they had done or blamed everyone and everything except themselves.

There is a salutary riposte to our tendency to push blame on to others in a book by the Harvard theologian Harvey Cox with the lovely title, *On Not Leaving It To The Snake*. This helped me to be a great deal less judgmental and to avoid gloating at the misfortune of others. It was particularly important in the Commission's encounter with the perpetrators of some of the most horrendous atrocities. So frequently we in the Commission were quite appalled at the depth of depravity to which human beings could sink and we would, most of us, say that those who committed such deeds were monsters because the deeds were monstrous. But theology prevents us from doing this. Theology reminded me that however diabolical the act, it did not turn the perpetrator into a demon. We had to distinguish between the deed and the perpetrator, between the sinner and the sin: to hate and condemn the sin whilst being filled with compassion for the sinner. The point is that if perpetrators were to be despaired of as monsters and demons then we were thereby letting accountability go out the window by declaring that they were not moral agents to be held responsible for their deeds. Much more importantly, it meant that we abandoned all hope of their being able to change for the better. Theology says they still, despite the awfulness of their deeds, remain children of God with the capacity to repent, to be able to change. If that were not true, we should, as a Commission, have had to shut up shop, since we were operating on the premise that people could change, could recognise and acknowledge the error of their ways and so experience contrition, or at the very least remorse, and would at some point be constrained to confess their dreadful conduct and ask for forgiveness. If, however, they were dismissed as being monsters then they could not by definition engage in a process that was so deeply personal as that of forgiveness and reconciliation.

In this theology we can never give up on anyone because our God was one who had a particularly soft spot for sinners. The Good Shepherd in the parable Jesus told had been quite ready to leave ninety-nine perfectly well-behaved sheep in the wilderness in order to look for, not an attractive, fluffy little lamb – fluffy little lambs do not usually stray from their mothers – but for the troublesome, obstreperous old ram. This was the one on which the Good Shepherd expended so much energy. When he found it, it is highly unlikely to have had a beautiful fleece. It would almost certainly have been thoroughly bedraggled and perhaps have fallen into a ditch of dirty water and thus be smelling to high heaven. That was the sheep the Good Shepherd had gone after, and when he found it he did not pinch his nostrils in disgust. No, he took it and placed it gently on his shoulders and returned home to throw a party because he had found this lost one. And Jesus says there is *greater* joy in heaven over one sinner who repents than over ninety-nine needing no repentance.

Christians are constrained by the imperatives of this Gospel, the Good News of a God who had a bias for sinners contrary to the normal standards of the world. This God in Jesus Christ scandalised the prim and proper ones, the orthodox religious leaders, because he associated not with the respectable, not with the elite of society, but with the scum and the dregs and those on the fringes of society – the prostitutes, the sinners, the ostracised ones. None of us could in my theology ever consign anyone to hell as being ultimately irredeemable. When Jesus was crucified it was in the company of two thieves. One of them became repentant and Jesus promised that he would be in paradise with him on that day. The thrust of that story is that not one of us could say with any certainty that so-and-so has gone to perdition, because none of us could ever know whether even the most notorious sinner and evildoer has not at the eleventh hour repented and been forgiven, because our God is pre-eminently the God of grace.

What we are, what we have, even our salvation, is all a gift, not to be achieved but to be received as a gift freely given. God's bias in favour of sinners is so immense that it is said we will be surprised at those we will find in heaven whom we had not expected to encounter there. (Conversely we would be surprised by those not there whom we had expected to find. That is if we got there ourselves!) Ultimately no person or situation in this theology is an irredeemable cause devoid of all hope.

God does not give up on anyone, for God loved us from all eternity, God loves us now and God will always love us, all of us, good and bad, for ever and ever. His love will not let us go, for God's love for all of us is unchanging and unchangeable. Someone has said there is nothing I can do to make God love me more, for God loves me perfectly already. And wonderfully, there is nothing I can do to make God love me less. God loves me as I am, to help me become all that I have it in me to become, and when I realise the deep love God has for me, I will strive for love's sake to do what pleases my Lover. Those who think this opens the door for moral laxity have obviously never been in love, for love is much more demanding than law. An exhausted mother, ready to drop into bed, will think nothing of sitting up all night with her sick child.

As I listened in the Truth and Reconciliation Commission to the stories of perpetrators of human rights violations, I realised how each of us has this capacity for the most awful evil – all of us. None of us could predict that if we had been subjected to the same influences, the same conditioning, we would not have turned out as these perpetrators. This is not to condone or excuse what they did. It is to be filled more and more with the compassion of God, looking on and weeping that one of His beloved had come to such a sad pass. We have to say to ourselves with deep feeling, not with a cheap pietism, 'There but for the grace of God go I.'

And, mercifully and wonderfully, as I listened to the stories of victims I marvelled at their magnanimity, that after so much suffering instead of lusting for revenge they had this extraordinary willingness to forgive. Then I thanked God that *all* of us, even I, have this remarkable capacity for good, for generosity, for magnanimity.

Theology helped us in the Truth and Reconciliation Commission to recognise that we inhabit a moral universe, that good and evil are real and that they matter. They are not just things of indifference. This is a moral universe which means that, despite all the evidence that seems to be to the contrary, there is no way that evil and injustice and oppression and lies can have the last word. For we who are Christians, the death and resurrection of Jesus Christ are proof positive that love is stronger than hate, that life is stronger than death, that light is stronger than darkness, that laughter, joy, compassion, gentleness and truth, all these are so much stronger than their ghastly counterparts.

We were seeing this unfolding before our very eyes as we sat in the Commission. Those who had strutted about arrogantly in the days of apartheid, dealing out death and injustice and apartheid's excesses with gay abandon, had never imagined in their wildest dreams that their involvement in abominations hatched out in secret would ever see the light of day. They had fondly expected to rule the roost for as long as they wished. Now it was all coming out, not as wild speculation or untested allegations. No, it was gushing forth from the mouths of perpetrators themselves: how they had abducted people, shot them, and burned their bodies or thrown them into crocodile-infested rivers. They helped us exhume more than fifty corpses of those they had abducted and then killed and buried secretly. Those ghastly and macabre secrets might have remained hidden except that this is a moral universe and truth will out.

During the dark days of the struggle, when the morale of our people was often low in the face of rampant evil, I used to say: 'This is a moral universe – the upholders of apartheid have already lost.' I also used to appeal to our white fellow South Africans, 'We are being nice to you. Join the winning side.' Those of us who struggled against apartheid have been vindicated in the most spectacular fashion. And the victory was for all of us, black and white together – the rainbow people of God.

CHAPTER SIX

Victims – or a nation of survivors?

In a way, the parameters established in the law that set up the Truth and Reconciliation Commission were arbitrary. We could quite legitimately have gone right back to the days of Jan van Riebeeck; or said that all who were not white qualified automatically as victims since they had run the gauntlet of apartheid's viciousness. But this would have meant dealing with literally millions of people. Clearly that would not have been manageable in any way that would have contributed significantly to the vital process of healing and reconciling a wounded and divided people. It would also have been hopelessly lopsided, with virtually all the victims being black. That would have put paid from the start to any chance of this becoming a bridge-building process.

Sensibly, those who were negotiating the delicate business of the transition from repression to democracy opted for a limited and thus manageable exercise. The time limits they imposed were not entirely arbitrary. The date of the Sharpeville Massacre, 21 March 1960, was indeed a watershed because significant black political organisations were banned thereafter and thus transformed into liberation movements which reluctantly jettisoned non-violence and chose to engage in the armed struggle. The end date, 10 May 1994, was also highly significant, for that was the day we celebrated Nelson Mandela's inauguration as President. If any event might be said to mark the advent of the new dispensation, it was that day which demonstrated an irrevocable break with the past of conflict, alienation and domination of the many by the few. The Commission was required to deal with this manageable portion of our history in the relatively brief period of two years, later extended to nearly three. In order that the country would not have to be bogged down for too long in the necessarily divisive process of delving into its murky past, we presented our Report in October 1998, although the amnesty process continued into 1999 while the rest of the Commission was put into 'suspension'.

To establish the parameters of the Commission's work, the Act which established the Truth and Reconciliation Commission had to define the term 'gross violations of human rights'. This was restricted to killing (premeditated or not), abduction, torture and severe ill-treatment – a rather arbitrary definition which had at least two advantages. First, by limiting the mandate to these four categories it gave the Commission a manageable task that could hopefully be accomplished within the timespan allocated. Thabo Mbeki, Nelson Mandela's successor as President of the ANC and later of South Africa, made an impassioned plea to the Commission not to leave the new government a legacy of unfinished business, especially regarding amnesty matters. When presenting the ANC's evidence to the Commission in August 1996, he said:

It is also important that, within its lifetime, the Commission should complete the amnesty process, to ensure that the democratic state is not left with the responsibility of instituting criminal investigations and the possible prosecution of people for actions that took place during the period covered in the mandate of the TRC . . . We believe that the TRC should conclude its work as quickly as possible so that we do indeed let bygones be bygones and allow the nation to forgive a past it nevertheless dare not forget.

But the Act's definition was important for another crucial reason. It meant that it would indeed be possible for the Truth and Reconciliation Commission to be even-handed in the matter of designating people as victims, because the political affiliation of the perpetrator was irrelevant in determining whether a certain act or offence was a gross violation or not. If a Nationalist abducted someone or tortured or killed someone, then that constituted a gross violation of the human rights of the victim, and it would fall within the ambit of our Act if it was as a result of the conflict of the past. If an ANC member were guilty of the same offences then those would also constitute gross violations of human rights as defined by the Act. Thus there was legal equivalence between all, whether they had been upholders of apartheid or had sought to overthrow it.

We were at pains to point out that legal equivalence was, however, not the same thing as moral equivalence. A woman shoots and kills a man who is threatening to rape her. The act constitutes homicide. A car-hijacker kills the owner of the vehicle he wants to hijack. That death is also homicide. The woman's act would be declared justifiable homicide, and she might even be commended for her bravery. The hijacker would be guilty of culpable homicide and would be roundly condemned.

We have been criticised for what has been termed 'criminalising the liberation struggle' and insulting those who engaged in it by placing them on the same level as the upholders of apartheid. Nothing could be further from the truth. We obeyed the provisions of the Act. A gross violation is a gross violation whoever commits it and for whatever motive. Torture by a Nationalist is a gross violation. Torture by a member of the liberation movement is equally a gross violation of human rights.

We stated categorically that apartheid was a crime against humanity. We asserted equally vehemently that the liberation movements were conducting a just war because they had a just cause. But the Geneva Convention and the principles of the just war are quite clear that there must be justice in war. A just cause must be fought by just means.

The ANC conducted inquiries into the abuses in its camps outside South Africa and has apologised for such abuses as have been revealed. There would have been no reason to do this if a liberation struggle sanctifies every act committed in its name. The end does not justify the means.

It was important to reach out to as many South Africans as possible. Our aim in fact was to reach out to all South Africans; to engage them in the work of their Commission and to ensure that none would lose out by default, that all would realise that they had the opportunity to tell their stories and might be eligible for reparations. Our advertising campaign focused especially on the radio, which was more effective in reaching illiterate people. We put out pamphlets and posters with a distinctive logo and with slogans such as, 'The Truth Hurts, But Silence Kills'. We were very greatly assisted by the faith communities whose networks reached into every conceivable nook and cranny of South Africa. We owe a great debt of gratitude to the NGOs that cooperated with us. The international community generously contributed in personnel, in kind and in cash. Our own resources, considerable as they were compared to what had been allocated for similar commissions elsewhere, would have been stretched to the limits without all this additional help. We have indeed been singularly blessed. The world has been intrigued because it has hoped that there might be something to learn from the South African experience that could help resolve conflicts elsewhere.

We employed specially trained statement-takers who travelled all over the country. They were aided by volunteers who helped to take statements from those who thought they might fall within the ambit of our Act. As it happened, in the end we received well over 20,000 statements, more than any other similar commission has been able to muster. Some of the statements recorded more than one alleged violation and involved more than one potential victim.

Our very first hearing was to be held in East London in April 1996. One other characteristic of the Truth and Reconciliation Commission that contrasted with other Commissions elsewhere was its very public nature. It was originally suggested that the Amnesty Committee would do its work in camera, but the human-rights NGOs agitated very strongly against this and their view prevailed, giving the Commission an openness that has been much admired by people of other countries. There was an enormous amount of hard work involved in getting the show on the road so quickly. The logistics of holding a hearing were formidable. Statements had to be obtained, but then there was no guarantee that people would actually want to come forward. They might have been intimidated by those who had abused them; they might refuse to be regarded as victims since they believed themselves to be combatants in a struggle; they might be disillusioned, not believing any longer that anything worthwhile could be expected from those who were forever making promises and being so painfully slow on delivery.

We need not have worried. People definitely *did* want to tell their stories. They had been silenced for so long, sidelined for decades, made invisible and anonymous by a vicious system of injustice and oppression. Many bottled their feelings up for too long and when the chance came for them to tell their stories the floodgates were opened. However, we were distressed that not many white people came forward. Those who did were remarkable people.

We were greatly privileged to be given that glimpse into the secret places of the souls of so many of our compatriots, where they held their most intimate anguish and pain. I never ceased to marvel, after these wonderful people had each told their story, that when you looked at them they were so ordinary, so normal. Before they gave their testimony they laughed, they conversed, they went about their daily lives looking to all the world like healthy people with not a care in the world. And then you heard their stories and wondered how they had survived for so long when they had been carrying such a heavy burden of grief and anguish so quietly, unobtrusively, with dignity and simplicity. The resilience of those we arrogantly dismissed as 'the ordinary people', in the face of daunting challenges and harassment that would have been the undoing of lesser mortals, was in the end quite breathtaking. In my theology, as I have said, there are no ordinary people. Each one of us, because we are God's representative, is a very special person – a VSP – far more important and far more universal than your normal VIP.

We owe to these people a great deal more than we will ever know or be able to acknowledge. We had to ensure that they were really willing to testify, because they would in a sense become public property. There was no way we could predict how the media and the public would react and how they would treat those who were foolhardy enough to expose their grief in public. We provided counselling to those who came to our offices before they testified – an experience that would be, even at the best of times, gruelling.

We also provided those whom we called 'briefers', who accompanied the witnesses, sitting next to them as they testified, providing them with the comfort of their presence and passing a glass of water and the ubiquitous tissues to them when they broke down, as so many frequently did. (Some cynics disparagingly called us the Kleenex Commission.) We were scrupulous about the seating arrangements. Pride of place was reserved for the witnesses. We had to avoid any impression that they were in the dock, so they sat on the same level as the Commission panel hearing their testimony.

It was important that the witnesses should feel comfortable and at ease, so we insisted that they were free to tell their story in the language of their choice. This meant that we had to provide simultaneous translation, which added to the complications of arranging for a hearing. The witnesses could also be accompanied by a relative, who could sit with them as they testified. It could be something of a logistical nightmare arranging transport, accommodation and meals for all those who might attend a Commission hearing. My colleagues and the Commission staff did a remarkable job in bringing this all off without too many hiccups, even in small towns and rural areas where venues and facilities were often conspicuous by their absence. Many different places were used for the hearings – town halls, civic centres and especially church halls. The faith communities are to be warmly commended for all they have done to facilitate this aspect of our work.

The Commission was not universally welcomed and popular. There were those who were passionately opposed to it, particularly those who felt the Commission threatened to expose their nefarious past, and those who had convinced themselves that it was really a smart ploy for engaging in a witchhunt against the Afrikaners. We feared that these people might very well want to sabotage the proceedings of the Commission, hence security was an important issue. As it happened our very first hearing was interrupted by a bomb scare. Proceedings had to be suspended whilst police dogs sniffed out the whole venue. Mercifully it turned out to be a hoax, but we could not take chances with people's lives, especially with so much depending on the successful completion of our task. Those who were opposed to the process of reconciliation would have gloated at any mishap that befell the Commission.

We wanted to ensure that people felt they had had ample time to tell their story and that they had been duly acknowledged. As a result, the committee members who ran hearings were able to choose only a representative cross-section of witnesses to hear in any particular area. On average, only one in ten of those who made statements was able to testify in a public hearing. Many of those who were not allowed to testify felt a little let down, and they had to be reassured that the story described in their statement would be taken as seriously as those of the witnesses who testified in public.

We might perhaps take it as a compliment that people came to regard the public hearing so highly. In large measure this was because the media played such a splendid role: radio, TV and news-papers gave the Truth and Reconciliation Commission and its victim and amnesty hearings saturation coverage. When SABC Radio live broadcasts of the proceedings in the eleven South African official languages stopped for lack of funds, there was an outcry even from whites who hardly attended the hearings but who were obviously following them over the radio. (They were later reinstated.) We were given good advice by TV consultants from overseas on how to use TV cameras in the public hearings. We arranged for them to be stationary and not obtrusive. The stills photographers complained, though, because the requirement that they remain in one spot was too inhibiting and frustrating.

The atmosphere at our first hearing was solemn. We knew it was going to be a crucial event – so much depended on our getting it right the first time since this would shape subsequent hearings positively or negatively as the case might be.

We were apprehensive. We held a deeply moving interfaith service in Mdantsane, a ghetto township near East London, where our first hearing was to be held. Asked by journalists how I felt on the eve of our first hearing, I said:

> I certainly have very considerable butterflies in the pit of the tummy. But I also have a tingling sensation just being in this service, seeing so many people and the wonderful generosity of the people; that they do want this thing to succeed and that the stories must be told and that this process must end.

We prayed for God's blessings on our land, on the victims, the perpetrators and on the Truth and Reconciliation Commission. I always prayed in English, Xhosa, Sotho and Afrikaans to underscore that the Commission belonged to all. I welcomed all in these same languages for the same reason, and to point up our diversity as a nation.

The City Hall was packed to the rafters – mainly with black people. The witnesses sat at a table facing the Commission panel and with their backs to the audience (a practice which we changed later). There were cubicles for the translators away on one side of the platform and the hall was aglow with flowers and pot plants. The police did a splendid job looking after security at the hearing, searching everybody at the checkpoints.

As we filed in, the audience rose to its feet and a deep hush fell over us all. I went to shake the hands of those who were to testify at that four-day hearing, together with their relatives who had accompanied them. In silence I then lit a candle in memory of all who had died as a result of the conflict of the past. One of my colleagues read out a roll of honour commemorating all those who had fallen. And then we sang '*Lizalis' idinga lakho*' ('Let your will be done') as we had sung it that day in Bishopscourt when Nelson Mandela and his ANC comrades met there on the day of his release from prison, and as it would be sung on countless other occasions of significance. And then I prayed:

Oh God of justice, mercy and peace, we long to put behind us all the pain and division of apartheid together with all the violence which ravaged our communities in its name. And so we ask you to bless this Truth and Reconciliation Commission with your wisdom and guidance as it commences its important work of redressing the many wrongs done both here and throughout our land.

We pray that all those people who have been injured in either body or spirit may receive healing through the work of this Commission and that it may be seen to be a body which seeks to redress the wounds inflicted in so harsh a manner on so many of our people, particularly here in the Eastern Cape. We pray too for those who may be found to have committed these crimes against their fellow human beings, that they may come to repentance and confess their guilt to almighty God and that they too might become the recipients of your divine mercy and forgiveness. We ask that the Holy Spirit may pour out its gifts of justice, mercy and compassion upon the Commissioners and their colleagues in every sphere, that the truth may be recognised and brought to light during the hearings; and that the end may bring about that reconciliation and love for our neighbour which our Lord himself commanded. We ask this in the holy name of Jesus Christ our Saviour. Amen.

Thereafter I welcomed all present:

We welcome all those who will be telling their stories, as well as their relatives and friends. We will want to hear their stories. That is the basic reason for these hearings: for the Human Rights Violations Committee to help the Commission determine whether particular persons have suffered gross violations of their human rights and for those persons then to be declared victims who will thereafter be referred to the Reparation and Rehabilitation Committee of our Commission, which then must make appropriate recommendations to the President of our country for the nature and size of reparations to be given. Thank you all of you here in South Africa and round the world who have prayed and are praying for the Commission and its work.

We are charged to unearth the truth about our dark past; to lay the ghosts of that past so that they will not return to haunt us. And that we will thereby contribute to the healing of a traumatised and wounded people – for all of us in South Africa are wounded people – and in this manner to promote national unity and reconciliation. We want to indicate that those who testify before this Commission will enjoy the same privilege as in a court of law for the testimony that they give, provided what they say is the truth as they understand it, and provided what they have done is done in good faith.

I then declared the first hearing of the Truth and Reconciliation Commission open. It felt momentous.

We had decided that the first public proceedings of the Commission would be victim hearings to underline the fact that those who for so long had been consigned to the edges of society as voiceless and anonymous could now emerge from the shadows and occupy, for a while during the lifetime of the Commission, centre stage. We hoped this would help in the process of restoring their civic and human dignity. We ensured that the victims who testified represented the broadest possible political spectrum, in line with the requirement for the Truth and Reconciliation Commission to be even-handed. These cases also had to cover as much of the thirty-four-year mandate period, and as much of the region, as possible. We included women as well as men, young people as well as old, so that the process could be seen to be broadly representative.

We chose to hold our first hearing in the Eastern Cape deliberately because of the very special place this area occupies in South African history. This is where whites and the indigenous people first waged full-scale wars as they competed for the same geographical space. The Eastern Cape is the birthplace of black resistance to the depredations of white expansionism. This is also where the first educational institutions of higher learning for blacks were established: thus it was also the birthplace of black learning. And this is where many of the black political leaders were born – Nelson Mandela, Winnie Madikizela-Mandela, Govan and Thabo Mbeki,

Steve Biko, and others. It was the birthplace of black resistance and political awareness. And because of this it seemed to have attracted some of the most notorious implementers of apartheid's viciousness. The authorities dumped some of their less restrained elements of darkness and repression in the Eastern Cape.

We wanted to engender an atmosphere that would be welcoming, friendly and affirming. We did not want the witnesses traumatised and upset by insensitive cross-examination, so we resisted the requests of alleged perpetrators to be allowed to cross-examine. We contended that they would have the right to put their side of the story if and when they received notice that the Commission was going to make an adverse finding against them. These were the same people who were used to manipulating the judicial process, often with the connivance of magistrates and judges. Two of the alleged perpetrators did manage to get court interdicts to stop some of the witnesses from naming them, much to the chagrin and anger of those attending the hearings, who had expected to listen to certain testimony from prominent people. Having frustrated some of our potential witnesses in this manner, they then almost cynically confessed in subsequent amnesty applications to the very things that they had stopped our witnesses testifying to. They had yet again been able to thumb their noses at the world, and show that legality had little to do with justice and moral rightness.

We were determined to provide our witnesses with a safe environment. Thus it was typical to have whoever might be presiding over a hearing speak words of warm and friendly welcome such as these, spoken to the first witness at our first hearing on 15 April 1996:

Dr Boraine: We invite Mrs Nohle Mohapi to take the stand. Mrs Mohapi, do you wish to take the oath or to make an affirmation?

Mrs Mohapi: Yes, I will take the oath.

Dr Boraine: Thank you very much. Do you solemnly swear that the evidence you will give before this Commission will be the truth, the whole truth and nothing but the truth, so help you God.

Mrs Mohapi: So help me God.

Dr Boraine: Thank you very much indeed. Do be seated. In welcoming you as the first witness in the proceedings of the Truth and Reconciliation Commission, we are mindful of the sufferings that you have endured in the past. Many of us remember as though it was yesterday when Mapetla [Mohapi] died in police custody. We remember the anguish and the horror of those days . . . We know . . . that you too have been detained and were in solitary confinement. And we salute you as someone who has witnessed to great courage. And you coming here today is a testimony to your commitment to truth, to justice, to reconciliation and to peace between you . . . and all South Africa. Tiny Maya, who is sitting on my right, will lead the questions which the Commission would like to ask as you give your testimony. You are very, very welcome.

Ms Maya: Thank you, Alex. Before we begin I would like to indicate that my witness would be more comfortable presenting her testimony in Xhosa. So I would like everybody who does not understand Xhosa to put on their headphones so that we can begin. Molo, Sis Nohle. [Good morning Sisi Nohle (Mohapi).] How are you today?

At the end of each of the days on which I presided I tried to capture the mood of the day and to sum up what had been its chief features. This was also an opportunity to affirm those who had testified as well as the communities from which they came, and to draw lessons for us all in this unusual journey which our nation was undertaking. I often appealed to our white compatriots not to shun the Commission but to embrace it as an opportunity that would not return once it was lost. I said that the extraordinary magnanimity that was so much in evidence in those who could easily have been lusting for revenge deserved an answering generosity of spirit from those who willingly or unwillingly had benefited from apartheid. These appeals seemed to fall largely on deaf ears, though more whites were following the Commission proceedings via the live radio broadcasts than was evident from their physical absence at the hearings. For instance, in the first days of the hearings I could say:

I want to read from two letters that I received yesterday . . . 'As an ordinary member of the public, I would like you to know that I have been intensely moved and inspired by the testimonies heard at the Truth and Reconciliation Commission in East London last week. My pain and inspiration have come from the awesome, horrific and humbling stories and the extraordinary forgiveness of those wounded people. We are all wounded. I wrote a poem to try and understand what all this means and I would like you to know that there are many people out there who feel with those people. The pain belongs to us all. Thank you, all of you, for your own humanity and for helping us all towards healing.' The poem reads:

The world is wept.
Blood and pain seep into our listening; into our wounded souls.
The sound of your sobbing is my own weeping;
Your wet handkerchief my pillow for a past so exhausted it cannot
   rest – not yet.
Speak, weep, look, listen for us all.
Oh people of the silent hidden past,
Let your stories scatter seeds into our lonely frightened winds.
Sow more, until the stillness of this land can soften, can dare to
   hope and smile and sing;
Until the ghosts can dance unshackled, until our lives can know
   your sorrows
And be healed.

At the end I summed up:

We have been shocked and filled with revulsion to hear of the depths to which we are able to sink in our inhumanity to one another: our capacity for sadistic enjoyment of the suffering we have inflicted on one another; the refinement of cruelty in keeping families guessing about the fate and whereabouts of their loved ones, sending them carelessly on a run-around from police station to police station, to hospital and mortuary in a horrendous wild goose chase. That is one side – the ghastly and sombre side of the picture that is emerging thus far.

But there is another side, a more noble and inspiring one. We have been deeply touched and moved by the resilience of the human spirit. People, who by rights should have had the stuffing knocked out of them, refusing to buckle under intense suffering and brutality and intimidation; people refusing to give up on the hope of freedom, knowing they were made for something better than the dehumanising awfulness of injustice and oppression; refusing to be intimidated to lower their sights. It is quite incredible the capacity people have shown to be magnanimous – refusing to be consumed by bitterness and hatred, willing to meet with those who have violated their persons and their rights, willing to meet in a spirit of forgiveness and reconciliation, eager only to know the truth, to know the perpetrator so that they could forgive them.

We have been moved to tears. We have laughed. We have been silent and we have stared the beast of our dark past in the eye. We have survived the ordeal and we are realising that we can indeed transcend the conflicts of the past, we can hold hands as we realise our common humanity . . . The generosity of spirit will be full to overflowing when it meets a like generosity. Forgiveness will follow confession and healing will happen, and so contribute to national unity and reconciliation.

That is what happened normally in the victim hearings that for eighteen months became the public face of the Commission. No one in South Africa would ever again be able to say, 'I did not know' and hope to be believed.

CHAPTER SEVEN

'We do want to forgive but we don't know whom to forgive'

As I sat listening to the testimony of those who came to the Commission to tell us their stories, often of unbearable suffering, and as I considered some of the evidence that had been revealed in the applications for amnesty by those who committed some quite horrendous atrocities, I caught myself asking whether God does not sometimes wonder why He ever created us.

I am writing this at the time of the NATO strikes into Kosovo and Serbia, as we hear of the efforts of the Serbs under the leadership of President Milosevic to rid Kosovo of ethnic Albanians in another episode of so-called ethnic cleansing. There are reports of unspeakable atrocities happening: women and children told to flee and not to open their mouths otherwise they will be killed; men herded together and then summarily executed. I don't think the world will easily forget the picture of a young man wheeling his mother-in-law to safety in a wheelbarrow. It is a defining image of the horrors God's children are suffering at the hands of other children of God. Maybe it will become as haunting an image of this carnage as that during the Vietnam War of the little girl fleeing naked, aflame from the napalm bombing.

In bold anthropomorphic vein I can picture God surveying the awful wrecks that litter human history – the bloody crusades and other wars that have been fought in God's name. The earth is soaked with the blood of so many innocent people who have died brutally. Two world wars in this century alone, plus the Holocaust, the genocide in Cambodia and Rwanda, the awfulnesses in the Sudan, Sierra Leone, the two Congos, Northern Ireland and the Middle East, and the excesses that have characterised Latin America. It is a baneful catalogue that records our capacity to wreak considerable harm on one another, and our gross inhumanity to one another. I can imagine God surveying it all and weeping, as Jesus wept over hard-hearted and unresponsive Jerusalem, where he had come to his own and his own would not receive him. If God wants to consider the folly of ever having brought us into being then we have provided God with ample cause to do so. In the book of Genesis it is recorded that, 'The Lord saw that the wickedness of humankind was great in the earth, and that every inclination of the thoughts of their hearts was only evil. And the Lord was sorry that he had made humankind on the earth and it grieved him to his heart.'[1]

Geoffrey Studdert Kennedy, a chaplain who lived during the horror of the First World War, reflected on the pain God felt because of human behaviour in his poem, *The Suffering God*:

> How can it be that God can reign in glory,
> Calmly content with what His Love has done,
> Reading unmoved the piteous shameful story,
> And the vile deeds men do beneath the sun?
>
> Are there no tears in the heart of the Eternal?
> Is there no pain to pierce the soul of God?
> Then must He be a fiend of Hell infernal,
> Beating the earth to pieces with His rod.
>
> Father if he, the Christ, were Thy Revealer
> Truly the First Begotten of the Lord,
> Then must Thou be a Suff'rer and a Healer,
> Pierced to the heart by the sorrow of the sword.

> Then must it mean, not only that Thy sorrow
> Smote Thee that once upon the lonely tree,
> But that today, tonight, and on the morrow,
> Still will it come O Gallant God, to Thee.[2]

I thought of God's sorrow many times as we listened to harrowing tales of the kind of things we are capable of doing to one another. Awful things that seemed to beggar description and called into question our right to be considered fit to be regarded as human at all. One could understand at such moments just how it was possible to describe those responsible for such terrible deeds as being monsters, not deserving to be considered as human beings any longer – their deeds filled all decent people in the community with a sense of outrage and revulsion. And these perpetrators came from all sides in the conflict that had convulsed our land for so long.

Five police officers, in amnesty applications which detailed the killings of dozens of people from the Pretoria region, described how they had tortured their 'terrorist' quarry and how they had then disposed of the bodies. Giving suspects electric shocks was such a widespread form of torture that one of the police officers could say matter-of-factly, 'We interrogated Sefolo in the same way as the other two . . .' It was as if it was an unsurprising routine, and in fact the Commission established that torture in some form or other was used as a matter of course by the security police.

Consider the evidence of one of the five, Warrant-Officer Paul van Vuuren of the former Northern Transvaal Security Branch – dubbed 'the electrician' by his colleagues:

We interrogated [Harold Sello] Sefolo in the same way as the previous two [Jackson Maake and Andrew Makupe] . . . We used a yellow portable Robin generator to send electric shocks through his body and to force him to speak . . . There were two wires. One was attached to his foot and the other to his hand. When we put the generator on, his body was shocked stiff . . . Sefolo was a very strong man and believed completely . . . in what he was doing, that he was right . . . After he was interrogated, he admitted to being a senior ANC organiser in Witbank . . .

He gave us even more information after Joe Mamasela shoved a knife up his nose. He was pleading for his life and asked if he could sing 'Nkosi Sikelel' iAfrika' ['God Bless Africa'].[3] Then he said we might as well kill him. He also said the ANC would rule one day and that apartheid could not survive . . . [After we shocked Maake to death] Mamasela covered his body with an ANC flag while Sefolo was singing 'Nkosi Sikelel' iAfrika'. We then shocked Makupe to death . . .

It was necessary to kill them in order to destroy the entire cell. No one knew what had happened to them. After this we blew them up with a landmine so that it would be impossible to recognise them . . . It had to appear that they were planting a landmine . . . We did not enjoy doing this, we did not want to do this, but we had to stop them from killing innocent women and children. It was additionally necessary to do this because we were at war with the ANC. I have tremendous respect for Harold Sefolo because of the way in which he behaved during the process of us killing him.

Dirk Coetzee was once head of 'Vlakplaas' near Pretoria, which turned out to be the notorious headquarters of police death squads. Coetzee, Almond Nofomela and David Tshikalanga applied for amnesty for murdering Griffiths Mxenge, a prominent Durban lawyer who defended political activists. Coetzee told the Amnesty Committee:

The decision was made by Brigadier [Jan] van der Hoven . . . from . . . Port Natal security police and he told me that he [Mxenge] was a thorn in the flesh . . . because he acted as instructing lawyer for all ANC cadres . . . and he stuck by the law. So they couldn't get to him . . . I had never heard of the name before, until that day, when I was instructed to make a plan with Griffiths Mxenge. It means one thing only. Get rid of the guy. Kill him. Nothing else . . . but murder him. Kill him.

Coetzee elaborated in an interview with Angie Kapelianis of SABC Radio on how the following black policemen were chosen to carry out the killing:

. . . Brian Ngqulunga was picked because he was the Zulu and knew the area and knew . . . the language . . . David Tshikalanga I've known since 1973 . . . He worked for me . . . and I helped him join the police and he was on Vlakplaas. So a well-trusted guy. Almond Nofomela was a sober guy, a fit guy . . . a tiger if it comes to guts. If you've got to do something, Almond won't hesitate. He's got guts. And Joe Mamasela was the super-fit, killer instinct . . . Didn't smoke, didn't drink at all and . . . You could see an absolute killer. He just never stops. I mean, same way with his gun . . .

The killing was planned so as to appear to have taken place in the course of a robbery and members of the unit attacked Mxenge with knives and a wheel-spanner:

. . . Tshikalanga stabbed first . . . and he couldn't get the knife out of the chest of Mxenge . . . Then apparently Mxenge . . . took the knife out himself and started chasing them with the knife and that is apparently when Almond knocked him down with the wheel spanner and . . . the stabbing frenzy started between Almond and Joe.

Judge Andrew Wilson, deputy chairperson of the Amnesty Committee, questioned Nofomela at the amnesty hearing:

Wilson: Can you give any reason . . . why he was stabbed so many times?

Nofomela: The reason I suspect is that . . . all the time, he was not falling to the ground. He was fighting.

Wilson: He fought to save his own life, didn't he?

Nofomela: That is correct, sir.

Wilson: Did he have any weapon?

Nofomela: No, not that I know of.

While this stabbing was going on, Coetzee said in the radio interview that he was 'drinking and driving around Durban . . . Partying and waiting for the rendezvous time to come up and meet them and say is everything still okay? Nothing funny happened? Okay. So [let's have] one big party.'

The radio interviewer reported the discovery by Mrs Victoria Mxenge of her husband's body in the government mortuary:

> Forty-five lacerations and stab wounds pierce his body, lungs, liver and heart. His throat is slashed. His ears are practically cut off. And his stomach is ripped open.

The killers were frenzied and yet in many ways it was just a job, carried out cold-bloodedly since they actually did not have a grudge against Griffiths Mxenge. They appeared to have no feelings at all. They were just part of an efficient, ruthless and unfeeling killing machine.

Here is Dirk Coetzee giving evidence in his application for amnesty for killing a young Eastern Cape man who had been abducted by police:

> Drops were administered to Sizwe Kondile in a drink . . . And the reason why the knock-out drops was [sic] administered is because I don't think any sober guy would have had the courage . . . to just . . . look a normal . . . person in the eye, sober, and shoot him at point-blank [range] in the head. One of Major Archie Flemington's men . . . took a Makarov pistol with a silencer on and whilst . . . Mr Kondile was lying on his back, shot him on top of the head. There was a short jerk and that was it . . . The four junior, non-commissioned officers . . . each grabbed a hand and a foot, put it onto the pyre of tyres and wood, poured petrol on it and set it alight . . . Whilst that happened, we were drinking and even having a braai [barbecue] next to the fire.
>
> Now that I don't say to show our 'braveness'. I just tell it to the Commission to show the callousness of it, and to what extremes we had gone in those days . . . A body takes about seven hours to burn to ashes completely. The chunks of meat especially the buttocks and the upper parts of the legs had to be turned frequently during the night to make sure that everything burnt to ashes . . . The next morning, after raking through the rubble to make sure that there was [sic] no big pieces of meat or bone left at all . . . we all went our own way.

You are devastated by the fact that it could be possible at all for human beings to shoot and kill a fellow human being, burn his body on a pyre and whilst this cremation is going on actually to be able to enjoy a barbecue on the side. What had happened to their humanity that they could manage to do this? How were they able literally to stomach it? Burning human flesh has a peculiar odour which is stomach-turning for most normal human beings. Is it that they had to be schizophrenic – split themselves into two different people – to be able to go on living? How was it possible for them to return from such an outing to their home, embrace their wives and enjoy, say, their child's birthday party?

In many cases in the Eastern Cape, people vanished without trace since their bodies were burned to ashes. But in the case of the 'Cradock Four' – activists abducted while travelling to the small town of Cradock from Port Elizabeth in the Eastern Cape in June 1985 – their horribly mutilated bodies were found a week after they had disappeared. Nevertheless the full story of the killing of Matthew Goniwe, Fort Calata, Sparrow Mkhonto and Sicelo Mhlauli, including the identities of the perpetrators, emerged only when the Commission was set up.

Advocate George Bizos, Senior Counsel appearing for relatives of the men, cross-examined Johan Martin ('Sakkie') van Zyl, one of the police officers who applied for amnesty:

Bizos: Mr Van Zyl, sixty-three stab wounds were inflicted on the four people you murdered on the night of the twenty-seventh? Do you agree with the District Surgeon's report on that?

Van Zyl: I cannot disagree with that, Mr Chairman.

Bizos: Do you agree that the sixty-three stab wounds is evidence of barbaric conduct?

Van Zyl: Mr Chairman, in retrospect, absolutely. The fact is though that the instruction was that this killing should look like a vigilante attack and that a more humane way of doing it would not have had the same effect.

Bizos: Does your answer mean that you were prepared to behave like a savage barbarian in order to mislead anyone that bothered to investigate the murders that you had committed?

Van Zyl: In effect, yes, Mr Chairman.

Captured ANC activists, under threat of imprisonment or even death, sometimes agreed to work for the police. They were called 'askaris' and Joe Mamasela was one such, stationed at Vlakplaas. By his own evidence, he was involved in dozens of killings of political activists, often infiltrating groups of youths and pretending to recruit them for military training before leading them to their deaths in police traps. Under the protection of the Attorney-General, who wanted to use him as a state witness in exchange for immunity from prosecution, he refused to apply for amnesty and was both defiant of the Commission and angry with his erstwhile masters. He gave evidence at a hearing where his former colleagues applied for amnesty for murdering the 'Pebco Three', leaders of the Port Elizabeth Black Civic Organisation, in May 1985:

In all my experience in this hell hole I have never come across a thing that is called clean killing. There is no such thing, it only exists in the minds of those who want to appear here as honest and decent gentlemen who don't want to subjugate other people into unnecessary pain. There's nothing like that – people are killed brutally, they die worse than animals and that is a fact . . . The purpose of the security police is not just to kill people and get out, they want . . . to dig as much information as they possibly can before you die. The idea is to inflict as much pain as possible. It was a sadistic, well-calculated method of killing people and they know it and I was part of it.

The Pebco Three, Sipho Hashe, Champion Galela and Qaqawuli Godolozi, were killed at a deserted police station near Cradock. Mamasela told the Committee that Mr Hashe had told his interrogator that the ANC, banned at the time, 'stands for a democratic South Africa'.

This reply more than anything else seemed to infuriate Lieutenant [Gideon] Nieuwoudt so much that he just grabbed an iron pipe and beat the poor old man several times on his head, and as he did so all the people joined in . . . The only thing he could [do to] help himself was just to scream out loud. I was then ordered by Lt Nieuwoudt to stifle his screams, to put my hands in his mouth and hold it hard so that his screams mustn't attract the neighbouring farmers. Myself and Piet Mogoai, we struggled to stifle the old man's screams while all the others that I've named waded into the old man with kicks, punches, fists, sticks.

As Lt Nieuwoudt was beating the old man several times on the head with the iron pipe, I noticed that the blood was oozing from the old man's nostrils and ears as well as the mouth. I saw the old man's eyes turning into white pupils. They were turning, it was as if he was fainting or just about to die . . . The beatings went on and on until I saw the old man lying prostrate on the ground with blood all over his head and face . . .

During the assault of Champion Galela, something brutal happened . . . Warrant-Officer Beeslaar took out the testicles of Champion Galela and squeezed them very hard until they became the size of almost golf balls. Then with his right hand he punched them severely, very hard. I saw the man changing, the colour of his face becoming pale and blueish and there was some yellowish liquid that spattered out from his genitals. That was the most brutal thing I ever witnessed in all my life of hell in Vlakplaas. I stayed for a long time in this devil's belly. I know how it looks but I've never seen anything like this in all my life as a prisoner of war of these people. I've never seen anything like that. It was the most dehumanising experience of my life.

One of the groups infiltrated and led to their deaths by Mamasela was one which came to be known as the 'KwaNdebele Nine'. The youngsters, who had fled from Mamelodi, a black township to the east of Pretoria, to the rural KwaNdebele homeland, were killed in July 1986. Mamasela told the Committee:

In the KwaNdebele Nine, the people were ambushed in a house and they were shot, all nine of them. They were shot and massacred with

AK-47s and then one Lieutenant [Jacques] Hechter . . . came with a big twenty-five-litre [drum] of petrol. He poured in [sic] all these corpses and then he lit the fire. Some of the people there were still alive, you could hear their shrill screams and they were all incinerated.

On the other side of the struggle, there were persistent allegations made about Mrs Winnie Madikizela-Mandela, former wife of Nelson Mandela, suggesting that the so-called 'Mandela United Football Club', which operated around her in Soweto in 1988 and 1989, was not a group of township youths looking to redeem themselves and working as her bodyguards. It was rumoured that they were a gang of thugs who terrorised people, burning their homes and abducting and killing those they regarded as 'sell-outs', those who in their view might be collaborating with 'the system' by spying for the police. Those who were suspected of falling within this category were allegedly tortured and frequently executed. People said they did this not only with Mrs Mandela's connivance but her positive support and encouragement and, even more disturbingly, on her instructions. One of the main accusations, a cause célèbre, concerned the fourteen-year-old activist Stompie Seipei, who had fled the police in his Orange Free State home and sought refuge in the Methodist manse of the Revd (later Bishop) Paul Verryn. Mrs Mandela was found guilty in 1991 of kidnapping Stompie from the manse. She claimed she had rescued him from Mr Verryn when she heard that he was sodomising the young boys who had fled to him for refuge. Stompie's decomposed body was found in the veld in January 1989.

We held a special hearing into the activities of Mrs Mandela's bodyguards. It lasted nine days, longer than any other Commission hearing focusing on a single political leader. Witness after witness implicated her in assaults and killings. The 'coach' of the Football Club was Jerry Richardson, who had been convicted of Stompie's murder and sentenced to life imprisonment some years before the Commission was established. He came from gaol and gave his version of how Stompie and three others abducted from the manse with him had been interrogated:

We started torturing the youths in the manner that the Boers used to torture freedom fighters. The first thing that I did to Stompie was to hold him with both sides, throw him up in the air and let him fall freely onto the ground. 'Mummy' [Mrs Mandela] was sitting and watching us.

A day or two later he and an associate he called 'Slash' took the battered Stompie away to a deserted spot outside Soweto:

. . . I slaughtered him. I slaughtered him like a goat. We made him lay on his back and I put garden shears through his neck and the garden shears penetrated to the back of his neck and I made some cutting motion . . .

I killed Stompie under the instructions of Mummy [Mrs Mandela]. Mummy never killed anyone, but she used us to kill a lot of people. She does not even visit us in prison. She used us!

Richardson also said he had killed Priscilla Mosoeu, known as 'Kuki Zwane', the girlfriend of a Football Club member who was allegedly thought to be an informer and who died of multiple stab wounds in December 1988:

I stabbed her. I slit her throat. We dumped her body . . . I reported to Mummy that: 'Mummy, I have now carried out your orders. I have killed Kuki' . . . Mummy embraced me and said: 'My boy, my boy'.

Mr Nicodemus Sono gave us a graphic description of the last time he saw his son, who had been brought to him, still alive, by Mrs Mandela in a minivan:

. . . He was beaten up, his face was bruised, it was actually pulped . . . as if somebody had beaten him up and crushed him against the wall . . . Mrs Mandela explained to me that Lolo is a spy . . . I started pleading with her. I said to her, please, leave Lolo with me because he has already been beaten. If it's for punishment, I understand that he's been punished, can't you please leave him with me, and she refused . . . She raised up her voice, she was speaking very loud, you know: 'I cannot leave him with you. He is a spy.'

After further pleas, and a trip around the block near Mr Sono's home in the minivan, Mrs Mandela allowed Lolo's parents to fetch him a jersey. Mr Sono then returned to the van to see his son:

> When I looked at Lolo he was in a terrible state, he was shaking . . . I started pleading again with Mrs Mandela: 'Please, won't you leave my son with me because he's already been beaten.' . . .And she totally refused that: 'This is a spy.' She said to . . . [the driver] again, 'Pull off,' so he pulled off. As he went I pleaded with her until she said to me: 'I am taking this dog away. The movement will see what to do.'

Bishop Peter Storey, leader of the Methodist Church in the Johannesburg area at the time, a past president of his church and a former president of the South African Council of Churches, gave us a step-by-step account of Church efforts to secure the release of Stompie and the other abducted boys and concluded:

> I believe Mrs Mandela knew what happened to Stompie, knew about the circumstances of his death . . . If Stompie was, indeed, killed or brought near to death in her house, I believe she knew about that . . .

Azhar Cachalia and Murphy Morobe, leaders of the loosely formed coalition of internal anti-apartheid organisations known as the Mass Democratic Movement, came and told us how it came about that they issued a public statement after Stompie's death distancing themselves from the conduct of Mrs Mandela and the Football Club. Mr Cachalia explained:

> At the time there were in our view certain objective facts. Firstly that four males including Stompie were forcibly removed from the manse to the Mandela home. Secondly they were viciously beaten at the Mandela home where they were kept against their will. Third, one young man, Kenneth Kgase, had escaped on January 7th and reported

his ordeal. Fourth, Stompie was not only tortured at the house, but then subsequently murdered in a savage fashion.

At best for Mrs Mandela . . . she was aware of and encouraged this criminal activity. At worst she directed it and actively participated in the assaults. Sixth [sic], Paul Verryn was framed and, seventh, all reasonable efforts by the Church, community leaders, Mr Mandela and President Oliver Tambo [of the ANC] to disband the gang of thugs by trying to secure Mrs Mandela's cooperation had failed.

Bishop Storey summed up:

The primary cancer may be, and was, and will always be, the apartheid oppression, but secondary infections have touched many of apartheid's opponents and eroded their knowledge of good and evil. One of the tragedies of life, sir, is it is possible to become like that which we hate most, and I have a feeling that this drama is an example of that.

The following is the story of Greta Appelgren, arrested with Robert McBride for the ANC car bomb placed outside the Why Not and Magoo's bars on the Durban beachfront in June 1986: three people died in the explosion and about sixty-nine were injured. Greta was a Roman Catholic who later became a Muslim and took the name Zahrah Narkedien. We pick up the story as Angie Kapelianis reported it in a documentary produced by SABC Radio:

Winter 1986. Zahrah Narkedien and Robert McBride are picked up in Nigel on the Far East Rand. Their hands are cuffed behind their backs. Thick, woollen balaclavas are pulled over their faces . . . back-to-front. They are driven like that for three hours until their blindfolds are damp with sweat. [At] CR Swart Police Station, Durban, Zahrah Narkedien is interrogated and tortured. Day in and day out for a week on the thirteenth floor. When they hurl abuse at her, she rolls the rosary beads in her hand . . . and prays silently.

Ms Narkedien, as well as appearing before the Commission to be questioned on her role in the attack, spoke at a hearing in

Johannesburg on the treatment of prisoners and those detained without trial. She first related the torture to which she was subjected, then her solitary confinement:

> For the first seven days they did torture me quite a bit because I felt that I didn't have to cooperate . . . I was proud of who I was as an MK [Umkhonto we Sizwe, the armed wing of the ANC] comrade and I was proud of the fact that I joined the struggle, that I was a revolutionary and I was willing to just suffer the consequences. They wanted me to say certain things so they tortured me for these seven days and the only thing that really made me break in the end was when they threatened to go back to my house where my sister was staying with me and kidnap my four-year-old nephew Christopher, bring him to the thirteenth floor and drop him out of the window.
>
> At that point I really was at my weakest because I felt I could risk my life and I could let my body just be handed over to these men to do what they liked, but I couldn't hand over someone else's body so at that point I fully cooperated. By then I was becoming weaker and weaker . . . [They] would take me out of my cell after breakfast at about half past seven or eight o'clock and interrogate me the whole day, the whole night right through until two or three o'clock in the morning. I'd be standing all the time and whole groups of them would be swearing and screaming at me but that was bearable because I could pray silently while they were doing that and not even hear the abuse.
>
> They started to realise that I was enduring that kind of abuse so they started to take a plastic bag . . . then one person held both my hands down and the other one put it on my head. Then they sealed it so that I wouldn't be able to breath and kept it on for at least two minutes, by which time the plastic was clinging to my eyelids, my nostrils, my mouth and my whole body was going into spasms because I really couldn't breathe . . .
>
> They always had a woman present when they were torturing me and they asked her if she would like to leave because they were going to intensify the treatment. All these days I was wearing the same clothing, just a dress, and I was also menstruating at that time . . . and I was bleeding a lot. They made me lay on the floor and do all kinds of physical exercises, lifting my body with my hands, what they call

press-ups, then reducing the fingers until I had to pick myself up with just two fingers. By then I couldn't because my body was tired, it was sore and I had to drop it and lift it up and I was hurting my knees every time I dropped it. While I was down they would kick me and tramp on me . . .

She then spent more than a hundred days in isolation:

What really bothered me was the rats . . . These were huge rats, the size of cats that were in the cells, in the passages all the time. I would sit and eat my food and three of these rats would just sit and look at me. I'd be in the yard praying, the rats would just be around me and I'd get up and chase them but they'd come back in . . . One particular evening one was crawling on me and I didn't quite mind until it got to my neck – I went totally berserk, I screamed the whole prison down . . . The guards came running . . . they found me in the corner and I was actually eating my T-shirt. That's how berserk I went.

While on trial in Pietermaritzburg, she was seen by prison wardresses as a dangerous terrorist and forced under prison regulations to strip twice a day:

I had to actually stand fully naked. I used to say: Never, I'm not going to take my panties off for you. You do all the searching and when you're finished, I'll pull them down quickly.

Sentenced to imprisonment, Ms Narkedien, classified 'Coloured' under apartheid, was blamed by African comrades for a fight by other prisoners and sent to an isolation cell for seven months:

So I had to pay the price just for being a coloured person. It was the first time that I had to face the fact that I was part of a minority . . . Even my comrades used the fact that I was not really an African in their eyes. It was painful . . . My parents have always taught me that my Zulu ancestors mean a lot to them so it hurt to also be tortured by your own comrades . . .

I don't even want to describe psychologically what I had to do to survive down there. I will write it one day, but I could never tell you. But it did teach me something . . . that no human being can live alone . . . because there's nothing you can do to survive all by yourself . . . I felt as the months went by that I was going deeper and deeper into the ground . . . As the months of isolation went by I used to feel that God had abandoned me, the whole world had abandoned me, I was totally alone in this whole universe . . .

I'm out of prison now for more than seven . . . years but I haven't recovered and I will never recover, I know I won't . . . The first two years after my release I tried to be normal again and the more I struggle to be normal, the more disturbed I become. I had to accept that I was damaged, part of my soul was eaten away as if by maggots, horrible as it sounds, and I will never get it back again.

A not dissimilar story was shown in a documentary on the Truth and Reconciliation Commission produced by Bill Moyers for the Public Broadcasting Service (PBS) in the United States entitled *Facing the Truth*. One of the people he interviewed was a woman from Soweto, Thandi, who was tortured whilst in detention. She was raped repeatedly. She said she survived by taking her soul and spirit out of her body and putting it in a corner of the cell in which she was being raped. She could then, disembodied in this manner, look on as they did all those awful things to her body intended to make her hate herself as they had told her would happen. She could imagine then that it was not she herself but this stranger suffering the ignominy heaped on her. She then uttered words which are filled with a deep pathos. She said with tears in her eyes that she had not yet gone back to that room to fetch her soul and that it was still sitting in the corner where she had left it.

From 1982 there was an increase in covert operations by the state security forces. For instance, in Operation Zero Zero, Joe Mamasela lured eight young East Rand activists with the promise of training them in the use of hand grenades that could be used against the police. The eight were supplied with booby-trapped hand grenades which blew them to smithereens when they pulled the pins. A young woman, Maki Skhosana, herself an activist in the struggle, had innocently introduced Mamasela to the youths. As a result she was suspected of being a sell-out, a spy. A mob attacked her and she became one of the early victims of the gruesome method of killing called the necklace, when a tyre is placed round the victim's neck, filled with petrol and set alight. This heartless way of killing another fellow human being was widely publicised in the media as an example of so-called black-on-black violence, and used to good effect as Nationalist Party propaganda.

Maki's family had to live with the shame and stigma of having had an informer as one of their number and for a long time they were ostracised and vilified for this. It was one of the more wonderful moments in the life of the Commission when, through its amnesty process, the truth was eventually disclosed that the death of the eight had been one of the state's 'dirty tricks' and that Maki was no informer. It was a tremendous act of communal reconciliation as Maki's family was vindicated and reintegrated back into the community. She could not be brought to life again but her memory would be an honourable one instead of that of somebody who had died in shame and disgrace.

Because apartheid was intrinsically evil and immoral, almost by definition it had to use equally evil and immoral methods to sustain itself. On 12 June 1988, the eve of the twelfth anniversary of the Soweto uprising, Stanza Bopape, General Secretary of the Mamelodi Civic Association, died in police custody after three days in detention. The then Minister of Police, Mr Adriaan Vlok, announced that Stanza Bopape had escaped from the police while he was being transported from Johannesburg to the Vaal, south of the city. Improbably, a handcuffed Bopape had apparently found the key to unlock his handcuffs and escaped, possibly to Lesotho, eluding three police officers who were busy changing a punctured tyre. How could this have happened when it is well known that the police were trigger-happy, and yet not one of the three had managed to shoot him? Mr Vlok was blatantly lying and cynically misleading the public. As a result, Bopape's family went on a wild-goose chase amongst the exiled community in the 'frontline states' bordering South Africa to the north. In one of the Commission's hearings his mother broke down several times and said she wanted 'the police who were with him [to] come here and tell us where the bones are'.

A cabinet minister and the commissioner of police had, without any qualms, conspired with their underlings in an elaborate cover-up to mislead the public. As emerged subsequently in amnesty applications, it turned out that Stanza Bopape had been tortured with electric shocks and had collapsed and died. Scared of the political fallout on the eve of such a sensitive anniversary in a volatile community, the police lied and were aided and abetted in this subversion of public morality by the minister and their commissioner. They took the body secretly to what was then the Eastern Transvaal, where it was thrown into a crocodile-infested river. All this would have remained in the murky crevices where apartheid hid such secrets had it not been for the amnesty process. The Bopape family could at least experience closure, knowing where the bones of their loved one had gone.

One day during our first victim hearings in East London the last witness to take the stand was Mr Singqokwana Malgas. He was now confined to a wheelchair but had in his prime been politically active as a member of the ANC and, predictably, had fallen foul of the law and been harassed by the police. He had, as was seemingly standard practice, been tortured and had also served time on Robben Island, where black political prisoners were jailed. The end result of all this was that he had a stroke which left him half paralysed and suffering from a speech impediment. He told us about the fact that he had been tortured. Dr Boraine then asked him to describe some of the torture he had undergone. I thought I had done quite well that day: though I had been close to tears at many moments as I heard one heart-rending story after another, I had not broken down and this was to be the last witness for the day. Dr Boraine was my undoing. Mr Malgas tried to describe some of the torture methods used on him. He spoke about one which we were to encounter many times afterwards – the so-called 'helicopter' method. The police handcuff your hands behind your back, your ankles are manacled together, then you are suspended upside down and spun around.

Mr Malgas tried to tell us all this. Whether it was that he could not bear to recall the memories of the torture or whether he was frustrated that his tongue could not articulate what he wanted to tell us, I will never know. (He died even before we had handed over our Report to President Mandela.) Whatever the reason, he just put his normal hand over his face and cried. I was too full from all that I had heard and it was all too much for me too. I could not hold back the tears, I just broke down and sobbed like a child. I bent over the table and covered my face with my hands. I told people afterwards that I laugh easily and I cry easily and that I wondered whether I was the right person to lead the Commission since I knew I was so weak and vulnerable.

Mercifully it was the last time that I cried in public during the lifetime of the Commission. I begged God not to let it happen again because the media then concentrated on me and took their attention away from those who should have had it, the witnesses. I have been close to breaking down many times but managed to stop myself actually doing so.

This was the kind of testimony that made me realise that there is an awful depth of depravity to which we can all sink, that we do possess an extraordinary capacity for evil. As I have already noted elsewhere, this applies to all of us. There is no room for gloating or arrogant finger-pointing. We have supplied God with enough evidence for Him to want to dispatch us all, to wipe the slate clean as He did before with the Flood, and try to make a fresh start. It is important to note that those guilty of these abuses were quite ordinary folk. They did not grow horns on their foreheads or have tails hidden in their trousers. They looked just like you and me. The philosopher Hannah Arendt refers to 'the banality of evil' – that those involved with this evil are certainly outwardly not grotesque. They are to all intents and purposes normal people like you and me.

Mercifully, wonderfully, that was only one side of the picture, the dismal part painted by the evidence revealed in the testimony before the Commission. Gloriously, there was another side that was revealed as well. There are moments when God would probably preen Himself as He surveyed His handiwork. When God had finished the work of creation it is recorded that He declared what He saw to be not just good, as He had indicated after each individual creative act, but *very good*. We can almost see God rubbing His hands in sublime divine satisfaction at the beauty and goodness of what He has brought into being. God asserts how good his creation is at the beginning of the Book of Job, where He addresses Satan, who has not yet degenerated into a source of evil constantly opposed to God. In this story, Satan is still a member of God's heavenly court, though it is becoming clear that he is evolving into a character who tests the credentials of God's servants much as a modern-day prosecutor in court would want to undermine the credibility of a witness, pointing mostly to the unflattering elements. God points with some pride to Job and asks Satan whether he has considered His servant Job. Really, God is showing off. God asks Satan, 'Don't you think he is quite something?' Satan is somewhat surly when he responds that of course Job would be righteous. What was so remarkable about that? After all, God had protected him against disaster and suffering, and made him prosperous. There could be no real merit accruing to someone who had been so mollycoddled by God. God then stakes His reputation on Job, who is exposed to all kinds of suffering, as Satan hopes and expects that Job will denounce God because of his suffering, which seems to be inflicted on him for no apparent reason.

There must be moments when God has beheld the nobility of His human creatures, their compassion and generosity to others; when He has looked at the integrity and courage of those who have stood up to tyrants, who have been willing to die for their faith. When God looked at the exploits of a Francis of Assisi, a Mother Teresa, a Martin Luther King Jr, an Albert Schweitzer, a Nelson Mandela, God must have said, 'No, it was worth taking the risk. They have

vindicated my faith in them.' And God has again rubbed His hands
in divine self-satisfaction and said of what He has seen that it was not
just good, but that it was all really very good.

The hearings in the Eastern Cape included a wonderful story of the
nobility of which the human spirit is capable. One of the liberation
movements, the Pan Africanist Congress, through its armed wing the
Azanian People's Liberation Army (APLA), decided to intensify its
armed struggle by declaring 1993 'The Year of the Great Storm',
even though negotiations between the apartheid government and its
opponents had already begun. An early target was King William's
Town golf club in November 1992, during a wine-tasting party. Four
people were killed. Ms Beth Savage was among those badly injured.
She underwent open-heart surgery and remained in an intensive-care
unit for several months. When she was discharged she was still so
badly disabled that it was her children who bathed her, clothed her
and fed her, helping her to do those things that you and I do without
ever thinking twice. It was an awful thing to have happened to her.
Her parents found it particularly baffling because they had been quite
scrupulous in bringing up their family to respect everyone, regardless
of race or status. In the South Africa of those days that was a
courageous thing to do, and they could not understand how a child
brought up in a family that opposed apartheid and all its madness
should end up being targeted by the very people whose lot they were
striving to improve. They were unable to accept that the attack was
arbitrary and random – any and every white person would be a target,
since in the kind of gathering that was being celebrated in the
clubhouse there was no way for anyone to differentiate between the
white person who supported the system and one who did not.

   Beth Savage thinks her father died of a broken heart. She told us
that even at the time of the hearing in 1996 she could not go through
the security checkpoint at an airport. All sorts of alarms and lights
would flash because she still had shrapnel embedded in her body.
What she said of the experience which had left her in this condition
was quite staggering and unbelievable:

All in all, what I must say, is through the trauma of it all, I honestly feel richer. I think it's been a really enriching experience for me and a growing curve, and I think it's given me the ability to relate to other people who may be going through trauma.

She said it had enriched her life! Now that really is breathtaking and shows once again that we are blessed with some remarkable people. If that was all she had said it would still have stood out as a most noteworthy comment. But then she went on to say, when asked how she felt about amnesty for the perpetrator:

It's not important to me, but, and I've said this to many people, what I would really, really like is, I would like to meet that man that threw that grenade in an attitude of forgiveness and hope that he could forgive me too for whatever reason. But I would very much like to meet them.

Her sublime attitude left many of us quite speechless and, in general, we were filled to overflowing with a sense of deep thankfulness that nearly all the victims, black and white, possessed this marvellous magnanimity. It did seem to augur well for our country.

At this same East London hearing we listened to the testimony of the widows of the Cradock Four including Nomonde Calata, Nombuyiselo Mhlauli, and the daughter of one of them, Ms Babalwa Mhlauli. Babalwa means the 'blessed one' and what she was to say at the hearing was indeed to bring the grace of blessing to those who heard her words.

These four men were dedicated to work for a new and just dispensation in their rural communities which, as was usual, suffered even more severely from the depredations of apartheid than their urban counterparts. (Though you could hardly convince urban dwellers of this: they all believed that their own existence was sheer hell.) The four had all been frequently detained, tortured, threatened and harassed by the security police before their abduction and killing.

Nomonde Calata, wife of Fort, one of the victims, testified at our first hearing:

> During the time when the [*Eastern Province*] *Herald* was being delivered, I looked at the headlines. And one of my children said: 'Mother, look here, the car belonging to my father is burnt.' At that moment I was trembling because I was afraid of what might have happened to my husband . . . Nyami [Goniwe, widow of another of the Cradock Four] was always supportive, I was still twenty at the time and I couldn't handle this. So I was taken to Nyami's place and when I got there Nyami was crying terribly . . .

At this point in her evidence, Mrs Calata broke down, uttering a piercing wail which in many ways was the defining sound that characterised the Truth and Reconciliation Commission – as a place where people could come to cry, to open their hearts, to expose the anguish that had remained locked up for so long, unacknowledged, ignored and denied. I adjourned the proceedings so that she could recover her composure and when we restarted, I led the gathering in singing '*Senzenina?*' ('What have we done?').

Later, Mrs Nombuyiselo Mhlauli described what they had done to Sicelo, her husband and Babalwa's father:

> I read the post-mortem documents . . . In the upper abdomen were twenty-five wounds. These wounds indicated that different weapons were used to stab him, or a group of people stabbed him. Now in the lower part he also had wounds but the wounds in total were forty-three. One other thing that we understood, they poured acid on his face. After that they chopped off his right hand below the wrist, I don't know what they did with that hand.

In fact, the hand was preserved in alcohol at police headquarters in Port Elizabeth. Detainees were intimidated with it – 'the baboon's hand' as the police called it. They were told *that* and worse could be their fate if they did not cooperate with the police and make statements.

Babalwa (Sicelo's daughter) knew all this. She lived through all the harassment and humiliation that her mother suffered at the hands of the security police. She told her story as the child of an activist, what it meant both in the warm support and affirmation of the township community and in having to run the gauntlet of police activity.

When she had finished telling her story, she said she wanted to know who had killed her father. She spoke quietly, and for someone so young, with much maturity and dignity. You could have heard a pin drop in the hushed city hall when she said, 'We do want to forgive but we don't know whom to forgive.'

At that time the identity of the perpetrators was still unknown. The apartheid government had held inquests and inquiries and appointed a judicial commission to try to get to the bottom of this gruesome episode. The police turned these into a sham and a charade, conspiring to perjure themselves until they were blue in the face. The truth was eventually to surface only when the perpetrators took advantage of the Commission's amnesty process and in their applications disclosed the ghastly truth, that it was the police who murdered the Cradock Four.

In September 1992, what came to be known as the Bisho massacre happened. Bisho was in the Eastern Cape, the capital of the 'independent' homeland of Ciskei, ruled by Brigadier Oupa Gqozo. At first he was friendly towards the ANC but relations soured especially when he decreed Ciskei a virtual no-go area for the party. The ANC decided to stage a march on Bisho to highlight its campaign for free political activity in all the homelands and particularly Ciskei, Bophuthatswana and KwaZulu. (These and other homelands were established under apartheid's divide-and-rule master plan, which sought to strip all black South Africans of their citizenship and make them citizens of a patchwork quilt of ethnically based Bantustans scattered around South Africa. KwaZulu resisted government efforts to make it take 'independence' but the leaders of all three felt threatened by the ANC.)

Thirty people died as a result of what happened on the day when the ANC marched for free political activity and Ciskeian Defence Force soldiers fired on unarmed demonstrators. Twenty-eight protestors died in the immediate aftermath of the shootings, together with a CDF soldier shot by his colleagues. Another ANC supporter died in 1995 from his injuries.

The Commission held two hearings on the Bisho massacre, the first of which took place in Bisho itself, not far from where it had happened. The hall in which we met was packed to the rafters with those who had either been injured in the incident or who had lost loved ones, as well as those who had participated in the doomed march. The tension in the room was palpable. Some high-profile ANC leaders, who had been on the march were going to testify – Cyril Ramaphosa, at the time of the march Secretary-General of the ANC and later Chairperson of the Constituent Assembly that gave us our much-admired constitution and Ronnie Kasrils, now Minister of Water Affairs.

One of the first witnesses was the former head of the Ciskeian Defence Force, Major-General Marius Oelschig. He incensed the audience perhaps not so much by what he said as by how he said it. It may have been that he was carrying himself as a soldier, with his feelings very much under control. This may be how soldiers should conduct themselves, not carrying their hearts on their sleeves, but when people have been traumatised and their feelings are raw then such an attitude comes across as hard, unsympathetic and cynical. The temperature went up a few degrees by the time he finished testifying.

The next witnesses were former CDF officers, one white and the others black. The white officer, Colonel Horst Schobesberger, was their spokesperson. He said that it was true that they had given the orders for the soldiers to open fire. The tension in the hall became so thick that, as they say, you could have cut it with a knife. The audience could not have been more hostile. Then he turned towards the audience and made an extraordinary appeal:

I say we are sorry. I say the burden of the Bisho Massacre will be on our shoulders for the rest of our lives. We cannot wish it away. It happened. But please, I ask specifically the victims not to forget – I cannot ask this – but to forgive us, to get the soldiers back into the community, to accept them fully, to try to understand also the pressure they were under then. This is all I can do. I'm sorry, this I can say, I'm sorry.

That crowd, which had been close to lynching them, did something quite unexpected. It broke out into thunderous applause – unbelievable. The mood change was startling. The Colonel's colleagues joined him in apologising and when the applause died down I said:

Can we just keep a moment's silence please because we are dealing with things that are very, very deep. It isn't easy as we all know to ask for forgiveness and it's also not easy to forgive, but we are people who know that when someone cannot be forgiven there is no future. If a husband and wife quarrel and they don't one of them say 'I am sorry' and the other says 'I forgive', the relationship is in jeopardy. We have been given an example by our president and by many other people.

No one could have predicted that day's turn of events at the hearing. It was as if someone had waved a special magic wand which transformed anger and tension into this remarkable display of communal forgiveness and acceptance of erstwhile perpetrators. We could only be humbled by it all, and deeply thankful that so-called ordinary people could be so generous and gracious.

A few days before Christmas 1985, South African forces raided Maseru, the capital of the mountain kingdom of Lesotho, landlocked and completely surrounded by South Africa. Nine people were killed in the raid. Four days later a limpet mine placed at a shopping complex in the KwaZulu/Natal coastal town of Amanzimtoti killed five up-country holidaymakers doing their Christmas shopping. The young ANC activist, Sibusiso Andrew Zondo, aged nineteen, maintained it was in retaliation for the raid on Lesotho. He was found guilty, sentenced to death and executed in September 1986. Two of his accessories were also executed by the police.

One of the fatalities of the bomb blast was Cornelius, the eight-year-old son of Mr Johan Smit, who testified to the Commission. (I have already referred to his extraordinary reaction at the time of his son's death.)

> I told the newspapers that I thought my son was a hero because he died for freedom for people who were oppressed. A lot of people criticised me for this. They thought I was a traitor and condemned me but I still feel that way. Everybody just branded the ANC as 'terrorists' and never saw the other side of the coin. I would also never have realised this if I didn't have my own business and saw with my own eyes how these [black] people really struggled.

Now that is quite remarkable. You would expect a father to be furious that the innocent life of his son had been snuffed out in such a brutal fashion. But here is a white father, an Afrikaner to boot, saying something that just leaves you speechless. It is the sort of thing we dreamed might happen but did not dare to hope that it could; here was a miracle unfolding before our eyes and we were not dreaming it all up; we were hearing him with our own ears and dared not believe what we were hearing.

In August 1993 the Pan Africanist Student Organisation (PASO) joined hands with the ANC-supporting Congress of South African Students (COSAS) in a campaign of street protests in Cape Town, much of it involving stoning cars. The students were undeterred by ANC condemnations of their activities. They used bloodcurdling slogans such as, 'One settler, one bullet', and 'Kill the farmer, kill the Boer', which some young black activists referred to in their amnesty applications as having incited them to their bloody actions.

Amy Biehl was a Fulbright scholar from California attached to the University of the Western Cape. Before she came to South Africa, she, had been involved for a long period in the anti-apartheid student campaign at Stanford University. On 25 August 1993 she gave a lift to student friends, taking them to Gugulethu township. Youths stoned the car and when Amy and her passengers got out, the mob chased them, stoning and stabbing her. She who was so committed to justice was ironically killed by people whose cause she had espoused.

Her family were obviously shattered. Yet instead of being embittered and seeking revenge, they did not oppose the amnesty applications of those who had killed their child so brutally. Mr Peter and Mrs Linda Biehl attended the amnesty application hearing and said that they supported the entire process of reconciliation and amnesty. They embraced the families of the murderers of their child.

But what is more remarkable is that they have established the Amy Biehl Foundation, whose objectives are to help young people in the township where some residents could very well have been involved in the murder of their daughter. The Biehls return to South Africa regularly to oversee the operations of the Foundation and they frequently pass the spot where their child met her gruesome death. They have testified to how their daughter's death has led them to deeper insights and they have invested a great deal of their time and energy as well as their money to help develop the township community where their daughter was killed. They are passionately committed to rescuing as many as possible of Gugulethu's youth from the dead ends that might well be their lot, salvaging them from the engulfing criminal violence, and setting them on the road to responsible adulthood.

In the 1980s the ANC embarked on a bombing campaign. It claimed that the targets selected were meant to be security force personnel or the buildings in which they worked, such as police stations or military installations. But contrary to the ANC's declared intentions, most of those who were killed in such explosions were in fact civilians.

The first such major bomb blast took place in Pretoria in Church Street on 20 May 1983. Twenty-one people were killed and 219 injured when a massive car bomb went off outside the city centre building that housed the South African Air Force headquarters. Eleven of those killed worked for the SAAF, two were members of the ANC's armed wing, Umkhonto we Sizwe and the rest were civilians.

One of the 219 injured was Mr Neville Clarence, who was blinded. He had had great difficulty obtaining a disability grant and pension from the Air Force, but he told one of our Human Rights Violations Committee hearings, 'I have absolutely no grudge whatsoever to bear, never have and never will, against the perpetrators of that car bomb explosion . . .'

He attended the amnesty hearing when those who had master-minded this attack were applying for amnesty. The main applicant was Mr Aboobaker Ismail. Neville Clarence did not oppose the application. Instead, he went over to Mr Ismail, who had apologised for causing the civilian casualties, shook hands with him and said he forgave him even if his action had cost him his sight and he wanted them to join forces to work for the common good of all. He later said that it was as if they did not want to let go of each other as they shook hands. The picture of the two shaking hands was blazoned on our TV screens and splashed on the front pages of our newspapers. It said more eloquently than words what the whole process of healing and reconciliation was about. It stood out as a superb icon for the Truth and Reconciliation process.

I have described the victims who testified to the Commission as *remarkable, extraordinary* and *special* and in a real sense they have proved themselves so. Yet in an important sense they are *not* extra-ordinary, special or remarkable, if those words are taken to mean that they were an exception; unique; out of this world. Then the South African way of trying to deal with a divisive, traumatic and awful past would not be useful as an example the world might care to emulate because it would be unrepeatable. Such an interpretation would also fly in the face of facts – as demonstrated in the case of the Biehl family. These are not South Africans. They are United States citizens. South Africans are therefore not peculiar. Perhaps it would be better to say that there are so-called ordinary people in each nation and land who are capable of some extraordinary accomplishments. People who can make a process such as the Truth and Reconciliation Commission a viable option for other countries that need to come to terms with their past. Just as those who have been capable of the most horrendous atrocities turn out to be ordinary human beings like you and me, who could so easily be the neighbour next door, so too those who have demonstrated noteworthy instances of the capacity to forgive, to be magnanimous, could easily be the man or woman living down the street. Wonderfully, forgiveness and reconciliation are possible anywhere and everywhere and have indeed been taking place often, unremarked and unsung.

The following story, for example, took place in the United States. Marietta Jaeger and her husband and five children spent a glorious month-long summer vacation camping in Montana. On the last night of their holiday her youngest child, seven-year-old Susie, went missing. Marietta hoped against hope that she would be found and thought this was going to happen one night when the man who had kidnapped Susie telephoned. But he only taunted her. Eventually the man was arrested, the body of her child was found and she met the girl's murderer and told him she forgave him. This is how she described her experience:

> . . . I had finally come to believe that real justice is not punishment but restoration, not necessarily to how things used to be, but to how they really should be. In both the Hebrew and Christian scriptures whence my beliefs and values come, the God who rises up from them is a God of mercy and compassion, a God who seeks not to punish, destroy, or put us to death, but a God who works unceasingly to help and heal us, rehabilitate and reconcile us, restore us to the richness and fullness of life for which we have been created. This, now, was the justice I wanted for this man who had taken my little girl.
>
> Though he was liable for the death penalty, I felt it would violate and profane the goodness, sweetness, and beauty of Susie's life by killing the kidnapper in her name. She was deserving of a more noble

and beautiful memorial than a cold-blooded, premeditated, state-sanctioned killing of a restrained defenseless man, however deserving of death he may be deemed to be. I felt I far better honored her, not by becoming that which I deplored, but by saying that all life is sacred and worthy of preservation. So I asked the prosecutor to offer the alternative sentence for this crime, mandatory life imprisonment with no chance of parole. My request was honored, and when the alternative was offered, only then did he confess to Susie's death and also to the taking of three other young lives.

Though I readily admit that initially I wanted to kill this man with my bare hands, by the time of the resolution of his crimes, I was convinced that my best and healthiest option was to forgive. In the twenty years since losing my daughter, I have been working with victims and their families, and my experience has been consistently confirmed. Victim families have every right initially to the normal, valid, human response of rage, but those persons who retain a vindictive mind-set ultimately give the offender another victim. Embittered, tormented, enslaved by the past, their quality of life is diminished. However justified, our unforgiveness undoes us. Anger, hatred, resentment, bitterness, revenge – they are death-dealing spirits, and they will 'take our lives' on some level as surely as Susie's life was taken. I believe the only way we can be whole, healthy, happy persons is to learn to forgive. That is the inexorable lesson and experience of the gospel of Marietta. Though I would never have chosen it so, the first person to receive a gift of life from the death of my daughter . . . was me.'[4]

It is a powerful story.

In similar vein, the President of the Irish Republic, Mary McAleese, in her book *Unreconciled Being – Love in Chaos*,[5] describes the remarkable reaction of Gordon Wilson to the brutal killing of his daughter:

It is a rare person who arrives at that state of perfect spiritual serenity. I suppose they are saints of sorts, not necessarily beatified and canonised saints but the kind of people in whose presence we intuit the nearness of God because they bring their best friend everywhere with them. God does not accompany them as a bodyguard or go in front of them like a Soviet tank clearing a path. He accompanies them like a soprano's pure voice accompanies a song, like a dewdrop sits on a rose.

One such was Gordon Wilson. He was a man so practised in the discipline of love that when his beautiful daughter Marie died, hard and cruelly, at the slaughter that was the Enniskillen bombing, her hand in his as she slipped away, the words of love and of forgiveness sprang as naturally to his lips as a child's eyes are drawn to its mother. His words shamed us, caught us off guard. They sounded so different from what we expected and what we were used to. They brought stillness with them. They carried a sense of the transcendent into a place so ugly we could hardly bear to watch. But he had his detractors and unbelievably his bags of hate mail. How dare you forgive, they shouted? What kind of father are you who can forgive your daughter's killers? It was as if they had never heard the command to love and forgive anywhere before. It was as if they were being spoken for the first time in the history of humanity and Christ had never uttered the words, 'Father forgive them for they know not what they do.' As one churchgoing critic said to me on the subject of Gordon Wilson, 'Sure the poor man must have been in shock,' as if to offer love and forgiveness is a sign of mental weakness instead of spiritual strength.

There may indeed have been moments when God may have regretted creating us. But I am certain there have been many more times when God has looked and seen all these wonderful people who have shone in the dark night of evil and torture and abuses and suffering; shone as they have demonstrated their nobility of spirit, their magnanimity as they readily forgive. They have dispelled the murkiness and fresh air has blown into that situation to transfigure it. It has filled people with new hope that despair, darkness, anger, resentment and hatred would not have the last word; hope that a new situation could come about when enemies might become friends again, when that dehumanised perpetrator might be helped to recover his lost humanity. This is not a wild, irresponsible dream. It has happened and it is happening and there is hope that nightmares will end, that seemingly intractable problems will find solution and that God has some tremendous fellow-workers, some outstanding partners out there.

We each have a capacity for great good and that is what must make God say it was well worth the risk to bring us into existence. Extraordinarily, God the omnipotent One depends on us – puny, fragile, vulnerable as we may be, to accomplish His purposes for good, for justice, for forgiveness and healing and wholeness. God has no one but us. St Augustine of Hippo said, 'God without us will not as we without God cannot.'

A rustic Russian priest was accosted by a brash young physicist who rehearsed all the reasons for atheism and arrogantly went on, 'Therefore I do not believe in God.' The little priest, not put off at all, replied quietly, 'Oh, it doesn't matter. God believes in you.'

God believes in us. God depends on us to help make this world all that God wants it to be.

CHAPTER EIGHT

'It feels like I've got my sight back'

There have been many scoffers who sniffed disparagingly at what some called the Kleenex Commission because there was so much crying in the public hearings when witnesses unburdened themselves. Others who wanted the Truth and Reconciliation Commission to fail gloated as they asked superciliously what reconciliation had this Commission effected and what truth had been unearthed since, as these sarcastic critics claimed, all we seemed to get were just wild, untested allegations by those playing to the gallery.

If we asked these cynics what precisely they themselves had done or were doing to promote reconciliation, they often mumbled some exculpatory, self-justifying tale. They seemed oblivious to the fact that had there been no such process as the Truth and Reconciliation Commission, which depended on the transitional agreement that there should be no retribution or revenge, and that South Africans should seek to create a new country unspoiled by racial or sectional conflict, they might very well not have been around to spew forth their distressing and dismissive observations. How quickly and how easily we get to take things for granted. So many white people in South Africa have come to see themselves as entitled to reconciliation and forgiveness without their having to lift so much as a little finger to aid this very crucial and demanding process.

(That is a broad generalisation, which in the way of generalisations does not do justice to those white people who have been outstanding in their commitment to justice and who were in the thick of things in the dark days of apartheid's repression. Many of those in this distinguished group had to run the gauntlet of the hostility of their white community. They faced ostracism and frequently had to suffer the sort of harassment and vilification, and sometimes detention and torture, that were the lot of those who dared to stand up to be counted, who were willing to swim against the current in a country where all this was anathema. Their contribution to our struggle was incalculable and indispensable and I want to pay them all a very richly deserved and very warm tribute.)

Having said that, I have to note sadly that a very large section of the white community have forgotten, far too easily and far too soon, that our country was indeed on the verge of a catastrophe which could have seen us overwhelmed by the kind of carnage and unrest that have characterised places such as Bosnia, Kosovo, the Middle East and Northern Ireland. We should all be filled to overflowing with immense gratitude that things turned out differently, that we have been blessed to have as President someone who has become an international icon of forgiveness and reconciliation, and that so many in our land have emulated their President. I have longed so eagerly and so desperately for a like generosity of spirit to have been evoked in the white community by the magnanimity of those in the black community who, despite the untold suffering inflicted so unnecessarily on them, have been ready to forgive their tormentors.

So there have been the detractors, mostly, though not exclusively, from the white community. If we were challenged on what we really achieved in the Truth and Reconciliation Commission, a valid reply would be that we were asked to try to provide as full a picture as possible of the gross human rights violations that occurred in our mandate period of thirty-four years. The Commission was expected to promote national unity and reconciliation. It is crucial to underscore that it was meant to *promote* not to *achieve* those worthwhile objectives. It was expected to make a contribution – perhaps it was hoped that it would be a telling, a strategic contribution – to a process that was envisaged as being a national project. The onus is on each single South African to realise that this is not a project to which anyone can be indifferent. It is a long-term and enduring process to which it is incumbent on every South African to make his or her contribution. Without being melodramatic, it is not too much to claim that it is a matter of life and death. On its success does hinge the continued existence of our nation, of all of us as a people and as separate individuals. It is ultimately in our own best interest that we become forgiving, repentant, reconciling and reconciled people, because without forgiveness, without reconciliation we have no future. So it is in a real sense premature to ask what the Commission has achieved. And yet there are some significant achievements that were notched up in the two and a bit years during which most of our work was undertaken.

The examples of reconciliation or willingness to forgive that I have described in the last chapter were not the only ones. We found that many who came to the Commission attested afterwards to the fact that they had found relief, and experienced healing, just through the process of telling their story. The acceptance, the affirmation, the acknowledgement that they had indeed suffered was cathartic for them. If this had happened to only one person, then we would have said that the Commission had more than justified its existence. The fact that many people said the same made us wish we could have afforded many more the opportunity of unburdening themselves of the heavy weight of their anguish.

In Chapter 2 I told the story of how the brother of Matthew Goniwe, one of the Cradock Four, told me of the sense of relief the family experienced after his sister-in-law, Nyameko, had testified to the Commission. In the way of *ubuntu,* her story was his story vicariously too, because *ubuntu* says they belong together, all of them who make up the Goniwe family. They are interconnected in this network of interdependence and togetherness, so that what happened to one, in a very real sense happened to them all. Nyameko means 'one who endures much', 'the patient one'. When Nyameko Goniwe testified to us she told how the family had been disappointed by the magistrate's finding at the first inquest on her husband's death that he and his comrades had been killed by persons unknown, when all the while it was an open secret that the security forces must have been involved:

> . . . The family was engaged in trying to get the first inquest to be opened up – they [the state] wanted to have just a closed matter and deal with it as quickly as possible. We fought over that, using our lawyers, and then it was opened up a little bit. But . . . nothing came out of that. Then we had to go through a [second] long inquest, and we were bruised by it, emotionally and physically, and I guess we had high hopes as well. I remember when the finding was announced, we were so disappointed. I don't know what we were expecting at the end, so I suppose we are approaching the Commission in the same sort of light . . . The . . . reluctance [about coming to the Truth and Reconciliation Commission] was over not knowing what it is that's going to happen here. I had little information. But now that I am here I'm humbled by the experiences of the others. I'm happy to say, I'm happy that I came.

We have been humbled at what people did seem to find when they exposed their vulnerability in public. I certainly should not claim that I had been expecting that those who approached the Commission would often find healing and closure in the process of recounting their often devastating stories. I am not a trained psychologist, though as a pastor I am supposed to know a little about how the human soul and spirit operate. It was a wonderful privilege to be there when people opened their hearts, and in that telling came to a new wholeness. I thank God that the Truth and Reconciliation Commission offered the kind of safe and welcoming environment that enabled some of this catharsis to take place.

Here is what a young man, Lucas Sikwepere, said after he had described how a notorious Cape Town policeman, Warrant Officer H. C. J. 'Barrie' Barnard, had shot him in the face, blinding him:

> I feel what . . . has brought my sight back, my eyesight back, is to come here and tell the story. I feel what has been making me sick all the time

is the fact that I couldn't tell my story. But now . . . it feels like I've got my sight back by coming here and telling you the story.

The privilege of being part of such a process more than made up for the mean-spiritedness of so many who impoverished themselves by shutting themselves out of something that would have benefited them in ways that they had never imagined.

One of our most difficult and contested hearings was the nine-day marathon sitting which enquired into the activities of Mrs Winnie Madikizela-Mandela's 'Football Club'. Despite the controversy, even this gruelling hearing produced some positive results. The saga began when, in response to statements from victims and in view of her conviction in the courts on charges of kidnapping and assault, the Commission subpoenaed her under Section 29 of the Promotion of National Unity and Reconciliation Act. This was the provision which allowed us, among other things, to summon people to investigative inquiries. In the normal course of events it would have been an in-camera inquiry. On her insistence, however, it was held as an open and public hearing, presumably so that she might be able to respond to all the suspicions, allegations and innuendos levelled against her.

There is no gainsaying that she is a remarkable and unusual lady. When her husband was serving his life sentence in gaol the apartheid system did all in its power to destroy her by all kinds of harassment. She was detained, she was kept under police surveillance, she was even banished from Soweto to Brandfort, nearly 480 miles away in the Free State, where she was dumped in a community that spoke seSotho, a language Mrs Madikizela-Mandela did not know at the time. This was all in an effort to break her spirit, by cutting her off from people. And she was a banned person. This means you are a prisoner at your own expense. She was not permitted to attend a gathering, which was defined as meeting more than one other person. She could not leave the magisterial district to which she was confined for the period of the ban, usually five years, without permission. She could not go to the movies, attend church or go to a picnic. She could not attend the wedding or funeral of even the closest family member unless she got permission, rarely granted. A banned person could not communicate with another banned person nor be quoted without the Minister's permission. You had to be at home from 6pm to 6am on weekdays and throughout the weekend – a veritable twilight existence. This was the lot of many opponents of the apartheid system, and they were banned without benefit of due process. The Minister was prosecutor and judge in his own case: you did not know what evidence was available to justify the ban, and thus you could not challenge it. It was a total abrogation of the rule of law and it was justified for the benefit of the West by the claim that it was necessary to combat Communism. Many of those who fell foul of these laws were committed Christians.

Winnie Mandela was quite marvellous: charismatic, attractive, a powerful speaker at those times when she was not banned. She played a crucial role in rallying people when most of our leaders were either in prison or in exile. The struggle against apartheid owes her an immense debt. She was a consummate politician who knew what made so-called ordinary people tick. She was there when they were hurting. She ran circles round most politicians when it came to gaining popular support and even now, when she has been disgraced by being convicted of the abduction of Stompie Seipei, she has a remarkable capacity to bounce back. Her popular support among the grassroots membership of the ANC has remained steady and by 1999 was growing again.

When she was in Brandfort I used to visit her and bring her Holy Communion, which we celebrated in my car in the street. You could see away in the distance on a hill overlooking the squalid township the security police in their car keeping strict watch on her movements. At weekends she was not allowed out of her yard, and on those occasions we used to celebrate Holy Communion with me on one side of the fence and her on the other. I often wondered at our country, preening itself before the world, claiming to be a Christian country – whatever that might mean – and here we were having to celebrate the Eucharist in this fashion.

Banishing her to Brandfort backfired on the system. She was soon raising the political consciousness of this rural, unsophisticated community by example. Brandfort is a small, dusty ghetto township. She planted a lawn and vegetable garden, and soon little vegetable gardens and pocket-handkerchief-size lawns began to sprout around Brandfort. She started a clinic and a library, and the white Afrikaner community began urging the authorities to remove her because they said she was an agitator: their natives were becoming uppity ever since she had landed in their midst. The people admired her – indeed, loved her. She wasn't someone to trifle with, and I think she was aware of her power and influence. She was self-assured and not a little arrogant. I was very fond of her, and her two daughters called me 'uncle'. She was the darling of the resistance overseas, especially in the African American community. She came to be known as 'The Mother of the Nation'.

The apartheid system applied massive pressure on her. One of the lessons I have learned as I have grown older is that we should be a great deal more modest in any claims we make about our prowess and our various capacities. Even more importantly, we should be generous in our judgements of others, for we can never really know all there is to know about another. I do not hereby want to exonerate Mrs Madikizela-Mandela from responsibility for the awful things she did or was believed to have been involved with, nor to condone any of it. But she did do a marvellous job as a leader in the struggle. None of us can ever predict with absolute certainty that we know we would not buckle under pressure. It is no good pointing out that others survived the same kind of pressures. We are all different, reacting and responding in uniquely different ways.

Nothing like that nine-day hearing was held for any other person. One can well imagine the howls that would have been forthcoming about the Truth and Reconciliation Commission not being even-handed had we subjected, say, an Afrikaner to similar treatment. Some who are forever looking for hidden agendas claim this was done at a time when the ANC leadership would have been glad for anything that might embarrass her and so undermine her popularity with the people. It is enough to point out that the Commission had wanted a hearing behind closed doors. We were intent on understanding a fascinating personality and her immense impact on significant events that were relevant to our concern about the violation of human rights. It was she who insisted on an open hearing with all the attendant publicity.

Security was stepped up at the venue in Mayfair, a suburb west of Johannesburg, in November 1997. The media were there in full force and Mrs Madikizela-Mandela, resplendent in her elegant designer outfits, did not let anyone down. Many of her supporters turned up – young men who danced and sang their hearts out as well as sedate matrons in the distinctive uniform of the ANC Women's League, of which she was president. Once these ladies staged a demonstration with posters inside the room in which the hearing was being held until I told them they were in contempt, for although the hearing was not a court trial many of the conventions of a court obtained. (Witnesses who perjured themselves, for instance, could be charged as if they had done so in a regular court case.)

There was a panel of lawyers representing various clients who had an interest in the proceedings. They were a little frustrated when we had to curtail their cross-examination because we were not a court seeking to establish guilt beyond reasonable doubt. We were seeking to establish as much of the truth as possible, and had to keep reminding everybody that we would not pass a verdict of guilty or innocent at the end of the hearing. It would be left to the Commission to announce in its main report just where it believed responsibility resided in the violation of human rights.

Mrs Madikizela-Mandela disdainfully dismissed almost all the testimony against her as 'ridiculous' and 'ludicrous'. She hardly turned a hair. Perhaps the only time she seemed to be affected was when Bishop Verryn turned to her during his evidence, directly after apologising to Mrs Joyce Seipei for not doing more to protect her son, Stompie, from being killed. Bishop Verryn, who had been unjustly smeared and libelled by her as an abuser of children, addressed her in these moving words:

We've met face to face briefly in my mission house once, and my feelings about you have taken me in many directions, as you can imagine. I long for our reconciliation. I have been profoundly, profoundly, affected by some of the things that you have said about me, that have hurt me and cut me to the quick. I have had to struggle to come to some place of learning to forgive, even if you do not want forgiveness or even think that I deserve to offer that to you. I struggle to find a way in which we can be reconciled for the sake of this nation and for the people that I believe God loves so deeply. And so I sit before you and want to say that to you.

At the end of the hearing, the Commission adjourned to consider its findings on the activities of Mrs Madikizela-Mandela and the Football Club, which we published in our Report in October 1998. However, before we did so, I made an impassioned plea to her. I began by telling the hearing about my family's relationship with her:

I just want to say that we have had a very close relationship with the Mandelas. We live in the same street in what is sometimes called Beverley Hills [Orlando West in Soweto], our children went to the same school in Swaziland . . . Mrs Madikizela-Mandela is godmother to one of our grandchildren, who was baptised on the Sunday of Madiba's [Nelson Mandela's] release.

I told of my visits to Brandfort and described her as an icon of liberation:

We can never forget her outstanding contribution to the struggle and her indomitable spirit. Everything was done to seek to break that spirit and she was an incredible inspiration to many and her contribution to the struggle can never be gainsaid. She was the most apt representative for her husband.

I then introduced an appeal to Mrs Madikizela-Mandela by reiterating what it was that we had been trying to do in the hearings and describing my mixed responses to the performance of prominent leaders of our people, who had given evidence at the hearing of their attempts to intervene to stop the abuses of the Football Club:

> We struggled to establish a new, a different dispensation characterised by a new morality, where integrity, truthfulness and accountability were the order of the day. We say that the current crime, domestic violence, not caring for our environment, corruption, selfishness, which are prevalent are there because we need the antidote of a new moral order, a respect for authority.
>
> Some of us were devastated, but also found it exhilarating what happened during this hearing: devastated by the performance of some eminent leaders of the struggle. The moral turpitude that came from them was unexpected and shattering. There were splendid exceptions who stood out in stark contrast, Azhar Cachalia, Murphy Morobe, the two Methodist bishops, Sydney Mufamadi [now the Cabinet minister responsible for the police] . . .
>
> We need to demonstrate that qualitatively this new dispensation is different, qualitatively morally, that we need to stand up to be counted for goodness, for truth, for compassion and not kow-towing to the powerful.

I then turned to my appeal:

> I acknowledge Mrs Madikizela-Mandela's role in the history of our struggle and yet one has to say that something went wrong, horribly, badly wrong. What, I don't know. None of us can ever be able to predict – for you have to keep saying, there but for the grace of God, go I. Something wrong, such that many leaders had to be involved in seeking to deal with a particular problem.
>
> It was marvellous seeing Winnie as she walked hand in hand with her husband . . . [in 1990] leaving the Victor Verster prison. It was wonderful seeing them walk together on the lawn of Bishopscourt on the day after his release.
>
> I was one of the Church leaders who was asked to come and speak to you [in 1988, when the activities of the Football Club forced Church and civic leaders to act]. I came all the way from Cape Town [to Soweto] . . . When I came and we tried to have the meeting, it was

impossible to have the meeting for you were not able to see us. You were studying, you said . . .

This is what I would have said to you, this is what I want to say to you: I speak to you as someone who loves you very deeply, who loves your family very deeply. I would have said to you: Let us have a public meeting, and at that public meeting for you to stand up and say there are things that went wrong, there are things that went wrong and I don't know why they went wrong. There are people out there who want to embrace you. I still embrace you because I love you and I love you very deeply. There are many out there who would have wanted to do so if you were able to bring yourself to say something went wrong . . . and say, 'I am sorry. I am sorry for my part in what went wrong.'

I believe we are incredible people. Many would have rushed out in their eagerness to forgive and to embrace you.

I beg you, I beg you, I beg you please – I have not made any particular finding from what has happened here. I speak as someone who has lived in this community. You are a great person and you don't know how your greatness would be enhanced if you were to say, 'Sorry, things went wrong, forgive me.' I beg you.

Mrs Madikizela-Mandela responded:

Thank you very much for your wonderful, wise words. That is the father I have always known in you. I am hoping it is still the same. I will take this opportunity to say to the family of Dr [Abubaker] Asvat[1], how deeply sorry I am; to Stompie's mother, how deeply sorry I am – I have said so to her before a few years back, when the heat was very hot. I am saying it is true, things went horribly wrong. I fully agree with that and for that part of those painful years when things went horribly wrong and we were aware of the fact that there were factors that led to that, for that I am deeply sorry.

On that note, I adjourned the hearing.

It may have been considered a lukewarm plea, but I am not sure that we are right to scoff at even what might appear a half-hearted request for forgiveness. It is never easy to say, 'I am sorry', they are the hardest words to articulate in any language. I often find it difficult to say them even in the intimacy of my bedroom to my wife. I can imagine how much more difficult it must be to utter them in the full glare of TV lights and media publicity.

The prophet Isaiah speaks of the servant of God who is gentle and does not blow out a flickering flame. I think this was the very first time Mrs Madikizela-Mandela had apologised in public, and that was something for someone as proud as her. During the course of the hearing she had been photographed with Mrs Seipei, and some suggested that it was the Commission that had somehow manoeuvred Mrs Seipei into such a picture because our stock would go up for having effected a reconciliation between these two people. As it happens, the initiative was Mrs Seipei's, herself an amazing person who nursed no grudge.

My colleague Yasmin Sooka, deputy chair of the Commission's Human Rights Violations Committee, described to SABC Radio journalists some of the public reaction to my plea, especially among whites:

> I think that his gesture was misinterpreted by a number of people who saw it as him trying to give her a way out, but for me that's the reality of what this is about – about saying things have gone wrong and we take responsibility for it. I think that was a very poignant and emotional moment. And I knew it was one of the sort of great cameos, I would call it, of the Commission.

I did not have time to think about the consequences of a rebuff from Mrs Mandela. My impassioned plea could so easily have fallen flat on its face. Mercifully, she responded reasonably positively and I could rush out to catch a plane for Cape Town for an urgent meeting early on the following day. I was relieved, to put it mildly!

The case of a policeman in KwaZulu/Natal, however, showed what could happen when someone took the initiative himself to go out of his way to ask for forgiveness. In December 1988, at the height of the bloody conflict between Chief Buthelezi's Inkatha Freedom Party

and the ANC-aligned United Democratic Front (UDF) in KwaZulu/
Natal, Brian Mitchell, a police captain, gave orders to a group of
special constables to attack UDF supporters. These constables were
referred to disparagingly as '*kits konstabels*' (*kits* being Afrikaans for
'instant', as in instant coffee) because they received only the most
rudimentary training and were then let loose on people. They were
often ill-disciplined and sometimes came on duty whilst under the
influence of alcohol; they were armed with shotguns. The township
youth taunted them and they were despised as collaborators, as were
most police officers. Thus they were likely to be quite unsympathetic
to those they saw as hostile to the 'system'. In this case, they
misunderstood their orders and attacked the wrong target. Instead of
hitting the intended UDF supporters (which would have been just as
reprehensible) they mowed down eleven people, mainly women and
children, who were at a vigil at Trust Feed Farm, devastating an
apolitical rural community. Mitchell was found guilty and sentenced
to thirty years' imprisonment. At his amnesty hearing he asked for
forgiveness from the community he had helped to destroy.

> And I can just ask the people that were involved directly or indirectly
> . . . and who have been affected by this case . . . to consider forgiving
> me . . . I have lost everything in life . . .

The Trust Feed Farm community said they were ready to forgive
him, providing he became actively involved in reconstructing the
community he had helped to destroy. Brian Mitchell did a
courageous and unusual thing. He asked the Commission to arrange
for him to visit the community. It could have gone badly wrong. It
was a difficult and tense meeting at the beginning, with everybody a
little awkward and the community understandably hostile. Haltingly,
he addressed the assembled community:

> I just want to express my gratitude towards the community for
> allowing me to come here today and for the goodwill that . . . I've
> experienced here so far. There were people that warned me that I

mustn't come here today. But, despite those warnings, I have come
here because I know it's the right thing to do . . .

I was led to understand that there are still a lot of people that left the
area in 1988, that have not been allowed to resettle in this area. I think
it's important that we must get these people to be allowed to return to
their land and to develop their land. And that there's reconciliation
between the political parties that were so divided in this area.

The atmosphere began to change, to ease, after a while. Whilst one
or two of the victims were still not too keen to forgive him, the
majority were glad he had come, and by the time he left things had
improved so much that they were waving him goodbye quite warmly.
This initially uneasy encounter which gradually warmed was shown
on TV and widely reported in South Africa and that could only be
good especially in an area that has been characterised by so much
violence and turmoil as KwaZulu/Natal. I am sure it served to
encourage others to try to walk the difficult but ultimately rewarding
path of destroying enemies by turning them into friends.

Brian Mitchell had paid a heavy price for his involvement with the
police in their underhand work in fomenting trouble between the
rival political groupings. His wife had divorced him and he had not
seen his son in a very long while. I admire him for wanting to
translate his remorse into something practical for the community he
had victimised. Perhaps this kind of reparation should have been a
required condition for amnesty to be granted. Then the criticism that
those who got amnesty had got something for nothing whilst their
victims languished in poverty, squalor and suffering would have
been unfounded.

A different story shows, again, the way the Commission was
sometimes able to reach the truth when other methods had failed. In
the early hours of 31 August 1988 a massive bomb rocked Khotso
House, in Johannesburg, the headquarters of the South African
Council of Churches, and reduced it to rubble. It is a miracle that no
one was seriously injured. A night watchman who was thrown down

the lift shaft suffered only light injuries. The occupants of a block of flats opposite that housed pensioners also escaped with relatively minor injuries when the force of the blast shattered window panes and sent debris flying like projectiles. During the day, the street that passes Khotso House is usually a hive of activity, a busy thorough-fare near the main railway station, with pedestrians hurrying by and street vendors plying their trades. When I visited the scene, a tapestry depicting Jesus standing guard over a city remained unscathed in the entrance lobby amidst all the dust and rubble – perhaps signalling that ultimately goodness and truth would prevail.

I had a fairly close link with that building because it was during my tenure as General Secretary of the SACC that we had procured it, through the generosity of the German churches. I came from Cape Town on the first available flight, now as Metropolitan of the Church of the Province of Southern Africa, to demonstrate our solidarity with the Council, whose staff had been traumatised by this awful episode. I joked with the then General Secretary, Dr Frank Chikane, as we toured the wrecked building, pointing out that I had handed over to him a sound edifice, how could he have let it come to such a pass. Most of us assumed that this was just the latest of the apartheid government's dirty tricks, even if we were not able to provide the kind of evidence that would have satisfied a court of law. Thus we were not taken in by the cock-and-bull story that the government's propaganda machine soon churned out. No less a person than Mr Adriaan Vlok, then Minister of Law and Order, announced that the ANC – which was still a banned organisation whose members were routinely described as 'terrorists' whose activities were 'Communist-inspired' – was responsible for the Khotso House bomb. He had the audacity even to name the person the police claimed had been the mastermind behind this latest outrage. He accused a Ms Shirley Gunn, who was detained without trial for about six months with her infant son.

Most of the white community, having been brain-washed by all the propaganda spewed forth by the government-controlled electronic media, took this at face value. They simply added it to their tally of terrorist deeds carried out by those savages who wanted to overthrow a Christian, God-fearing government that was providing whites with one of the highest standards of living in the world, and keeping the natives properly in their place. Most whites believed Mr Vlok and were proud of their police, who could apprehend these terrorists so quickly. They could sleep soundly in their beds knowing that their security was in such competent hands. Had I been white I would almost certainly have felt the same way. You needed grace to reject a system that assured you so much privilege, so many benefits and advantages. I constantly marvel at those white South Africans who did in fact oppose a system that benefited them so significantly.

The world and South Africa would perhaps have never been the wiser about what had actually happened to Khotso House had it not been for the Truth and Reconciliation Commission. The police could hardly be expected to blow the whistle on themselves, so the world would have gone on believing that the ANC had been the culprits – though some might have wondered how the ANC could have done this to an organisation that was so passionately anti-apartheid that it had often been described as 'the ANC at prayer', and accused of being really a front for the ANC's terrorism. The government sometimes claimed the SACC's headquarters were used as a staging post for the ANC and that ANC arms were stored in the building. Again, there were many in the white community who believed this arrant nonsense. They did not ask the obvious question: if the police had this incriminating evidence, why did they not raid the building, expose the SACC to the world and shatter irrevocably its credibility as an organisation working by peaceful methods for change? (Had this happened, almost all overseas churches and governments would have jettisoned the SACC as a huge embarrassment and it would have lost its most important financial backers.) But whites believed what the government told them. They did not want to ask awkward questions – why rock the boat when it was so comfortable floating along in it?

Then the former cabinet minister, Mr Vlok, who had announced so categorically to the media that the bombing was the handiwork of the

ANC, revealed the truth in his amnesty application. This act of terrorism, as he had accurately portrayed it when making his announcement, was in fact the work of his own department. His own police officers, meant to uphold law and order and to apprehend terrorists, had themselves carried out a very serious act of urban terrorism. This clearly demonstrated the moral bankruptcy of the apartheid system, which had to use such evil methods to sustain itself.

This is why the police had been unable to solve so many of the mysteries that abounded in our history – who had killed Steve Biko? Who had lured the Pebco Three to their gruesome deaths? Who had killed the Cradock Four? Who had bombed the headquarters of the Congress of South African Trade Unions and the Roman Catholic headquarters? The police could not solve these crimes because they themselves were the culprits, who sought to hoodwink the public by engaging in charades. Such crimes were not aberrations, the work of so-called 'bad apples', as defenders of the apartheid government later called them. They were an integral part of apartheid's tenacious efforts to survive by undermining the rule of law. The system had no integrity and was rotten to the core. It was doing what came naturally.

Mr Vlok revealed that Khotso House was bombed on the instructions of the then state president, Mr P. W. Botha, after a meeting of the State Security Council, which he had chaired. Mr Botha and others claimed that this incident did not constitute a gross violation of human rights and so was not a proper concern of the Truth and Reconciliation Commission. But the perpetrators were just lucky that no one had been killed. One of the operatives, Colonel Eugene de Kock, told the Commission they were ordered to shoot to kill even fellow police officers had they interfered in any way with the bombing. In any case, it is totally unacceptable that the state should subvert the very law which it is its duty to uphold and to safeguard.

To his credit, after applying for amnesty Mr Vlok apologised handsomely to Ms Gunn for having maligned her so disgracefully. Whilst nothing could compensate for the loss of personal freedom and gross injustice that she had suffered, it is good to know that she successfully sued the government for damages for this outrage.

Dr Chikane had survived bomb attacks, torture in detention and being one of the accused in a treason trial during the years in which he stood up to apartheid. One day whilst on a trip to Namibia he became violently sick. He recovered, and later realised this had happened after he had changed his clothes. He forgot about this odd occurrence until the next time, in the United States, when he nearly died whilst at dinner. This proved to be his salvation, because he was visiting his wife at the University of Wisconsin, where an academic had been doing research on poisons. It turned out that he had absorbed an organic poison that had been sprayed on his clothes. Most people suspected that this was yet another example of the deadly games the government played to remain in power – this time, assassinating its opponents. We could have gone on nursing our resentments and suspicions, and our frustration at not having hard evidence to back our hunches had it not been for the amnesty process.

Now we know what happened, because the Commission held a public hearing in June 1998 on the previous government's Chemical and Biological Warfare programme. What was revealed in these public sessions was devastating. The new democratic government was unhappy about a public hearing, worried that public revelations of some of the secret projects might put it in breach of the non-proliferation treaties it had signed. We worked out a satisfactory arrangement: when they applied to have restrictions placed on the hearing, I ruled that we were seeking to help cultivate a new culture of transparency, accountability and respect for human rights, so we would hold the hearings in public but would also put in place safeguards to prevent the release of information that would undermine national security or breach non-proliferation treaties.

It soon became clear that, contrary to previous claims by the apartheid government, its Chemical and Biological Warfare programme had certainly not been only for defensive purposes. It had major offensive characteristics. What was so shattering for me was that it had all been so scientific, so calculated, so clinical. We had listened to gruesome details in evidence that had come before the Commission before then. Those attacks had not, however, been well thought out by white-coated men in clinically spic-and-span laboratories, subverting science for such nefarious ends as came to light at the hearings. Commission staff who were involved in the prior investigations deserve a very warm commendation as do those University of Cape Town academics who assisted our staff to decipher intricate scientific formulas.

The evidence that emerged at our hearing showed that scientists, doctors, veterinarians, laboratories, universities and front companies had propped up apartheid with the help of an extensive international network. Scientific experiments were being carried out with a view to causing disease and undermining the health of communities. Cholera, botulism, anthrax, chemical poisoning and the production of huge supplies of Mandrax, Ecstasy and other drugs of abuse (allegedly for crowd control) were some of the projects of this programme. We wonder now that there is such a huge supply of drugs in the Coloured community of the Cape Flats in Cape Town. Is it an unfortunate social phenomenon or does it relate to part of a Chemical and Biological Warfare programme to undermine the morale of that community?

There was a bizarre air about all this, with some aspects taking on the appearance of something from a James Bond film. There were special umbrellas, screwdrivers and other implements which could become lethal weapons as poison applicators. But the use of science against innocent people reminded me of the horrors of Dachau. For me, the Chemical and Biological Warfare programme was the most diabolical aspect of apartheid. I was ready to accept that its perpetrators would do almost anything to survive but I never expected them to sink to this level. The programme was headed up by a cardiologist, Dr Wouter Basson, whom the media dubbed 'Dr Death'. He was quite nonchalant and played a cat-and-mouse game when he had to appear before the Commission, claiming that as there was already a criminal case pending against him he could not testify before us for fear that he might incriminate himself. He behaved provocatively, appearing at the hearing wearing what have come to be called 'Madiba shirts', the brightly coloured shirts much loved by our President Nelson Mandela.

The programme had cost an exorbitant amount of money. Its research was often pedestrian and the operatives attained levels of incompetence and ineptitude that were breathtaking – mercifully for some of the targets of the programme's machinations. The truth emerged about the mysterious attacks that had nearly killed Dr Chikane. His suitcase was tampered with on one of his travels and his underpants were impregnated with poison but not quite enough of it. Thus he owed his life to the ineptitude of the operatives who had tried to administer the poisons. The programme included a project that allegedly attempted to reduce the fertility rate of blacks by finding bacteria that would target blacks only.

One of those who gave evidence was scientist Dr Schalk van Rensburg, who told the hearing:

> There were also plans to contaminate medication used by President Mandela at Pollsmoor [Prison] with the untraceable, heavy metal poison Thallium. In a conversation with [another researcher] André Immelman shortly after Nelson Mandela's release . . . he was very confident that Nelson Mandela's brain function would be impaired, progressively, for some time.

Thank God they were so incompetent. Our country owes its survival very largely to Mr Mandela for being such a passionate advocate of forgiveness and reconciliation.

I had received an invitation to preach at a posh white Dutch Reformed Church in Lynnwood, Pretoria on 14 June 1998, the Sunday after the Chemical and Biological Warfare hearings. This was the parish church of some of the members of the former government. It was an important, prestigious congregation, and my second foray into that particular lion's den.

Until fairly recently the white Dutch Reformed Church (Nederduitse Gereformeerde Kerk) had been steadfast in its support of apartheid. It had provided the theological rationale for apartheid and had even preceded the politicians by proposing certain legislation to bring effect to the God-sanctioned separation of the races. The story of the Tower of Babel and the subsequent dispersal of the races, which were unable to communicate because they could not understand one another's languages, and the curse of Ham (whose descendants were condemned to be the 'servants of servants') were used to put the natives properly in their place. It was an odd interpretation to take divine punishment for the human sin, in the case of the story of the Tower of Babel, to reveal the divine will, ignoring the fact that the story of the first Christian Pentecost, recorded in Chapter 2 of the Acts of the Apostles, was seen in the Church as a dramatic reversal of all that had happened at the Tower of Babel. Most churches had condemned apartheid as a heresy, whereas the DRC harassed and declared to be heretics those of its members who criticised its stance – among whom were outstanding people such as Dr Beyers Naudé, who succeeded me as general secretary of the SACC.

But then this Church that had upheld apartheid theologically for so long abandoned this position. It invited those it had previously persecuted, those who had witnessed prophetically, to its general synod and apologised handsomely and publicly for all it had made them suffer. It was wonderful to see God's stalwarts such as Beyers Naudé being publicly vindicated and rehabilitated. Very few churches have been as forthright in acknowledging the error of their ways. My own Anglican Church was always opposed to apartheid in its formulations and in many of its conferences and synod resolutions, yet it lived out an apartheid form of existence. Of course South Africa was racially segregated, so it would have been difficult to have non-racial parishes, but the Anglican Church was painfully slow in acknowledging that it was living out a lie at variance with its pronouncements. Many white congregations were opposed to receiving Holy Communion alongside their domestic workers, although there was no reason, even under apartheid, why they should not. The first black Anglican bishop was appointed only in 1960, more than a century after the establishment of the Church. It was no government decree that made the Church pay different stipends to its clergy according to race, with white clergy being paid a great deal more than their black counterparts. So we Anglicans can't be smug when we look at the Dutch Reformed Church.

I was feeling tense and apprehensive as I prepared to go to Pretoria because many in the white community, especially Afrikaners, had regarded me as an ogre, barely Christian, and they wondered whether I was not really presiding, in the Truth and Reconciliation Commission, over a witch-hunt against Afrikaners. I received a very warm welcome, however, in a church that was quite full. The music was superb. A group of children processed in with symbolic candles. My text was Romans 5:8, my special favourite: 'Whilst we were yet sinners, Christ died for us'. I preached my only sermon – that God loves us freely as an act of grace, that we do not have to impress God in order for God to love us as a reward.

And then I said that Afrikaners imagined that they had only two options in South Africa's political, social and community life – either to be top dog, domineering, or to be underdog, subservient, the doormat of others. I said there was an exciting third option, that of embracing the new dispensation enthusiastically and using their enormous resources in money, skills and experience to help make the new ordering of society succeed for everyone's sake.

I told them how devastated I had been by the revelations of the Chemical and Biological Warfare hearings and prayed that there might arise leaders in the white community, specifically in the Afrikaner community, who would help us to come to terms with all of this and who would unequivocally apologise without trying to be too clever by half and qualify their apology out of existence. It was an electric moment. A few people in the congregation, it appeared, were weeping and one of the 'dominees' or pastors, Ockie Raubenheimer, came to stand next to me in the pulpit. His eyes were filled with tears as he spoke, sobbing. He said he had been an army chaplain for thirty years and had not known that such things were being planned or done. In a broken voice he asked me for forgiveness and as we embraced in that pulpit of that church, the congregation gave us a standing ovation.

God has done some strange things in the history of our land. That was one of the more unusual. That it should have happened in a Pretoria suburb in a Dutch Reformed Church made it particularly poignant. It was as if in the United States a white Southern Baptist had apologised for Jim Crow segregation in his church when a black was preaching, or the former Israeli Prime Minister, Benjamin Netanyahu, had gone to the West Bank and apologised for Jewish settlements among the Palestinians. There really was hope for our common motherland. Only the most cynical would have remained unmoved. This was another example of the extraordinary reconciliation that God was accomplishing through the work of the Commission.

Earlier in the Commission's life, we held a hearing in Paarl, not very far from Cape Town. One of the more significant, indeed deeply moving, moments at the hearing was the presentation by the white Dutch Reformed Church Presbytery of Stellenbosch, where that Church had one of its major theological seminaries. The confession of having been less than faithful to the demands and imperatives of the Gospel of Jesus Christ was one of the most direct and unequivocal we have had from that quarter. The Presbytery did not mince words in condemning its collusion with an unjust socio-political dispensation and for not identifying with the poor, downtrodden, and oppressed. It was like a breath of fresh air where there was frequently a great deal of self-justifying cant.

There was a special exhibition at the venue in Paarl, depicting key moments in the history of racism and resistance to apartheid. It had a section on military conscription and one of the exhibits was the uniform and equipment that had been used by Private Wallace MacGregor, who had served on the Namibian-Angolan border during the struggle for Namibian independence. He came from an Afrikaans-speaking family. His mother, Anne-Marie, had not really come to terms with the fact that her son had died at the border. She told us in a written statement:

> I was told that my son was killed a few kilometres from Oshakati [in northern Namibia]. He was brought home wrapped in a thick, sealed plastic bag. The instruction was that the plastic bag should not be opened. The only thing I know about the state my son was in is that all his limbs were intact. And this I heard from his uncle, who could only establish this by running his hands over this plastic bag . . .
>
> I accepted this as military law. You are not allowed to have the last glimpse of your own child – even as he lay there, lifeless. On the day of Wallace's funeral, his coffin wasn't opened. It is ten years since I last laid eyes on my child – nine years since he was laid to rest. But in these nine years, I've been struggling to complete the process of mourning for Wallace.
>
> A part of me wonders if in fact it was him in that plastic bag. How can I lay him to rest within my heart, if I didn't see him go? When I lost my mother, whom I loved very much, I saw her, I touched her and therefore I was able to separate from her, release her and move on. But with Wallace, there are so many questions that are still unanswered.
>
> In my struggle with my grief, I would like to know where exactly he died. How it had happened. Who was there with him when it happened? Did anybody help him to prevent it from happening? Who was the doctor who attended to him? I've never had the opportunity to ask these questions. Nobody has ever explained anything to me about my son's death . . .
>
> I sometimes see Wallace in the streets. I remember two distinct occasions, when I thought I was seeing him. And it turned out to be somebody who looked like him. My grief becomes more intense on the anniversaries of my son's death and on his birthday. He would have turned thirty in January. I've kept an album of all his photographs, as a way of dealing with the many feelings I have about the loss. But it is very hard, when there are so many things you are not sure about.

The Commission was able to arrange a meeting between the MacGregor family and someone who had seen action with their son.

He described how Wallace had been killed and Mrs Anne-Marie MacGregor kept repeating under her breath, '*Hy is rerig dood*' ('He is really dead'). Once this fact had been established beyond doubt for her, she seemed to be able to come to terms with its trauma and starkness, and to experience closure. She would no longer suffer the torture of hoping against futile hope that the Army had made a mistake and that her son was still alive.

I will not easily forget the plaintive cry of a mother who came to testify to the Commission at one of our hearings. She told us how her son had disappeared. She believed that perhaps he had died. She was not sure, but she had come to a point when she thought it was unlikely that he could still be alive, for there had been no word from him, no rumour that he might be in exile, to break the eerie silence about him that haunted her so much. And so her heart-rending *cri de coeur*, 'Can't you find me even just a bone that I could give his remains a decent burial.'

Part of the awfulness of the struggle against apartheid was the skill with which its operatives, under cover of darkness, would abduct those they suspected of being 'terrorists' or who were the underground cadres of the liberation movement inside the country, or leading lights of the still legal anti-apartheid movement. Then they would take their hostages to remote police stations or farms, where they tortured them and almost always ended up killing them. Quite frequently they ventured across South Africa's borders into foreign countries, violating without compunction the sovereignty and territorial integrity of those lands in order to spirit off those they wanted, and do with them whatever they felt like doing. Many people had disappeared in this fashion, which is why a mother could make that heart-rending appeal. Without the Commission such cries would have been carried by the wind to end uselessly as a plaintive sigh.

There must be well over 200 disappeared people. Armed with the information garnered from amnesty applications, our investigators set out to inspect various farms in different parts of the country. The police and other members of the security forces appear to have had great success in enlisting the cooperation of a few farmers and undertakers who helped them keep their dark secrets by burying quite a few people in largely unknown graves. Apartheid would have failed a great deal earlier than it did had there not been so many ordinary white citizens apparently willing to collaborate with the state. Possibly they genuinely believed they were contributing to a struggle to resist the onslaught of Communism. Otherwise it is difficult to understand why seemingly normal, law-abiding citizens should have been so ready to collaborate in such horrendous activities, in some cases not once but many times over. No wonder some in the liberation movements should have thought that farmers, especially in the farms adjacent to the borders with foreign countries, were legitimate targets for military action, that they were not strictly civilians but an integral part of the military machine. The Truth and Reconciliation Commission rejected this view but one can understand why it could be seriously canvassed.

Some of these farms became death farms, where several people were buried in this mysterious fashion. In one case the Commission investigators opened three graves, expecting to find one corpse in each. Instead they found four in each – twelve bodies in total. This was a deeply distressing occasion. The exhumations were carried out by people skilled at discovering where the earth had been disturbed, often with the help of police tracker dogs. We had pathologists and other forensic experts to help us in reconstructing the skeletons.

Members of the victims' families, who often attended the exhumations, must have hoped that the graves would be empty so that they could perhaps cling to the hope that their loved ones were still alive somewhere; that they would hear again a remembered lilt in the voice and the special way that person had of laughing or holding hands with them as they talked. We have so many ways of giving ourselves hopes that deep down we know are really false; if we didn't, perhaps we would find life intolerable.

Then families must have wondered how they could be sure it was their loved one whose remains were exhumed. Fortunately in most cases the police had kept records of these awful things. The apartheid

system is notorious for having destroyed many incriminating documents but they had not managed to destroy everything, and so
sometimes we could be reasonably certain about identification. They
had also frequently buried their victims with their identity
documents. In one heart-tugging instance there could have been no
doubt at all about the identity of the person buried there. When the
grave was opened a man said, 'This is my brother. I know those
shoes. I bought them for him.'

Speaking of records, I recall how towards the end of the life of the
Commission our investigative unit had scoured various police
stations to retrieve any records still surviving and uncovered a file of
some quite gruesome pictures. It looked as if the security police used
to bring their quarry to this police station near the border, where they
tortured and then killed them. The pictures seemed to indicate that
they had used blowtorches on their victims, the sort used by welders
– they showed horrendous scenes of burned-off limbs. If this is what
happened, what an excruciating way to die. How could the torturers
stand the stench and the screams of unbearable agony? They probably used the pictures to intimidate subsequent victims. I nearly
broke down looking at those pictures. Those who could do this must
have been tough.

Our teams opened several graves. This is what Richard Lyster, the
Commissioner who headed our KwaZulu/Natal office, had to say
about one of them:

The most enduring moment, the one that will stay with me . . . for the
rest of my life . . . is the first exhumation which was done in
KwaZulu/Natal. It involved a young woman [Phila Ndwandwe] who
had been a senior ANC MK [Umkhonto weSizwe] member in
Swaziland. She was abducted by a man called Andy Taylor, a
notorious security branch policeman. She was taken to a farm which
was rented by the security branch in a remote area of the Natal
Midlands. She was kept naked in a small concrete room. We know this
because the people who killed her have applied for amnesty. The
purpose of keeping her there and torturing her, because they did say

that they tortured her, was to persuade her to become an informer.

And then when they had no further use for her, they made her kneel down and shot her in the back of the head. They had dug a fairly deep grave, but a short grave and they had to bend her knees up to put her in and she was on her back. When we uncovered her body she had a blue plastic bag on her waist. We asked the people . . . what it was. They said she had put this plastic bag over her to try and maintain some sense of feminine dignity while she was being interrogated and tortured. For me it just said so many things about the people who killed her and it said so many things about people like her, people who died. They said things like: 'She was very brave.'

In the fifty or so cases where we managed to conduct exhumations before our mandate ran out, the families were able to give the remains of their loved ones a decent burial. In the case of ANC cadres, they received a funeral with appropriate military honours, often with a cabinet minister or deputy in attendance. All the families who were able to do this thanked the Commission profusely for finding the bones so they could bury them decently. Now they knew what had happened to their loved one and they experienced closure.

CHAPTER NINE

Why am I doing this thankless job?

There were many moments when I thought I should have had my head examined for agreeing to take on the job of chairing this particular Commission. This soliloquising despondency was always brought on by those moments when I realised that relationships in the Commission left a great deal to be desired. I have already pointed out that it was a good thing for us to be as representative of South African society as possible with regard to gender, race, political affiliation or lack of it, age, social status, religious adherence or lack of it, as well as in our professions or avocations. But this admirable attribute of the Commission did mean it took us a while to gel into a coherent group who were ready to work by consensus and who had confidence and trust in one another.

For quite a while each of us tried to impress the others as being someone not to be trifled with. We spent a long time carving out our bit of turf and making sure we would not be taken for granted, that we were people in our own right who had to be taken seriously. This is all well and good when you have heaps of time to engage in team-building exercises. But since we had such a formidable agenda to contend with, and had to hit the ground running to establish all the massive infrastructure necessary for such an impressive operation as ours turned out to be, this jostling for position made one want to tear one's hair out. However, most of my colleagues worked extremely hard. One of them was so committed to the objectives of the

Commission that she gave very considerably of her time and energy voluntarily to deal with some of the backlog of work that remained after we handed the Report to President Nelson Mandela and her formal appointment ended.

Because we were working under considerable pressure, our nerves were frequently frayed. It is remarkable that we did not buckle more often and that we did manage to complete our assignment as a much more coherent group than when we first started out. But we really were like a bunch of prima donnas, frequently hypersensitive, often taking umbrage easily at real or imagined slights.

Perhaps we had not realised just how wounded and traumatised we all were as a result of the buffeting we had all in various ways taken from apartheid. This vicious system has had far more victims than anyone had ever thought possible, because it is no exaggeration to say that we have all in different ways been wounded by apartheid. It has only been as we engaged in the process of the Commission that this has dawned on me and others. Sometimes it would be more accurate to say the realisation hit one like a pile driver in the solar plexus. In one way or another, as a supporter, a perpetrator, a victim, or one who opposed the ghastly system, something happened to our humanity. All of us South Africans were less whole than we would have been without apartheid. Those who were privileged lost out as they became more uncaring, less compassionate, less humane and therefore less human; for this universe has been constructed in such a way that unless we live in accordance with its moral laws we will pay a price. And one such law is that we are bound together in what the Bible calls 'the bundle of life'. Our humanity is caught up in that of all others. We are human because we belong. We are made for community, for togetherness, for family, to exist in a delicate network of interdependence. Truly, 'it is not good for man to be alone',[1] for no one can be human alone. We are sisters and brothers of one another whether we like it or not, and each one of us is a precious individual. This does not depend on things such as ethnicity, gender, or political, social, economic or educational status. Each person is not just to be respected but to be revered as one created in God's image. To treat anyone as if they were less than this is not just evil, not just painful – it is veritably blasphemous, for it is to spit in the face of God. And inevitably and inexorably, those who behave in this way cannot escape the consequences of their contravention of the laws of the universe.

Those who opposed apartheid could also end up, as Bishop Peter Storey so poignantly described it in the Winnie Madikizela-Mandela hearing, becoming like what they most abhorred. Tragically, they themselves frequently became brutalised and descended to the same low levels as those they were opposing. The victims often ended up internalising the definition the top dogs had of them. They began to wonder whether they might not perhaps be somehow as their masters and mistresses defined them. Thus they would frequently accept that the values of the domineering class were worth striving after. And then through the awful demons of self-hate and self-contempt, a hugely negative self-image took its place in the centre of the victims' being, corrosive of proper self-love and self-assurance, eating away at their core. This is the pernicious source of the destructive internecine strife to be found, for instance, in the African American community. Society has conspired to fill people with self-hate which they then project outwards. They hate themselves and destroy themselves by proxy when they destroy those who are like this self they have been conditioned to hate.

One of the chief, the most blasphemous consequences of injustice, especially racist injustice, is that it can make a child of God doubt that he or she is a child of God. South Africa became the site of a conflict between gravely wounded, badly traumatised combatants. Perhaps those who claimed not to be so wounded or traumatised were the most to be pitied.

The work of the Commission was to try to help heal such a wounded people. The Commission members were not some superior breed pontificating about the lot of poor, hapless victims. We were also wounded and traumatised. We each came burdened with our own baggage. We were conditioned by this thing that had defined South Africa to the world, turning her into a house divided against herself, at war with herself and a pariah to the rest of the world. Mercifully for us, the world did not leave us to our own devices but prayed for us, loved us, was exasperated by us, boycotted us, applied sanctions against us and just went on supporting us until the wonder of 27 April 1994 held the world in awe.

I was not too smart. Had I been smart I should have known we were going to start on the wrong foot in our first meeting because, stupidly, all the staff appointments we made or recommended were white. We were all anxious to get started as quickly as possible and I suggested that my personal assistant and secretary from my time as Archbishop, who knew my foibles and, most important, could read my handwriting, should be appointed as my personal assistant at the Commission. In addition, my former media secretary was made media director, because we would need to liaise with the media as quickly as possible. Dr Boraine made the same points in proposing his current secretary as his personal assistant at the Commission. These appointments were approved with little discussion. When Dr Boraine and I suggested that a young white lawyer, who had begun to distinguish himself as a human rights lawyer, be appointed as the executive secretary of the Commission, then the cat was truly set among the pigeons. Using coded language, Commissioners made it clear that there was very considerable unease about who was really going to head the Commission. Was I going to run the show, or was I just a token black fronting for Dr Boraine, who was an outstanding stalwart with an impeccable 'struggle' record but who would be suspected of being that hated species in South African anti-apartheid politics, the white liberal with all sorts of hidden agendas who would want to manipulate the Commission to his advantage? How this was to happen no one said explicitly. But the waters were properly muddied and it took nearly two years after that to get people to begin to think that we were really all on the same side with much the same kind of concerns.

Along the way we had a few other hiccups. Soon after our first staff appointments we were faced with a very serious problem. One of the first appointments in our Western Cape regional office was of the spouse of a Commissioner. That in itself would not necessarily have been a major problem. The trouble is that the Commissioner was on the panel which interviewed applicants and she should, with the perfect wisdom of hindsight, have excused herself from the panel or declared her interest when it interviewed her spouse. Most of her colleagues in the same regional office had no doubts about her integrity and were not particularly concerned that she would be an interviewer, not fearing that she would let her judgement be affected by nepotism. It was not so with other colleagues. Right in the middle of our first hearing in East London, when we had so many other things to be concerned about, this particular bombshell was revealed. It certainly did not help that the couple was white. It really was extraordinary, though, that people ignored the fact that there had been others on the panel who would certainly have rejected a candidate who was not suitably qualified.

Thus our attention was divided at a crucial time when we needed to put our best foot forward, since this was our opportunity to display the Commission as effectively and attractively as possible. Whatever impact we made at this first hearing and the impressions it had on the media and the public would have important repercussions about whether victims would be willing to come forward to testify. Thus it was a thoroughly inopportune time to be distracted by this kind of concern. I was worried too that it was the sort of tidbit that certain sections of the media would find difficult to resist, especially the constituency that had long ago dismissed the Commission as a witch-hunt against Afrikaners and a stick for the ANC to clobber its political opponents with. There were some within the Commission who were naive in their dealings with the press, enjoying a new sense of power and importance in seeing themselves in print and on television and finding it difficult to maintain the confidentiality enjoined by the law.

We discovered to our chagrin that the Commission leaked like a sieve. Information which the Act under which we operated enjoined should be kept confidential, at least until a hearing was convened, kept finding its way into the public domain, and this added to the sense of distrust. You were not sure that sensitive material might not find its way into the public domain at inappropriate times. I had to hone my skills at juggling a number of balls in the air at the same time – taking pastoral responsibility for all the members of the team; seeking to make everyone feel that they were indeed valued and special and that they brought indispensable attributes to the process; and providing the media, who could undermine the whole process if they were to become hostile, with that information to which they were entitled.

Fortunately I had a good media director, who was held in high regard by the practitioners of a trade in which he had himself been trained, and I had on the whole a very good relationship with the journalists covering the Commission. I decided long ago in my public life to be as accessible as possible, particularly in the dark days of the struggle when we did not have many resources and needed the media to tell our story to combat the sophisticated and well-funded propaganda of the apartheid state. I also decided that it was always better to be straightforward and transparent, so that when sometimes I had to say 'no comment' or 'please wait for a while', the journalists tended to trust that I was not trying to pull a fast one on them. We also learned that it was always best to get your version of events out first because that usually determined the nature of the discourse after-wards. Nothing was more debilitating than to be caught wrong-footed, having to be defensive and trying to explain and to justify. You had lost the round if you had to be defensive and so I tried to avoid having too many things that were confidential. We all like power. There are few things as exciting as having a secret, and what is the point of having a secret if others on the outside do not get to know that you possess this precious thing? We tried to pre-empt this temptation to show off by taking the media into our confidence as much and as frequently as possible. Even so we did experience some awkwardness when now and again something was leaked.

So at that first hearing we were apprehensive about having to field questions about the appointment of a Commissioner's spouse when we should have been concentrating on the absorbing and distressing business of the hearing. Mercifully either the leak did not happen or the press decided that it was really of very little significance in the face of the terrible drama that was unfolding in the heart-rending testimonies being given before the Commission. If we appeared calm and in reasonable control of things then we must have been consummate actors, for there were certainly ripples below the surface.

Perhaps I should be more appreciative of those moments in the early morning when I try to be quiet, to sit in the presence of the gentle and compassionate and unruffled One to try to share or be given some of that divine serenity. It was a mercy too to have the joyful privilege of a daily Eucharist – normally in my office or hotel room with my personal assistant, the media director and the policeman appointed to see to my security, and on Fridays in St George's Cathedral whenever we were in Cape Town. It was comforting too to know that we were being upheld by the fervent intercessions of so many in South Africa and around the world. Without all this I know I would have collapsed and the powers of evil, ever on the lookout to sabotage efforts to attain good, would have undermined this extraordinary attempt to heal a wounded people. We could have been overwhelmed by the forces that make for disintegration and failure. We were fortunately kept in touch with the source of Good not just by our own efforts, but even more by the loving concern of so many others.

On one occasion, as related in the Old Testament, the prophet Elisha and his servant were surrounded by a host of enemies. The prophet remained strangely calm and somewhat unconcerned whilst his servant grew ever more agitated. The prophet then asked God to open the servant's eyes and then he saw that those who were on their side were many times more than those against them. We South Africans have experienced this in our lives – that the forces of good turn out to be many times more than the forces of evil. We experienced it on a few occasions in the Commission, and the controversy over the appointment of the Commissioner's spouse was one such, when a potentially explosive situation was ultimately resolved amicably. But it was an episode in our life as a Commission that I would much rather not have had. Perhaps that is being naive, given what I have said about our composition and what a malevolent effect apartheid has had on us – if it had not been this particular problem then it would have been something else, as almost a necessary stage in our process of coming to terms with our various pasts and that of our country. It was perhaps utopian and ultra-idealistic to have expected us to sail along smoothly, given the turbulent nature of the seas we were navigating.

On another occasion I received reports, widely published in the press, that a Commission panel had been less than even-handed in its dealings with witnesses at one of our hearings on the Bisho Massacre. I told the media that we were very much aware of the statutory requirement that we should be even-handed, so that people coming from all sides in the conflict in our land would feel that they had had a fair hearing and were not discriminated against. I said we could not afford to jeopardise the success of our enterprise by being perceived to be biased in favour of one or other side.

The members of that particular panel felt that I had given them a public rebuke. They raised the whole matter at a formal meeting of the Commission soon afterwards, where they said they did not feel they had done anything for which to apologise. They felt that their questions and their attitude to those who had supported the apartheid dispensation had been fair and appropriate, though they indicated that they were aware of the suffering that these people had helped to inflict on those who had been the victims of apartheid. I sought to emphasise that they were free to have whatever feelings they deemed appropriate but that they had to be scrupulous in handling all as fairly and as even-handedly as possible. I pointed out that criticism of the way they had done things had come not from those journalists who were usually hostile to the Commission but came from those who wanted to see us succeed. My colleagues were adamant that they had done nothing wrong and that they were suspicious of any media which had either not always been objective in the past, or had not been supportive of the struggle. We were clearly not on the same wavelength in this meeting and the dissenting Commissioners made a written presentation which in one paragraph questioned my integrity. I regarded the whole matter so seriously, feeling it was likely to damage irreparably our whole work, that I said I could not work in an environment where my bona fides were attacked. I said I would resign if they did not reconsider their statement and acknowledge the seriousness of what they were perceived to have done. Eventually we did get to a happy ending – the offending paragraph was withdrawn and this was one instance in which an internal crisis and resignation threat did not leak to the media. But the crisis took its toll in all kinds of different ways, physically and psychologically.

The upheavals and difficulties that we encountered as we tried to learn to trust one another more and to become a more coherent and united body pale in significance when compared with the turmoil that we experienced when a Commissioner was accused at an amnesty hearing of having been involved, as at the very least an accomplice, in the incident which was the subject of the public hearing: the Azanian People's Liberation Army (APLA) attack on the Heidelberg Tavern in Observatory, a Cape Town suburb, on 30 December 1993. Three women were killed and six people injured when two APLA operatives fired at the Tavern patrons. A nail-filled hand grenade was also thrown into their midst but mercifully failed to explode, otherwise the number of casualties would have been higher. Three of the six accused had been found guilty and sentenced to long terms of imprisonment. It was during the hearing to consider the application for amnesty of these three – Humphrey Luyando Gqomfa, Vuyisile Brian Madasi and Zola Prince Mabala – that a witness identified Mr Dumisa Ntsebeza, a Commissioner and head of our Investigative Unit.

In the course of its investigations into these amnesty applications, the Investigative Unit had found an affidavit from a Mr Bennet Sibaya in an earlier police dossier. The affidavit alleged that Sibaya had seen a group of armed men in Gugulethu, a black Cape Town township, shortly after the Heidelberg Tavern attack, in a car registered in Mr Ntsebeza's name. Mr Sibaya claimed that he had picked up a piece of paper which was a rudimentary map to the

Heidelberg Tavern. The Commission investigators interviewed Mr Sibaya, who confirmed his earlier affidavit. He testified to this affidavit at the October 1997 amnesty hearing. It was an electric moment when Mr Sibaya was asked whether he could identify Mr Ntsebeza, whom he alleged had been near the car that he had seen in Gugulethu: he walked slowly round the room, past Mr Ntsebeza, and then returned to say he was the man he had seen on that evening.

Everything else that had happened in the Commission was a Sunday school picnic compared to the impact of this testimony and identification. When I went back home after the hearing I hoped against hope that it really was all only a bad dream, a horrible nightmare and we would all wake up and find that the Truth and Reconciliation Commission was all in order and that things were proceeding reasonably smoothly. But no – this was brutal reality. The banner headlines blared it forth and television news carried dramatic pictures of Mr Sibaya walking slowly round the room and coming to a stop in front of a bemused Mr Ntsebeza, who to his great credit did not do anything rash. I held on to a shaky belief in his integrity and innocence. Mr Sibaya withstood vigorous and searching cross-examination by Mr Ntsebeza's very able lawyer. Many people said that he had impressed them with his demeanour. Despite being an uneducated gardener, he was very self-assured and not easily ruffled. He appeared to be speaking the truth and we were in very real trouble. Our investigators had first got wind of the affidavit some months earlier but, mistakenly, we thought that an internal investigation – from which Mr Ntsebeza was excluded – would clear the matter up before the amnesty hearing. This had not happened, the matter was now in the public domain and the whole Truth and Reconciliation Commission process was in jeopardy.

This particular case was a bit like the Commission's own O. J. Simpson case, especially at staff level. It split the staff virtually down the middle and almost on racial lines. Those who were convinced that Mr Sibaya was telling the truth thought he was too unsophisticated to have thought up something as elaborate as the story he had told, that there was only one explanation: that he had not made it up. And most of these Sibaya supporters were white. With equal fervour there were those who believed Dumisa Ntsebeza to be speaking the truth when he declared his innocence; and they were mainly black. Apartheid has a lot to answer for.

You can imagine how the enemies of the Commission were feeling. They were having a field day while we were labouring under a heavy blanket of gloom. It shook us to the foundations, and I believe that had it happened at the beginning of the life of the Commission it would without any doubt have destroyed us. But by this time, two years into the life of the Commission, we had grown to have a great deal more trust in one another. Hence the Commissioners almost unanimously accepted that Dumisa's integrity was unimpugned, and we believed his side of the story. There were some mercies for which to be thankful. But the turmoil and distress were considerable.

A few days after his dramatic performance in pointing out Ntsebeza, an agitated Mr Sibaya sought an audience with me. He confessed that both his affidavit and testimony were false. He said that at the time of the Heidelberg Tavern attack he had been arrested for illegal dealing in crayfish, or rock lobsters. He had then been tortured and coerced by the police into making a false statement implicating Mr Ntsebeza who was at the time the target of a series of allegations by the police who believed he had APLA or PAC connections. He had been their lawyer in a number of political trials, which had made him *persona non grata* with the police, just like Mr Griffiths Mxenge, the Durban lawyer murdered by them in 1981.

To say we were relieved is the understatement of the year. We did not waste time in letting the world know: I appeared at a press conference with Mr Sibaya, who was accompanied by his lawyer to safeguard his interests. We could not have had a better ending to our nightmare. It was the perfect rejoinder to those who were yapping at our heels and basically writing our institutional obituaries. Poor Dumisa had lived through sheer hell during all this time: it was small comfort to have the support of a few colleagues when half the staff of your organisation and most of the world out there had already condemned you. You saw the vultures hovering and you knew it was just a question of time before they swooped down on your carcass.

Despite Mr Sibaya's confession, the Commission decided to request President Mandela to appoint a judicial Commission of Inquiry as a matter of extreme urgency to conduct a thorough investigation. The President responded with commendable alacrity and appointed the highly regarded Constitutional Court judge, Richard Goldstone, who had to report as soon as possible. I thought it would have been politic for Mr Ntsebeza to excuse himself from Commission business until the matter was resolved when Judge Goldstone issued his report. He refused because he said it would mean he had already been found guilty and he protested his complete innocence.

Judge Goldstone acted with commendable speed and produced his report wonderfully quickly. He found that the allegations were false and declared Mr Ntsebeza to be innocent. He criticised the Commission for not calling for an independent inquiry when the allegations first surfaced. I must take the blame for this because I did hope we would have been able to get to the bottom of it all through an internal inquiry. I suppose I was also driven by a desire to spare the Commission as much embarrassment as possible and to shield our colleague. It was not a wise decision and demonstrated how crucial transparency can be: it is a great deal better for all concerned. But the entire episode showed yet again the lengths to which the system, even when already moribund, was ready to go to remove awkward customers from circulation. No holds were barred and we are still paying heavily for a police system with such an ethos.

Former President Mandela is really a remarkable man. Now that has become such a commonplace observation that it could be dismissed as hackneyed. He was aware that Mr Ntsebeza would be on tenterhooks, apprehensively awaiting the outcome of the Goldstone inquiry. Thus as soon as the judge's report was handed to him, he was eager to let Dumisa Ntsebeza know that he had been completely vindicated and telephoned to share this good news with him. I was upset at this breach in protocol, however, so I telephoned the

President's secretary and said she should let the President know that I was upset: I was the Commission Chairperson and thus should have been the first on the Commission to know the contents of Judge Goldstone's report. Within minutes of my call the President was on the line. He said, 'Mpilo [my African name], you're quite right. I am sorry, I should have told you first, but I was concerned for that young man. I apologise.' I don't know that there are many so powerful who are so ready to humble themselves. But then he is acknowledged everywhere in the world as a very special kind of person.

Whenever I was tempted to throw in the towel, things like this happened – goodness and truth prevailed and I realised what an incredible privilege it was to be part of this extraordinary experiment and soldiered on with renewed vigor and enthusiasm until the next crisis hit us between the eyes.

Before you could say 'apartheid' the next crisis came quite unexpectedly on the eve of our handing our Report over to President Mandela on 29 October 1998. Now I know a little better the wisdom of the saying, 'do not count your chickens before they are hatched'.

The Act that set up the Truth and Reconciliation Commission required that the Commission should send notices to those persons, institutions or organisations against whom we intended making an adverse finding. Such notices had been sent to various individuals as well as to political parties. Each was given the opportunity to provide additional evidence for the Commission's consideration in order to persuade the Commission to amend that particular adverse finding. All to whom such notices had been sent were given the opportunity of engaging in a dialogue with the Commission but only in writing, not orally, because there just was not enough time to hear oral evidence from the large number of potential perpetrators. In the ANC's case, the issues in question had already been canvassed at three separate hearings involving both their political and military leaders. They were given ample time to respond to the notices.

The ANC requested a special meeting with the Commission in order to discuss the contents of the notice that it had received. I must say that some of us were taken aback, since we believed that the notice was a mere formality as far as the ANC were concerned. The contemplated finding had been based on the ANC's own very substantial, full and frank submissions that included eloquent expressions of regret for the violations that had happened when the liberation movement's operatives had carried out the ANC's policies or when they had not quite adhered to the organisation's guidelines, or when cadres had acted in angry retaliation for the activities of the apartheid regime.

The ANC had apologised, for instance, that there had been civilian casualties in its landmine campaign (which was ended because of this), and also in episodes such as the Church Street bombing in Pretoria. The ANC had also admitted that some of its women members had been sexually abused in its military camps in Angola and elsewhere and the leadership had accepted moral responsibility and political accountability in a most exemplary manner. The top echelons of the party hierarchy had carried this principled stand to its logical conclusion when it applied collectively and symbolically for amnesty. This was a noble and commendable gesture, saying eloquently that they were not deserting their foot soldiers but were ready to take the rap. Unfortunately, there was no provision in the Promotion of National Unity and Reconciliation Act for such a corporate and collective application – but the motive behind the gesture was highly commendable. Thus we did not expect any trouble whatsoever from that quarter.

The Acting Chairperson of the Commission, Commissioner Dumisa Ntsebeza, entered into extensive correspondence with the ANC, pointing out that all those who had received notices had been urged to respond in writing if they wished to communicate with the Commission on any issue relevant to the matter at hand. He pointed out that the ANC was wasting precious time and ought to get on with the business of providing the Commission with its written reactions. He was under the impression that the matter had now been dealt with amicably because the ANC Secretary-General promised to supply the Commission with the party's written response. However, the ANC missed both our and its own deadlines for delivering its response, eventually providing it at the last moment, after the Report had gone to the printers.

Whilst all this was happening Dr Boraine and I were in the United States, having taken up university visiting professorships, he at the New York University School of Law and I at Emory University's Candler School of Theology. We were due to return in time for a final Commission meeting prior to the climactic event of the hand-over. This was intended to be a grand occasion where representatives of the victims would be present as well as the diplomatic community and representatives of the various religious bodies and NGOs. The SABC was going to broadcast it live on TV and radio. The Truth and Reconciliation Commission was going out with a real bang.

Our last meeting should have been more or less a routine business meeting. It would probably have been emotional, being the last formal meeting of a group of people who *had* grown close, who had been through a gruelling time together, and there would probably have been some nostalgia as well as a tinge of bereavement. We began by announcing that two Commissioners serving on the Amnesty Committee had been appointed as deputies to the new National Director of Prosecutions, very important posts for which they were very warmly commended, and other more mundane announcements were made. Then, like a bolt from the blue, one Commissioner suggested reopening the issue of the ANC's request for a meeting, since some of the Commissioners felt that they wanted to urge that such a meeting should in fact take place. The matter was re-opened even at that eleventh hour. I and other Commissioners tried to point out that it would be disastrous in the extreme to do any such thing because it would be interpreted as kow-towing obse-quiously to the governing party – no other individual or organisation had been granted a similar concession. Some Commissioners urged that we should consider the ANC's out-of-time representations – this two days before a five-volume, 2,700-page report was to be delivered by the printers and presented to President Mandela.

Considering the ANC's last-minute representations, made after the expiry of our final specified period of grace, could have led to even more disastrous consequences. Even if they had presented cogent and rational reasons why the Commission should amend its contemplated finding, the end result of us changing the Report would have been that nearly everybody out there would have said that here was proof positive that the Truth and Reconciliation Commission was the ANC's lackey, and that the whole process was an elaborate charade set up to do the ANC's bidding. It all seemed so obvious, but those colleagues urging the reopening of the whole matter remained unmoved and adamant that a meeting with the ANC should happen or that its representations should be considered, even on the very eve of the hand-over of the Report.

I really could not believe what I was hearing. The integrity and credibility of the Commission were so obviously on the line: surely no right-thinking, sane person could ever have wanted to risk wiping out all that extraordinary work and jeopardising the crucial work of trying to heal our nation. I suppose a blind spot is called that precisely because it is a blind spot – what seems so obvious, sticking out like a sore thumb, is invisible to those who will not or cannot see it. I had a hollow sensation in the pit of my stomach as I saw the whole enterprise sinking without trace. It would have been the most awful trick ever played on the hapless victims, who had been so generous and so dignified in their willingness to forgo their rights for the sake of our nation – and now we were ready to spit in their faces as our thanks for their magnanimity.

We had usually not voted much on issues, but on this occasion we had to put the issue to the vote in a very tense atmosphere. The vote for granting the ANC an audience was narrowly lost. Then we voted on whether to consider their representations. The votes for were seven, and those against seven. A deadlock. I had never before had need to use my casting vote and on this occasion I voted to say 'No' to the ANC. It had been a very close call at a final meeting which should have been a slightly more amicable and certainly a non-controversial affair.

It seems that some of our colleagues were privy to the ANC's decision to take us to court in the event of our refusing to grant the party an audience, and it may be they wanted to avoid that particular embarrassment. I was devastated by the news, the day before the scheduled presentation of the Report, that that was what the ANC had done – they applied to the High Court for an interdict to stop us from publishing any part of the Report which implicated the ANC in human rights violations until we had considered their submissions. It was so surreal. Mr F. W. de Klerk had also put in an application to have the finding against him removed. His behaviour we could understand, and even say it was in character. But the ANC, which had been so supportive of the process – this was totally unexpected and thoroughly out of line with its character and attitude.

I was heavy-hearted as we left Cape Town for Pretoria where the handing-over ceremony was due to take place. Our legal department and other lawyer Commissioners worked through the night to prepare the relevant papers for the court, which would deliver its verdict a very short time before the scheduled start of the hand-over ceremony. We continued with preparations as if we did not have an enormous sword of Damocles hanging over us. Venues were prepared where journalists from all over the world would be locked away so that three or four hours before the actual event they would have had a preview of the five-volume Report in order that they could prepare their copy to meet their various deadlines.

When the court verdict came through that the ANC application had been dismissed with costs, our celebrations were very muted. I was thankful that we had not let the victims down and the ceremony, though tinged with a great deal more sadness than would otherwise have been the case, was a wonderful blend of solemnity and celebration, sadness and joy, tears and dancing. The President and I danced what has come to be called the 'Madiba shuffle' to the melodious sound of one of our premier choirs, Imilonji kaNtu.

I was deeply thankful as I handed President Mandela his leather-bound volumes – thankful that God had been so good to us, that we had survived some very difficult and testing times; thankful that we had been able to uncover as much truth as we had done; thankful that we had been the agency to bring some closure, some healing, some reconciliation; thankful that we had indeed looked the beast in the eye; thankful for the tremendous colleagues God had given me; and above all thankful for all the wonderful people who had come before the Commission and generously stripped themselves before us and the world, making themselves vulnerable, helping us to regain our humanity as they had their dignity rehabilitated.

We were frail and fallible, veritable earthenware vessels as St Paul puts it, so that it was clear that the super-abundant glory belonged to God.

CHAPTER TEN

'We did not know'

How was it possible for normal, decent, God-fearing people, as white South Africans considered themselves to be, to have turned a blind eye to a system which impoverished, oppressed and violated so many of those others with whom they shared the beautiful land that was their common motherland? Apartheid could not have survived for a single day had it not been supported by this enfranchised, privileged minority. If they 'did not know', as many later claimed, how was it that there were those within the white community who not only knew of the baneful results of official policy but who condemned this vicious policy and worked to end it? And why was this courageous group often vilified and ostracised by the rest of the white community, if it was not that those who enjoyed the massive benefits that apartheid assured them at the very least condoned the evil system and might have made an uneasy peace with it?

It needs to be noted that many white people grew up knowing no other system and they acquiesced in it because it was a status quo that brought them much comfort. The system was not naive. In fact it was exceedingly sophisticated. The black townships were usually out of sight of whites, and it was an easy step from being out of sight to being out of mind. You had to want to put yourself to considerable inconvenience to visit a black township if you were white. There were those who did, but for the bulk of whites it was a great deal more comfortable to remain in your salubrious, affluent suburb. We, black and white South Africans, suffered from an acute form of schizophrenia – we inhabited two separate and alien worlds, physically and psychologically. When I was Archbishop I lived in the decidedly up-market suburb of Bishopscourt in Cape Town. It was as affluent a suburb as you could find anywhere in the world, with large estates, beautiful gardens, swimming pools and sumptuous residences – quite a distance physically and in all kinds of other ways from Langa or Gugulethu, the nearest black townships. You would not normally go to, or even through those areas unless you really wanted to see them. And why would a normal white person want to be put to so much bother?

Today, of course, you can't find anyone who ever supported apartheid. But the Commission wanted to have some insight into why it had been possible for such an unacceptable system to have survived for so long. We were mandated by our founding Act to seek to understand the 'antecedents, circumstances, factors and context' within which gross violations of human rights occurred. To try to help us, we held what we called 'institutional hearings', where representatives of the major social institutions came and described how they perceived their relationship to apartheid to have been.

We had positive responses from most of those we invited in the legal profession, the health-care sector, business, faith communities, trade unions and the media. Some who promised to come and to provide statements failed to do so. Others refused point-blank to attend, including the South African Agricultural Union, which represented white farmers, and the white Mineworkers' Union. The multinational oil companies, massive investors in South Africa, did not respond. We held hearings on youth, military conscription and on prisons, and we also held a women's hearing.

In most of these hearings, the perspectives differed along racial lines. Blacks naturally tended to be critical of the role that some of these institutions played in supporting and maintaining apartheid, whereas whites in the same institutions were defensive about their role in upholding that oppressive status quo. What your perspective would be really depended on who and where you were. Many whites had supported conscription – limited under apartheid to whites – because they had bought into the government's view that they were threatened by a Communist onslaught on the last bastion of civilised, decent existence. Most whites considered those young white men who wanted conscription abolished to be cowards and traitors, while the objectors saw it as participation in defending a system they abhorred. We were thus warned to be wary of generalisations – the situation tended to be more complex than was apparent at first sight, and required sensitive and acute analysis.

The institutional hearings revealed a country in which the vast majority was systematically and of set purpose excluded from any real participation in the political decision-making process. That in turn meant they were excluded from all other kinds of spheres of influence and power – economic, social, you name it. The most notable feature was the glaring absence of those who were not white from any worthwhile position in society which would ensure that they would be heard and that their point of view would be taken seriously. Most whites saw things from their own perspectives, which is not surprising. Their values were seen as universally valid: everyone had to measure up to those Eurocentric values or be considered inferior, a maverick, odd, an outcast. These were unexamined assumptions shared by most whites and they were likely to be best preserved by the status quo that protected white vested interests so efficiently.

The way in which many of our institutions operated under apartheid can be illustrated by the evidence of our hearing on the media. Ownership of newspapers was vested in white hands. News was described from a white perspective. Even newspapers that might be said to be anti-apartheid, which saw themselves as liberal, saw nothing wrong in persisting for a very long time in describing an accident, for instance, as one in which 'one person and four natives were injured'. It did not seem to occur to the white journalists and their editors that this was embarrassingly revealing of their visceral attitudes – deep down somewhere in their unconscious, not really articulated except in this fashion, a black person was not quite a person in the way that a white person was. There might be howls of protest, but that is how it seemed to those at the receiving end.

And the way so many other things were ordered in the country confirmed that racism ran deep in the ordering of South African life. Thus it was not surprising that these same newspapers consistently used the term favoured by the government for referring to those whom blacks called 'freedom fighters' – 'terrorists'. They could have used more neutral terms such as 'insurgents' or 'guerrillas'. The South African government knew that it was important to de-legitimise the struggle by styling it terrorism, knowing this would provoke Pavlovian conditioned responses from whites and from many in the international community.

Newspapers which claimed to be against apartheid nevertheless applied it in their newsrooms, with socially segregated facilities such as canteens and toilets. Black staff got the short straw in training opportunities and salaries. The newspapers were not averse to censoring themselves in order not to rouse the wrath of the government and ostensibly to avoid statutory control. When the apartheid government closed the black newspaper *The World*, the white papers in the same newspaper company were lukewarm in their protests, suggesting that *The World* had been playing with fire and had got what had been coming their way. It was not unusual for a white reporter's copy to be preferred to that of a black reporter, even if the latter had first-hand experience of what he or she was reporting on. When black reporters described the appalling conduct of the security forces against blacks, their copy was normally toned down as perhaps maligning these forces. Now we know, of course, that the black reporters were telling it as it was. The editors would have angrily denied that they were being racist. No, they wanted 'objective' writing. They did not care to define from whose perspective 'objective' was to be judged, because the assumption was that their standards were universal. They would be appalled to be accused of racism, but the fact of the matter is that they had refused to accept the word of a black person when it collided with what they believed about their own people and their adherence to 'decent standards'. They had no peers from the other group who could argue for that rejected perspective. These newspapers even got to the stage where they published township editions, which seems to demonstrate that they acquiesced in the view that there were different perspectives and views about what should be considered newsworthy. Many blacks especially were ambivalent about these separate editions because their existence seemed to be following apartheid's dictum about each ethnic group developing along its own lines.

The government was able to get much of its own way by its threat to take drastic action against 'undisciplined' newspapers which might cause trouble and agitate the blacks. The owners of the papers were suitably chastened and did the government's dirty work to the extent of allowing the death of an outstanding newspaper that had courageously championed the cause of the oppressed. This was the *Rand Daily Mail* which had had some remarkable editors. It was a persistent thorn in the government's flesh, and with pressure from that quarter, was allowed to fold. The government knew the value of having a relatively free though somewhat pliant press. It made for good propaganda abroad: 'South Africa can't be so bad, after all it has a critical and free press.' The Afrikaans press was unabashedly sycophantic and supportive of the apartheid government. The Afrikaans papers made no bones about it. They were four-square behind the National Party and government, most being party organs.

This was equally the case with the electronic media. The South African Broadcasting Corporation was under the thumb of a secret society, the Afrikaner Broederbond (Brotherhood), founded in 1918 to promote the interests of Afrikaners, which had tentacles in every single sphere of life – the Church, schools, business, culture, universities, professions, the Defence Force, sport, the media and, of course, politics. Its policies became government policy. If you wanted to make it in the Afrikaans world in any sector of human activity your chances were nil if you were not a member of this powerful, all-pervasive secret society. You could not gainsay its decrees and decisions and hope to prosper.

Thus the highest virtue in South Africa came to be conformity; not bucking the system. The highest value was set on unquestioning loyalty to the dictates of the Broederbond. That is perhaps why people did not cultivate the capacity to ask awkward questions. For most, something had to be so because someone in authority had declared it to be so. They found it singularly difficult, if not impossible, to distinguish between *authoritative* and *authoritarian*. In the end even the most bizarre thing could be accepted because the herd instinct was invoked. Visiting Japanese businessmen, because of the power of the yen, became 'honorary whites'. A person of Chinese origin born in South Africa would be a non-European, but if born in China then he or she was naturally European! It would have been utterly ridiculous except that it did have ghastly repercussions. Sometimes people committed suicide because of wrong racial classification, since worth and privileges hinged so much on what racial group you belonged to. It determined where you could live, who you could marry, what schools your children could attend, what job you could do, and even where you could be buried.

At the SABC, the chairman was at one time head of the Broederbond, and Afrikaners were in charge. Even the advisory board to supervise services for those not white had a completely white membership. Blacks employed in the SABC, we were told, were given inferior training, inferior equipment and awkward working hours. They were prohibited from looking at white women, and risked punishment if they contravened this rule. In the corridors blacks had to give way to whites. Unbelievably, under the rules providing for the disciplining of workers, workers could choose to be sacked or alternatively whipped with a *sjambok* (leather whip). Our media hearing was the first time that this shocking information was made known. And it was black workers who were the victims of this barbarism.

All this was possible because of the prevailing racist ideology. It was possible for a television news bulletin to be interrupted because the state president did not like a particular item and so it had to be changed. That was not thought to be odd. This was South Africa and the government was in charge, and no one who could really dared to question things. Mr P. W. Botha was the state president and being the irascible, difficult and stubborn man that he was, he had a short fuse.

It was said that he reduced grown men, his cabinet ministers, to tears with his caustic tongue, and no one dared to cross him. What he wanted he got.

During our hearings, the faith communities were generally far more forthcoming than members of other institutions in confessing their shortcomings and their collusion with the apartheid status quo. They admitted that they had often been very vocal and sharp in their criticism of apartheid but had nevertheless practised it in the ordering of their institutional lives. Some had split into racial groupings. Dr Frank Chikane had been interrogated and tortured by a group of security police who were commanded by a member of the white section of his denomination, the Apostolic Faith Mission, a man who had gone straight from a torture session to a church service. (The two sections of this denomination have since amalgamated at a deeply moving service where the whites asked for forgiveness from their black counterparts.) During the Truth and Reconciliation process the faith communities realised that they had a special responsibility in the whole business of healing a wounded people, in encouraging reconciliation and reparation among their adherents.

White farmers and those involved in commercial agriculture had benefited from both the original conqest of the land and then the racist and infamous Land Act of 1913, which allowed them to acquire huge tracts of farmland. They received state subsidies and loans, in later years from the Land Bank, on very favourable terms. They had available an inexhaustible supply of cheap labour – the pass laws were designed to prevent blacks from competing as food producers with cosseted white farmers, for there had been a time when blacks had been successful peasant farmers who had posed a real threat to the white farmers. The government pushed blacks off the land to become contract labourers in the mines. It was suggested that the Churches, particularly, should examine how they had acquired their land and return it to its rightful owners if it had been acquired in ways that were less than fair. The Churches were also urged to see how they could ease the huge desire for land among the landless.

The health sector had also organised itself along racial lines. Before the Second World War no blacks had been trained as doctors in South Africa. Before 1990 there was gross discrimination at our medical schools against black medical students. They often had separate classes, were hardly permitted to work on white cadavers, and almost never examined white patients in the obstetrics and gynaecology wards. After earning the same qualifications they were paid different and lower salaries to those of their white counterparts. But it was in the matter of collaborating with the security police as district surgeons that the medical profession behaved most reprehensibly. Some district surgeons contravened most of the rules of medical ethics. When examining detainees they frequently did not observe doctor-patient confidentiality. They examined their patients in the presence of the police or a prison official. They handed over medical records to the police without obtaining the patient's permission, bowed to police pressure, and did not make the welfare of their patient their priority. The most notorious case was, of course, that of Steve Biko, described earlier in this book, where the doctors had allowed the police to decide what was to be done. Some district surgeons advised police torture teams on techniques that left no traces, and on how much more someone being tortured could take. Others had sometimes refused to give medical treatment to injured activists, contending that the police had to get their information, or that terrorists should not be helped.

The legal profession was no better. One regional bar council refused to allow blacks to become members until 1990, thus making it difficult for them to practise. One apartheid-era law prohibited blacks from having chambers in a white area. Our present Chief Justice, Ismail Mahomed, used to eat his lunch in the toilets of his white colleagues' law chambers whilst they used their all-white canteen. When he wanted to work, he had to find out which of his white colleagues was in court so that he might use the vacant office. As a person classified under apartheid as Indian, he was not allowed to stay overnight in Bloemfontein, the seat of the Appellate Division of the old Supreme Court. So when he argued cases before South

Africa's highest court, he would have to travel between Johannesburg and Bloemfontein daily for the duration of his case – a distance of some 400 miles each way. (In the ironical ways that things happen, he now has his official residence as Chief Justice in Bloemfontein!) For most of the period that the Truth and Reconciliation Commission looked at, nearly all the judges were white and male, and whether they admitted it or not they brought their own baggage as white people with them to the Bench.

Unfortunately, judges in South Africa have normally been placed on an unassailable pedestal, almost deified. They are regarded almost as infallible beings. Yet very few of them would have been able to enter imaginatively into the world of most of the accused who appeared before them – because they were black, and the world of black experience, of black humiliation, deprivation and disempowerment under apartheid, was virtually closed to them. Very few judges could therefore have understood or had sympathy with the political aspirations of blacks. Outside court most only met those blacks who worked as servants in their homes. They are unlikely to have asked them how black people felt. Thus when blacks were charged with political offences the white judge, moving in the circles that approved white privilege and hegemony, would rarely be sympathetic to those who wanted to overturn a dispensation that provided him and his community with that to which they had become accustomed. A white judge was highly unlikely to think that there might be even a modicum of justification for agitation against such a system. Thus in the eyes of most blacks they were part of the oppressive dispensation. Judges and lawyers participated, apparently without too much demur, in a patently unjust judicial system. Most of the laws did not even try for subtlety. They were fundamentally unjust.

White South Africans under apartheid made the big mistake of confusing 'legal' with 'morally right', and thus would get very hot under the collar when I and others said unjust laws did not oblige obedience. They were very upset with the Churches and the Mass Democratic Movement, and their campaign to disobey unjust laws.

Many white South Africans thought that *illegal* was identical with *immoral*. When you pointed out that there were laws that made it a crime for a man to sleep with his own wife, they did not seem to understand that the obligation for the Christian was to obey God's law rather than that of man, and God's law said what God has joined together let no man put asunder. (Under laws designed to control the movement of blacks, a black woman and her husband would be breaking the law if she joined him in the single-sex hostel he occupied as a migrant labourer in the white man's town.)

When we asked the judges and lawyers why they cooperated with laws that were contrary to justice, they often said that parliament was sovereign and gave little room for judicial discretion and choice. When we asked why they did not refuse to collaborate with injustice by resigning, they said they feared that the government might very well appoint people even less sympathetic to true justice and that some possibility of justice was better than none at all. In my view, the doctrine of parliamentary sovereignty is valid only in a truly democratic state, where parliament can credibly be said to represent the people. This was patently not the case in South Africa. While it is true that it might be better to have judges who were reasonably well disposed to the rule of law, if they had resigned perhaps the ghastliness of apartheid would have been exposed to the world a great deal sooner and more starkly. Such a stand might have hastened the demise of apartheid. The South African government made capital out of its independent judiciary.

Some judges made very good submissions to the Commission, but regrettably refused to appear before us. They claimed that doing so would undermine their independence. With respect, that is quite untenable. The Commission was a unique institution hardly likely to be repeated, and so not able to set precedents. The judges, like everyone else who came before the Commission, would not have been placed in the dock. They would, with us, have been trying to find out what went wrong and how the judiciary might be shaped to assist in creating a culture where the rule of law and human rights are respected. Perhaps we erred in not using our powers to subpoena the judges, because they maintained this fiction of being largely unaccountable. Most blacks believe the judiciary colluded with a foul system, giving it a legitimacy it did not deserve and thus bringing the entire judicial system into disrepute.

We blacks have taken it as read that a black person was greatly disadvantaged in a South African court. There have been outstanding exceptions among the judges, people who tried to squeeze some justice for the most disadvantaged, who had no part in making these reprehensible laws. But most refused to accept the testimony of detainees, usually black, that they had been tortured. They almost always believed the police, even when there was medical evidence to support the complaint. A senior police officer confirmed to the Commission what most of us believed almost instinctively about the level of collusion between the prosecution and the police, especially at inquests investigating the mysterious deaths of activists, where the magistrates almost always found no one was to blame. He declared that at one inquest the prosecutor had provided him with the questions he would be asked as well as the answers he should give.

The judiciary is now being transformed, with more women and blacks being appointed. But four recent cases make many say that it is still controlled by apartheid attitudes. Our President, Nelson Mandela, contrary to all previous conventions, was required to testify in a case where his state of mind when appointing a judicial commission to investigate what was still largely white-controlled rugby was called in question, and the court found against him. In another case a white farmer was given a suspended sentence after killing a black baby. The third was when two white police officers got very light sentences after an incident where they had wielded pickaxes against a group of black men, two of whom died. The fourth case involved a suspended sentence given to a white man who killed a black woman whilst brandishing his gun to scare her off his property. This sort of thing does not inspire people's confidence in a system they have never trusted.

With regard to the business sector, the perception of most black people is that almost all business participated in racial capitalism, colluding with the apartheid rulers to extract as much profit as possible for themselves. Business, especially the mines, benefited from the pass laws, which by strictly controlling the movement of blacks prevented them from selling their labour freely in an open market. These vicious laws turned the Bantustans (black homelands) into inexhaustible reservoirs of cheap labour. Migrant workers were permitted into the white man's towns only for as long as they had work, and they were forced to live in debilitating single-sex hostels, a system that played havoc with black family life. This law and others enabled white business to accrue large concentrations of capital and to monopolise the stock exchange.

A United Nations report[1] indicates that South Africa has the most glaring gap between rich and poor in the entire African continent. The Commission said this situation was a disaster waiting to happen and the gap had to be closed urgently. Suggestions made to the Commission included a wealth tax, a one-off levy on corporate and private income, or a one-off donation by the private sector of one per cent of market capitalisation on the Johannesburg Stock Exchange, all to finance black development. The Commission left it to experts to determine the feasibility of these ideas, but we made the point in our Report that unless there is real material transformation in the lives of those who have been apartheid's victims, we can kiss reconciliation goodbye. It just won't happen without some reparation.

The gender hearings that we held revealed the extraordinary resilience and courage of women. We established statistically that when women came to testify to the Commission they almost always told the story of what had happened to somebody else; whereas when men testified, almost equally invariably, they told about what had happened to themselves. Thus it was felt that there was justification for hearings focused on women as victims and for us to hear about gender-specific abuses and violations. It seems women suffered more poignantly than men when they were deprived of company and were a great deal more vulnerable when their torturers used their relationships to hit at them – lying to them about sick or dying children, for instance. Many told of sexual assaults and how their gender was something that was used to dehumanise them through rape, or not being able to wash when they were menstruating, or being taunted by the security police that they were in the liberation struggle as combatants only in order to make up for not being able to get men and so were really unpaid prostitutes of the male soldiers.

It struck me forcibly for the first time in our victim hearings that we owed a great deal to our womenfolk; that we would never have got our freedom without them. I want to salute them for their remarkable part in our struggle. One day Leah, my wife, pointed out with unconcealed glee a car bumper-sticker that read, 'Any woman who wants to be equal to a man has no ambition.' Women in South Africa have been magnificent.

Good in parts

There are quite unexpected and truly beautiful things that have happened as a result of our Commission. At one of our Human Rights Violations Committee hearings in Port Elizabeth, Ms Ivy Gcina described the kindness of her white wardress, Ms Irene Crouse:

> The same night I saw a light and my cell was opened. I did not see who was opening my cell. I did not look at the person. She said to me, 'Ivy, it is me. I am Sergeant Crouse. I have fetched your medicine.' She rubbed me. She made me take my medicine. I told her that I could not even hold anything but I can try. I told her I was going to try by all means. She said, 'It is fine, do not worry yourself. I will help you.' So she made me take the medicine and then she massaged me. Then after that I could at least try and sleep.

A few days later the local newspaper, the *Eastern Province Herald*, carried a large front-page picture of Ivy Gcina hugging Irene Crouse, accompanied by the following report:

> Tortured activist Ivy Gcina was yesterday reunited with her Angel of Mercy – the kind jailer who held her hand and tended her wounds after hours of brutal interrogation by security police. 'I never thought you'd remember me,' said Irene, 37, as the two women threw their arms

around each other on the stoep [verandah], crying and laughing at the same time. Ivy, 59, replied: 'But after I was assaulted it was you who was there to help me, who entered my cell at night. Can you ever forget someone like that?

'We met as human beings, as women,' Ivy recalled. 'There was such communication there. Ensuring I had a clean towel, asking me how I was. The relationship was so good.' Irene felt she was 'only doing her duty' when she helped Ivy.

It would be less than honest and entirely counter-productive to pretend that the Truth and Reconciliation Commission was perfect, or that it was serviced by people who were infallible. That was patently not the case. We were flawed, mere mortals with some gifts and some faults, like other human beings. No one could have accused us of being paragons of virtue. To our chagrin and considerable frustration, we were anything but. It is an entirely unprofound observation to note that the Commission was, like the celebrated curate's egg, good in parts. There were splendid things about the Commission and it has notable achievements to its credit, but there were, alas, things we might have done differently, and things we might have done a great deal better. But that is in the nature of things. We were traversing uncharted waters and often having to improvise as we went along. It is to the credit of all who were part of our process that so much was achieved.

For me, one of the greatest weaknesses in the Commission was the fact that we failed to attract the bulk of the white community to participate enthusiastically in the Truth and Reconciliation process. This might very well be due to faults on our side, but was certainly a mistake on the part of our white compatriots. It paralleled the way in which they have refused to embrace the new dispensation whole-heartedly. They have spent far too much time, in my view, whining, being quick to find fault, and gloating shortsightedly at the imagined and real shortcomings of those at the helm nowadays. They are filled with far too much resentment at the fact that they have lost some political power. The trouble is that they have believed that there are only two positions possible in any socio-political set up. You are either the top dog or you are the underdog. There is no place in this kind of scenario for participatory, shared power.

White South Africans, tragically, have no white leader – for it has to be one of themselves ethnically – of any substance who could say to them: 'Wake up, fellow whites! You may indeed have lost political power, if you mean exclusive political control, but you have a heck of a lot of power still at your disposal. You have the bulk of economic power – you have lost little of your money; you have not been kicked out of your beautiful homes; you don't live in shacks. You have a great deal of power deriving from the superior education you received, which was a great deal better than that of blacks. You can embrace the new dispensation enthusiastically and offer your considerable skills, your resources, your money, to make this thing work. We have been very, very fortunate. Let us invest all we have to make this thing succeed, otherwise one day the blacks will really get angry that political change has brought no change for them materially and there will not be a Mandela to help control them. It is in our best interests that this whole enterprise succeeds. Without our cooperation it will fail dismally and we will go down with the sinking *Titanic*.'

Despite our sustained efforts, we were also unable to gain the committed participation of the Inkatha Freedom Party. We really did try. Their official participation was lukewarm at best, and far more frequently it bristled with hostility. They told their members they should approach the Commission only after we pointed out to Chief Buthelezi that ordinary members of his organisation would not qualify for the reparations to be paid from the President's Fund unless they first testified to the Human Rights Violations Committee, which would then determine whether they were victims as defined by the Promotion of National Unity and Reconciliation Act. If they did, they would be passed on to the Reparation and Rehabilitation Committee to recommend the precise reparations for which they were eligible. We were then confronted with an avalanche of last-minute applications to deal with in a very short space of time. Some victims could be referred to the Reparation and Rehabilitation Committee directly by the Amnesty Committee, but the vast majority came normally through the Human Rights Violations Committee. This failure to get the Inkatha Freedom Party to participate earlier was yet another of our shortcomings.

There were also weaknesses in the reparation and rehabilitation process. First there was our distress at the fact that successful amnesty applicants walked free immediately, while victims had still not received final reparations nearly a year after the Report was presented – a concern to which I have already referred. I have also said how many victims regarded appearing before the Commission as a turning point, something that enabled them to achieve a measure of closure. But there were critics, among them members of our own staff, who were upset that we were unable to provide long-term counselling and support. We of course had our briefers, who provided far more support and sympathetic assistance than is usually available to, for instance, victims who testify in the criminal courts. But it is possible that there were people who, because they reopened their wounds before us and did not receive sufficient professional help to deal with the anguish, went away more traumatised than before. The difficulty we had was that our legal mandate was to research and make recommendations to the government on rehabilitation and reparations measures, not to implement them. As a result, we were unable to secure state funding to provide those who came to the Commission with more extensive psychological and other forms of counselling and support than the briefers could provide. We are deeply indebted to NGOs and faith communities, who have tried to step into this yawning breach, but it would have been so much better had this important service been an integral part of the therapeutic process of the Truth and Reconciliation Commission. And of course those who appeared at public hearings constituted no more than a representative cross-section of victims who came to the Commission – about one in ten testified. In the final analysis, it will be up to government and civil society to respond to our recommendations with rehabilitation and reparations programmes which take care of the interests of all victims.

Although the Commission and the Amnesty Committee usually worked together well, there were sometimes difficulties. When our governing Act was drafted, the National Party feared that the Commission would be biased against the old dispensation. So it ensured that the Amnesty Committee would be headed by a judge and that its decisions on amnesty could not be reviewed by the rest of the Commission. Thus this committee had very considerable autonomy. Its decisions could be reviewed and set aside only by a court of law. In the middle of the hearing on the Mandela United Football Club and Mrs Winnie Madikizela-Mandela we received word that thirty-seven ANC leaders had been given amnesty. They had a very commendable motive for having applied – they wanted to demonstrate that they took collective responsibility for the actions of their cadres. Unfortunately, there was no provision in the Promotion of National Unity and Reconciliation Act for this kind of corporate amnesty, where no specific crimes had been itemised. Even those of us who were not lawyers raised our eyebrows at the Committee's decision. But our hands were tied. All we were able to do was to challenge the decision by taking our own Committee to court. We tried to negotiate an agreed settlement with the ANC to avoid protracted litigation. The Nationalists knew we were engaged in this process, but they were eager to score political points and went to court before our matter could be heard. Eventually both our and the National Party's applications were heard on the same day and the Committee's decision was set aside. I was disgusted with the unprincipled action of the Nationalist Party, which went on to trumpet its success as what had goaded us into action, knowing full well that the truth was otherwise. We never heard the end of what was claimed to be yet another demonstration of the Commission's bias towards the ANC. I am relieved that I am not smart enough to be a politician. Some people would not recognise integrity even if it was staring them in the face.

One of the successes of the Commission was that many members of the old regime's police force came forward to apply for amnesty and reveal what they had done. Much of the truth that we were able to uncover came from the mouths of the perpetrators. This was a massive rebuttal to the criticism that most of what was being publicised was the untested allegations and accusations of those who testified in our victim-oriented hearings. What those who testified in the victim hearings said was nowhere near as startling as the shocking details that the amnesty hearings revealed about the kind of atrocities that were perpetrated routinely. A mother such as Mrs Joyce Mtimkulu might say that her son was changed physically after detention, that he became confined to a wheelchair, that his hair had fallen out, and that he had later disappeared without a trace. She might speculate that perhaps the security forces were somehow involved. The police, who knew the truth all the while, might win a court interdict stopping her from naming them in her testimony. But in the end it was not she who revealed what had actually befallen her child. It was the culprits themselves when they applied for amnesty, the very same people who had deliberately lied in court to obtain their interdict. No one ever admitted to poisoning her son in detention – for that, according to doctors, was what had crippled him and caused him to lose his hair. But those responsible for killing him confessed and disclosed the sickening details – that they had abducted her son, Siphiwe Mtimkulu, they had drugged his coffee, and they had then shot him in the head and burned his body. Whilst his body was burning, which took six hours in order that the flesh at the top of the thighs might be rendered to ashes, they took it in turns to stoke the fire to keep it going. They then collected the cremated remains and scattered them on the nearby Fish River. They told the Truth and Reconciliation Commission this. Up to that point they had maintained their conspiracy of silence at inquiries into the disappearance of Mtimkulu. And they had done this under oath. Senior police had subverted the very rule of law they were meant to uphold by blatantly perjuring themselves. In the Truth and Reconciliation Commission process the perpetrator had to make a full disclosure to qualify for amnesty, whereas in court he tried to defend his innocence by lying.

We were fortunate that many police came seeking amnesty, but sadly the military, represented in the old South African Defence

Force (SADF), hardly cooperated with the Commission at all. This left a considerable gap in our truth-gathering process. The major figures who did apply for amnesty were forced into it by applications from the policemen who were involved with them in joint operations. There is much truth that the nation still needs to know if our healing and reconciliation are to be lasting and effective.

The Total Strategy

The SADF was part of the 'total strategy' that Mr P. W. Botha devised to respond to what he and the military establishment designated the revolutionary 'total onslaught' of Communism. South Africa was effectively ruled by the State Security Council. This body was in law subordinate to the cabinet, but the reality at that time was that the country was ruled by what we called the 'securocrats', who dominated government thinking in those days. Our country was placed almost on a war footing as we moved into the 1980s. We experienced a further erosion in human rights. From then on it would be unpatriotic to call in question the decisions of the government, which were really the decisions of the State Security Council. Everything was subordinated to the security of the state as determined by those in power. It made white South Africans feel that there was a bad world out there, eager to get them, to destroy their privileged 'South African way of life'. This hostile world wanted to overthrow a Christian government and replace it with an ungodly, atheistic, undemocratic, Communist dictatorship. The apartheid government's propaganda machine was adept at pointing out the disasters that had befallen countries to the north of us in Africa that had adopted socialism – basically, it claimed that they had come to a sticky end because these unreliable, feckless blacks had taken over.

This was a time when the superpowers, the United States and the Soviet Union, waged the Cold War. They did this in all kinds of ways, but especially through surrogate client states in different war zones, where they sought to flex their muscles and establish their hegemony. This was the era when the US enthusiastically supported any government, however shabby its human rights record, as long as it declared itself to be anti-Communist. Thus the apartheid government benefited hugely from President Ronald Reagan's notorious 'constructive engagement' policy. The US paid lip-service to anti-apartheid sentiments, claiming that maintaining relations with such wayward governments as the apartheid regime provided a better chance of influencing them to change for the better than isolating and ostracising them.

I tried without any success to persuade President Reagan and Prime Minister Margaret Thatcher of Britain to adopt a peaceful strategy to bring about change in South Africa through imposing economic sanctions. I met President Reagan and his cabinet at the White House soon after being awarded the Nobel Peace Prize in 1984, but to no avail. He was a bit shocked when I showed him my travel document, because I was not allowed a regular South African passport. What shocked him was how they described my nationality in that document: 'Undeterminable at present'. I had tea with Mrs Thatcher. We spent nearly an hour together at 10 Downing Street, and she oozed oodles of charm. I was really quite impressed with just how charming she was in contrast to her image as the Iron Lady who had zero tolerance for the weak. But I failed to get her to see the importance of sanctions. As she later said of herself, in relation to another issue, the lady was not for turning. Mercifully the people in both countries eventually heeded our pleas, and some sanctions were imposed, especially by the United States, and that contributed very substantially to the demise of apartheid. But up until then these two major Western leaders were dead set in their opposition to sanctions.

The Reagan administration funded the Contras in Nicaragua to subvert the Sandinista liberation movement. They supported President Ferdinand Marcos and his repressive regime in the Philippines, and showed unyielding consistency by supporting Dr Jonas Savimbi's Unita rebels in Angola in a deadly civil war against the MPLA government, at the time Marxist inclined. South Africa joined that fray, supporting Unita because South Africa was also fighting against SWAPO, the Namibian liberation movement, which had been given bases in Angola by the MPLA.

South Africa engaged in a policy of hot pursuit. The military raided what it called terrorist bases and camps in the so-called frontline states – Botswana, Lesotho, Swaziland, Mozambique, Angola, Zambia, Tanzania and Zimbabwe. In doing so, it violated the territorial integrity of many of these countries in order to force them not to give refuge to exiles or provide sanctuary to South African liberation movements. The raids were buttressed with a policy of destabilisation, supporting opposition groups in the different countries as its surrogates. It helped Mr Afonso Dlakama's Renamo movement in Mozambique in its quite heartlessly cruel war against the ruling Frelimo party. Renamo was known for the horrific atrocities it perpetrated against fellow Mozambicans – mutilating hostages by cutting off their ears, noses, lips and other parts of their bodies; abducting entire villages including children and women who were often sexually abused; and forcing young boys to become child soldiers. Mozambique and Angola have been devastated by these civil wars, which in part were due to apartheid's destabilisation policies.

In the report entitled *Apartheid Terrorism*, released in October 1989,[2] it was estimated the SADF destabilisation action during 1980 to 1988 had resulted in:

- the deaths of 1,500,000 people
- 4,000,000 refugees
- economic destruction of US $60 billion
- the deaths of 100,000 elephants and rhinos whose tusks and horns 'compensated' South Africa for supplies of weapons for Renamo and Unita

Angola and Mozambique continue to pay a heavy price: much of their arable land is unsafe for farming because of the landmines still buried in the ground. President Joaquim Chissano told a conference on landmines in Maputo in May 1999 that it would take Mozambique sixty years to get rid of the two million mines buried there. About 60,000 mines had been rendered safe since 1993, at the staggering cost of US $1.6 million. The SADF contributed to that devastation, which in the case of Angola continues in its unending civil war.

The Truth and Reconciliation Commission found the SADF responsible for various gross violations of human rights. Six hundred Namibians were massacred in Kassinga camp in Angola in an SADF raid in 1978. SWAPO claimed Kassinga was a refugee camp but the SADF disputed these claims, maintaining that it was a military camp and thus a legitimate military target. In our Report, we found the raid to have resulted in gross human rights violations against civilian occupants of the camp.

The Commission would have liked to have had more SADF personnel to testify and a great deal more cooperation in its efforts to unravel the mysteries of the total onslaught ideology and what it led to in practice. What we do know is that it led to policing within South Africa becoming increasingly militarised from the mid 1980s.

The aim of an army is to kill enemy personnel and knock out enemy equipment. It exists to destroy, to kill the enemy. As resistance to apartheid intensified in the 1980s, this philosophy was increasingly applied internally. Thus instead of apprehending suspects and culprits it became more and more the practice to eliminate them. This happened, for instance, to four members of the Congress of South African Students (COSAS): three teenagers, Bimbo Madikela, Ntshingo Matabane and Fanyana Nhlapo were killed and a fourth, Zandisile Musi, was injured. The security police lured them to an old pump-house at an abandoned mine near Krugersdorp to the west of Johannesburg, in February 1982. Those who applied for amnesty for the killing were former security policemen Willem Schoon, Abraham Grobbelaar, Jan Coetzee and Christian Rorich. They told the Amnesty Committee that an *askari* had told them the students wanted arms and training to kill a security policeman, one Warrant Officer Mkosi. Coetzee said he decided it would be best to kill the activists instead of arresting them. The incident was set up to make it appear as if these young men had blown themselves up. In the amnesty hearing the applicants were asked if they had known the ages of the teenagers, whether they were indeed terrorists and if the police had considered alternatives to murdering them. The perpetrators were headed by a senior officer: a brigadier gave the nod to the scheme. Clearly the decision was taken because it was too difficult to follow the legal way of dealing with suspects: to apprehend them and seek evidence to prove beyond reasonable doubt in an open court that they had engaged in, or contemplated and planned, subversive activity. No, that would be too time-consuming, and so it was deemed better to kill them than to arrest them.

The minutes of the State Security Council from the 1980s bristle with quite extraordinary vocabulary – 'neutralising' and 'eliminating' people, for instance – which leaders of the apartheid government disingenuously wanted us to believe was really quite innocuous language meaning nothing more sinister than to detain or to ban. Those who carried out these orders almost consistently understood them to mean to kill, murder and assassinate.

In our Report, we identified some of the phrases we found both in the Security Council documents and in politicians' speeches on public platforms and in parliament (English translations of the original Afrikaans are from the Report):

- 'elimineer vyandelike leiers' ('eliminate enemy leaders')
- 'neutraliseer' ('neutralise')
- 'neutralise intimidators by using formal and informal policing'
- 'destroy terrorists'
- 'fisiese vernietiging – mense, fasiliteite, fondse, ens.' ('physical destruction – people, facilities, funds, etc.')
- 'uithaal' ('take out')
- 'uitwis' ('wipe out')
- 'verwyder' ('remove/cause to disappear')
- 'maak 'n plan' ('make a plan')
- 'metodes ander as aanhouding' ('methods other than detention')
- 'onkonvensionele metodes' ('unconventional methods')

In public, this was the kind of language apartheid leaders used:

The security forces will hammer them [the ANC], wherever they find them. What I am saying is the policy of the government. We will not sit here with hands folded waiting for them to cross our borders. We shall carry out ongoing surveillance. We shall determine the correct targets and we shall crush those terrorists, their fellow-travellers and those who help them.[3]

This was the backdrop against which policemen and soldiers interpreted their orders. Some political, military and police leaders, faced with the absurdity of their position, conceded that some of the phrases listed might have been 'ambiguous', but protested that they had not intended that their operatives should break the law. One is tempted to retort, 'Oh, come off it!' If all they wanted to authorise was to detain, arrest, ban, deport, why did they not issue clear, unambiguous and explicit orders saying so?

General Johan van der Merwe, head of the police under Mr de Klerk, a member of the State Security Council and a former commander of the security police, who applied for amnesty for a range of murders, was more forthcoming. Our Report quoted his evidence to our armed forces hearing:

All the powers [given to security forces] were to avoid the ANC/SACP [South African Communist Party] achieving their revolutionary aims and often with the approval of the previous government we had to move outside the boundaries of our law. That inevitably led to the fact that the capabilities of the SAP [South African Police], especially the security forces, included illegal acts.

And:

If you tell a soldier 'eliminate your enemy', depending on the circumstances he will understand that means killing. It is not the only meaning, but it is specifically one meaning.

He was pressed at one point in his evidence:

Commission: . . . I am saying would you agree that that unfortunate use of that language, *'vernietig'*, *'uitroei'*, *'uit te wis'*, *'elimineer'* ['destroy', 'eradicate', 'to wipe out', 'eliminate'] and so on . . . resulted in deaths, would you agree with that?

General van der Merwe: Yes, Mr Chairman.

The closer we got to those who carried out the orders, the more blunt their replies. Brigadier Alf Oosthuizen, former head of the intelligence section of the police security branch, told us:

There was never any lack of clarity about 'take out' or 'eliminate', it meant that the person had to be killed.

Some former Cabinet ministers suggested to us that a small clique around P. W. Botha had been responsible for the direct orders to kill and destroy. But Mr Leon Wessels, a reformist who had been the first high-ranking Nationalist to apologise for apartheid after Mr de Klerk opened negotiations in 1990, said this was no excuse: 'I further do not believe the political defence of "we did not know" is available to me because in many respects I believe we did not want to know.'

These quotations show that it is very hard to sustain the position that at no time did the apartheid government sanction the assassination of its opponents. It is almost untenable. Evidence brought to us indicated, and we found in the Report, that the state resorted to unlawful methods of dealing with its opponents from about the time of Mr P. W. Botha's accession to power, first as Prime Minister in 1978 and later as State President. This criminal conduct stretched from then into the period of his successor, Mr F. W. de Klerk. The state entered the realm of criminality and could hardly be considered as being a legitimate authority. Mr Botha, according to Mr Vlok, who was a Cabinet minister at the time, ordered the bombing of Khotso House, headquarters of the South African Council of Churches, in August 1988.

The Commission found that it was highly improbable that members of the State Security Council did not foresee the possible consequences of adopting an increasingly military strategy. We found they did nothing to distinguish between people involved in military operations and those opposing apartheid peacefully. The term 'terrorist' was widely used and not defined precisely. All opponents were treated as legitimate targets to be eliminated.

We found the Security Council documents were a good illustration of 'plausible deniability' – that politicians deliberately phrased their instructions in such a way that they, the intellectual authors of security force atrocities, could transfer responsibility to their subordinates.

Saying sorry

When evidence emerged during an amnesty hearing late in 1996 that Mr Botha had personally given the orders to bomb Khotso House, it was our Deputy Chairperson, Dr Alex Boraine, much maligned as anti-Afrikaner and biased against the National Party, who suggested that I should visit the former state president at his retirement home in the town of George, on the southern Cape Coast.

Down the years, I had had a number of personal encounters with Mr Botha. The first one was in 1980 when, as General Secretary of the South African Council of Churches, I took a delegation of Church leaders to see him and other members of his cabinet at the government offices in Union Buildings, Pretoria. Some of our peers criticised us strongly for having dealings with the head of an illegitimate regime. However, my view was that Moses approached Pharaoh several times, even when he knew that Pharaoh's heart was hardened. I was as strongly committed to reconciliation then, when it was not popular, as I am now. At that meeting, I made a number of proposals to Mr Botha which, had they been accepted, could have laid down the basis for peaceful negotiations to bring about a settlement in our country. It was a fairly amicable meeting, but our efforts to open a dialogue collapsed when we resisted his attempts to get us to go on a propaganda jaunt to what the South African Defence Force called the 'operational area' on the Namibian-Angolan border. Later, we found out that, while talking to us, his government had been subverting us behind our backs – it had used secret government funds to support a private right-wing body, the Christian League of Southern Africa, to campaign against the South African Council of Churches.

I tried to go the second mile with Mr Botha again in 1986, after I and those working with me in the South African Council of Churches had been awarded the Nobel Peace Prize, and I had been elected Archbishop of Cape Town. I hoped that by some miracle I might just be able to convince him to shift enough to open up the possibility of a peaceful settlement. It was a one-on-one meeting, again fairly amicable, but I brought away from it no concessions. Although he shook hands warmly with me for the press afterwards, the photographs show me with an uneasy expression on my face.

The third, and most difficult, meeting with Mr Botha happened in 1988. I went to appeal to him to spare the lives of six people facing death sentences as a result of the killing of an alleged collaborator in Sharpeville, the same township in which the 1960 massacre had taken place. The first part of the meeting was friendly, two people having a fairly reasonable discussion over whether he would invoke his presidential prerogative. A court stopped the executions later that week and the sentences were subsequently commuted. Then he switched the subject and launched into a bitter attack on me over an illegal march which I and other Church leaders had led to Parliament in protest at restrictions which had been placed on a number of political organisations. He gave me a letter on the subject which had already been distributed to members of parliament and the media, so I protested at his breach of protocol. Then he hammered me for marching under a Communist flag at a funeral, so I challenged him to produce the evidence because I knew he wasn't speaking the truth. As I sat there in his office in Cape Town, I had this discussion with myself – should I be deferential or do I respond? He had a reputation for driving even his cabinet members to tears when he was in a rage. I thought to myself: these guys have made our people suffer; if I burn my boats, so be it, but he is not going to hector me like this. I told him that I was not a small boy, and he had no right to speak to me as he had done. I was his guest and he ought to observe the conventions and treat me as such. Unfortunately we ended up like small boys, wagging our fingers at each other. The meeting ended with me saying that I took strong exception to what he was saying; him retorting 'Then take your exceptions and go,' and the meeting breaking up with me leaving the room. Soon afterwards, the Churches launched the programme of civil disobedience we called the Standing for the Truth Campaign and later that year Khotso House was bombed.

Since that meeting in 1988, Mr Botha had suffered a stroke, been pushed out of office against his will by his cabinet colleagues, led by Mr de Klerk, and had retreated to his retirement home. Now over eighty, he had withdrawn from public life. The last time he had been seen in the news was when he was visited by President Mandela and told journalists he would have nothing to do with the Truth and Reconciliation Commission.

Dr Boraine's suggestion that I go and see Mr Botha was a bid to encourage him to cooperate with us, since he had presided over the affairs of our nation at a time when apartheid's repression was at its most intense and the 'total strategy' was at its height. He had also chaired sessions of the State Security Council. I need not have gone to see Mr Botha – the Commission could subpoena whoever we wanted and had powers of search and seizure – but I agreed to the trip in the hope it might reassure Afrikaners that we were not obsessed with the notion of humiliating them nor of engaging in what some of them claimed was a witch-hunt against them. I flew to George, where we had a very friendly meeting at his daughter's home. His daughter was a solicitous hostess, serving us tea and Afrikaner delicacies – the setting was one that bore no relationship at all to the gruesome activities with which our meeting was concerned. After presenting me with a written submission, Mr Botha agreed to cooperate with the Commission in providing us with written answers to the questions we wanted to pose to him. He pointed out that he would require experienced lawyers to assist him and would need access to state papers. He asked if I would use my good offices with President Mandela to secure both financial assistance for the considerable legal fees and access to the necessary documents.

After returning to Cape Town, I went to see President Mandela on both issues and got his immediate concurrence. We bent over backwards to accommodate Mr Botha, constantly postponing our deadline for his submission. During this period, his wife died. It seemed to me to be important to demonstrate again both to Mr Botha and to his supporters that I had no personal animosity against him, so I again travelled to George to attend her funeral. I was aware that many in the black community would at the very least find my behaviour odd, and at another level offensive. Indeed, a black radio journalist came up to me afterwards and asked me please to explain to his listeners why I was present.

It took nearly ten months for Mr Botha to complete his responses to our questions. In the meantime more information was emerging from the minutes of the State Security Council, so we decided we should invite a range of former political and military leaders, including Mr Botha, to a hearing. Written replies are satisfactory up to a certain point but they are not the same thing as a face-to-face meeting, where an answer might lead to a supplementary question. We were told Mr Botha was not well and we agreed to postpone his appearance. We even suggested that we could hold it in George to spare him the physical strain of travelling to Cape Town (although he had become engaged to a youngish lady whom he visited in a journey that was as long as that to Cape Town). This would be costlier for the Commission and inconvenient, as we would have to carry our trans-lation equipment all the way to George. After protracted discussions between the Commission and Mr Botha's lawyers, he announced that the Commission was a 'circus' and refused to attend the hearing. He was subpoenaed, but on the day he was first meant to appear he sent his lawyer instead with a written response.

The Attorney-General of the Western Cape decided to arraign Mr Botha on charges of refusing to obey the subpoena. Still we did not give up – as his trial began in the local magistrate's court in George, we continued negotiations aimed at finding a compromise which would ensure his appearance before us. We offered to hold the hearing in a nearby hotel, and to supply him with the questions we wanted to ask ahead of the hearing. We also said he could have his doctor present and whenever it might be deemed medically necessary we would adjourn the hearing until he was declared comfortable. Such a hearing would not have lasted more than one day. There was a great deal of haggling between our lawyers and those representing Mr Botha. We could not have been more accommodating, but in the end he rejected our proposals and the trial continued. Only the malicious could say we were hounding a sick, old man. We had bent over so far that many in the black community accused us of double standards when they compared the way we had dealt with Mrs Mandela to the kid-glove treatment we were giving a man whom many felt had been responsible for a great deal of the pain and suffering they experienced.

In the past, Mr Botha had got his way through his obduracy and irascibility. Nobody had dared cross swords with him. He thought the same rules still applied, but things had changed. He could have appeared at an investigative inquiry held behind closed doors, in the comfort of a hotel suite, being asked questions he had previously had sight of. He chose to be his old stubborn, granite self and received a big shock. He was not above the law. So something he would not have imagined in his worst nightmares occurred. He, the former state president who had made cabinet ministers quake in their shoes, stood as the accused in a court presided over by a black magistrate. There was a certain moral appropriateness in that scenario. The prosecution was able to call several witnesses including Colonel Eugene de Kock, former head of Vlakplaas, headquarters of a police death squad. De Kock was quite scathing in his contempt for political leaders: 'Myself and others in the security forces . . . have been sold out by cowardly politicians – in the National Party especially,' he told the court. 'They want the lamb but they don't want to see the blood and guts; they are cowards.' All this was carried prominently by the media.

It was feared that Mr Botha might become a focus for right-wing agitation and violence. Nothing came of it. It was only some members of his family who attended the court sessions, which with postponements lasted more than two weeks, when the matter could have been over and done with in a day had he accepted our offer.

I was among those called to give evidence against him, for he claimed that I had given him an assurance he would not be summoned to a Commission hearing. At the end of two days of vigorous cross-examination by his lawyers, I felt I could not leave the witness box without making one last plea to him. I appealed to the court:

> May I just say one thing, your worship? I believe that we still have an opportunity – although this is a court of law, and without suggesting that the accused is guilty of any violations. I speak on behalf of people who have suffered grievously as a result of policies that were carried out by governments, including the government that he headed. I want to appeal to him. I want to appeal to him to take this chance provided by this court to say that he may not himself have even intended the suffering to happen to people; he may not have given orders or authorised anything . . . I am just saying that the government that he headed caused many of our people deep, deep anguish and pain and suffering. Our people want to be part of this country and to be part of reconciliation. If Mr Botha was able to say, 'I am sorry that the policies of my government caused you pain.' Just that. Can he bring himself to say I am sorry that the policies of my government caused you so much pain? That would be a tremendous thing and I appeal to him. Thank you.

Mr Botha only showed anger at my appeal. He was convicted and sentenced to a suspended gaol sentence and fine by the magistrate, but was subsequently acquitted on a narrow technicality. (We had bent over so far backwards to accommodate him that we left issuing our subpoena too late. On the day we issued it, our mandate to do so had run out and President Mandela had not yet signed the new mandate.) Morally and politically, he had been called to account, faced with victims and perpetrators of his policies, and politically he had been isolated. He looked such a pathetic figure in court that I felt deeply sorry for him. His stubbornness provided some people with what they had been wanting to see – the leaders of the old dispensation getting a dose of retributive justice – but it happened against the Commission's wishes.

I have already paid my warm and deserved tribute to Mr F. W. de Klerk for the epoch-making and courageous decision he announced in Parliament on 2 February 1990. Nothing will ever take away from its monumental significance. We could so easily have been overwhelmed by a bloodbath. He had the chance of true greatness had he from that point been willing to apologise unreservedly for apartheid. He would then have gone down in history as a truly great South African statesman. Sadly, during the negotiations for a new constitution between 1990 and 1993, perhaps deluded by his success in the all-white referendum held to approve his policies in 1992, he believed he could find a way to keep power by trying to erode that of his major negotiating partner, Mr Mandela, who increasingly became his opponent. That was when so-called 'black-on-black' violence escalated and various horrendous massacres took place. He may claim that the security forces had no hand in fomenting this, or that if it did happen then 'bad apples' were responsible for the aberrations. I am afraid I cannot believe that. I cannot believe that the involvement of at least one cabinet minister and two former commissioners of police in human rights violations in the 1980s represented nothing more serious than aberrations by mavericks.

I have no animus against Mr de Klerk. The Norwegian Nobel Committee telephoned me on the eve of their announcement of the winners of the 1993 Peace Prize, to ask my opinion of their intention to make a joint award to Mr Mandela and Mr de Klerk. I supported this enthusiastically. Presumably the committee would have reassessed their decision had I expressed opposition to it, otherwise there was not much point in consulting me. Had I known then what I know now, I would have opposed it vehemently. Mr de Klerk in fact made a very handsome apology for apartheid when he appeared before the Commission in 1996, but then spoiled it all when he qualified the apology virtually out of existence. What a great man he would have been had he spoken as openly and with as much passion as either one of his former cabinet colleagues, 'Pik' Botha, the long-serving Foreign Minister, or Leon Wessels. He was incapable of seeing apartheid for what it was – intrinsically evil. He is a very bright lawyer who qualifies his answers carefully to protect his position, but in doing this he has steadily eroded his stature, becoming in the process a small man, lacking magnanimity and generosity of spirit. I hope he has the sensitivity to realise that his idea of establishing an institute for reconciliation, which he announced in 1998, would rub salt into the wounds of the victims of a policy over which he presided.

But for the grace of God . . .

During the Commission's institutional hearings, one realised just how powerful the forces were that had exerted an influence on people. We should not be shocked that so many in the white community were able to live normal lives, enjoying all the freedoms of citizenship, plus huge privileges and benefits. What should surprise us is not the fact that so many whites ended up accepting conventional racist attitudes and values, and did not really think much about the impact of racist policies on their fellow human beings. What *is* amazing is that there should have been those, and I keep acknowledging their significant numbers, who did not succumb to the insidious pressures of an ethos that permeated every aspect of life. This remarkable group not only resisted the enticing blandish-ments of conforming to the dominant racist culture; most wanted to end the system. That surely is extraordinary when you look at the forces that were ranged on the side of apartheid, forces that were so potent in forming the attitudes, the entire mindset and world-view of white people. We have seen how virtually every institution, every aspect of life, came under the control of this ideology. Everything conspired to condition white people to think and act in a particular kind of way. We might say they were programmed.

On my first visit to Nigeria in the early 1970s I had a sense of how programmed I had been too. I was travelling in a plane piloted by

Nigerians. Coming from South Africa, where blacks did not do such work, I experienced a strong feeling of pride in black achievement. The plane took off smoothly. Then we hit turbulence. At one moment we were at one altitude and the next you had left your stomach up there as the plane shuddered and dropped. I was shocked at what I discovered – I found I was saying to myself, 'I wish there was a white man in the cockpit. Can these blacks manage to navigate us out of this horrible experience?' It was all involuntary and spontaneous. I would never have believed that I had in fact been so radically brainwashed. I would have denied it vigorously because I prided myself on being an exponent of black consciousness, but in a crisis something deeper had emerged: that I had accepted a white definition of existence that assumed that whites were somehow superior to and more competent than blacks. Of course, those black pilots were able to land the plane quite competently.

We shouldn't underestimate the power of conditioning. That is why I hold the view that we should be a little more generous, a little more understanding, in judging the perpetrators of human rights violations. This does not mean we will condone what they and the white community in South Africa did or allowed to happen. But we will be a little more compassionate in our judgement as we become a little more conscious of how we too could succumb as easily as they. It will make our judgement just that little less strident and abrasive and possibly open the door to some being able to forgive themselves for what they now perceive as weakness and lack of courage. It might then persuade them perhaps to be a little more willing to acknowledge their frailty and make them more ready to accept accountability more easily. And it might make us say to ourselves as we sit in judgement, 'There but for the grace of God, go I.'

In other words, there is hope. There is hope because the perpetrators – as well as those who benefited from apartheid – are revealed as human beings, frail but with the capacity to do better if they get out of the self-justifying or denial mode and are able to say quietly, humbly, 'I am sorry, forgive me.'

After the gruelling work of the Commission I came away with a deep sense – indeed an exhilarating realisation – that though there is undoubtedly much evil about, we human beings have a wonderful capacity for good. We can be very good. *That* is what fills me with hope for even the most intractable situations.

o

CHAPTER ELEVEN

Without forgiveness there really is no future

A year after the genocide of 1994 in Rwanda, when at least half a million people were massacred, I visited that blighted land. I went as the President of the continental ecumenical body, the All Africa Conference of Churches. In my ten-year, two-term presidency I had tried to take the AACC to its member Churches through pastoral visits, especially to those countries that were experiencing crises of one sort or another. So I and other AACC office-bearers had visited Nigeria, Liberia during its civil war, Angola and others. We also went to celebrate successes when, for instance, democracy replaced repression and injustice in Ethiopia. But we usually went to be in solidarity with our fellow Christians in lands that were experiencing some trial or another. And the AACC leadership had gone to Rwanda.

We visited Ntarama, a village near the capital Kigali, where Tutsis had been mown down in a church. The new government had not removed the corpses, so that the church was like a mortuary, with the bodies lying as they had fallen the year before during the massacre. The stench was overpowering. Outside the church was a collection of skulls of some of those who had been brutally done to death – some of the skulls still had *pangas* (machetes) and daggers embedded in them. I tried to pray. Instead I broke down and wept.

The scene was a deeply disturbing and moving monument to the viciousness that as human beings we are capable of unleashing against fellow human beings. Those who had turned against one another in this gory fashion had often lived amicably in the same villages and spoken the same language. They had frequently intermarried and most of them had espoused the same faith – most were Christians. The colonial overlords had sought to maintain their European hegemony by favouring one main ethnic group, the Tutsi, over the other, the Hutu, thus planting the seeds of what would in the end be one of the bloodiest episodes in modern African history. (The third group was the Twa, much smaller in numbers.) That genocide made one pause in blaming racism for every conceivable ill that has befallen humankind, because whilst whites had a hand in fomenting the ethnic internecine strife, the actual perpetrators were blacks against fellow blacks.

A few kilometres from this church, some women had begun to build a settlement which they named the Nelson Mandela Village. It was to be a home for some of the many widows and orphans created by the genocide. I spoke to the leaders of the women's movement that had conceived this project. They said, 'We must mourn and weep for the dead. But life must also go on, we can't go on weeping.' How wonderfully impressive, how indomitable. Over at Ntarama, we might say, there was Calvary, death and crucifixion. Here in the Nelson Mandela Village was resurrection, new life, new beginning, new hope. Again it was noteworthy how women have this remarkable resilience and an instinct for nurturing life.

I also visited the overcrowded Kigali Prison, packed to the rafters with those suspected of being involved in the genocide. Almost all were Hutu. There were women, men and even young children, people of every age and from every social group – including priests and nuns, teachers and lawyers. Some people had died from suffocation. I told President Pasteur Bizimungu that that prison was a disaster waiting to happen and that it would add to the bitter memories and exacerbate the resentment of the Hutu towards the Tutsi.

During my visit I also attended a rally in the main stadium of Kigali. It was amazing that people who had so recently experienced such a devastating trauma could sing and laugh and dance as they did at that rally. Most of the leading politicians were present, from the President down. I had been asked to preach. I began by expressing the deepest condolences of all their sisters and brothers in other parts of Africa, for people elsewhere had been profoundly shocked at the carnage and destruction. (It turns out now that had the international community heeded the many warnings that were being given at the time, perhaps the United Nations might have had the resources to intervene and the genocide might very well not have happened. The Rwandese felt a deep anger against the UN. The victims and survivors felt they had been let down very badly, with disastrous consequences.) I said that the history of Rwanda was typical of a history of 'top dog' and 'underdog'. The top dog wanted to cling to its privileged position and the underdog strove to topple the top dog. When that happened, the new top dog engaged in an orgy of retribution to pay back the new underdog for all the pain and suffering it had caused when it was top dog. The new underdog fought like an enraged bull to topple the new top dog, storing in its memory all the pain and suffering it was enduring, forgetting that the new top dog was in its view only retaliating for all that it remembered it had suffered when the underdog had been its master. It was a sad history of reprisal provoking counter-reprisal. I reminded the Tutsi that they had waited for thirty years to get their own back for what they perceived to be the injustices that had been heaped on them. I said that extremists among the Hutu were also quite capable of waiting thirty years or more for the day when they could topple the new government, and in their turn unleash the devastation of revenge and resentment.

I said there was talk about tribunals, because people did not want to tolerate allowing the criminals to escape punishment. But what I feared was that if retributive justice was the last word in their situation, then Rwanda had had it. There is no way that most Hutu are going to be persuaded to believe that the courts are finding them guilty because the evidence is incontrovertible – that any court, anywhere in the world, confronted with such evidence, would pronounce them guilty. They would, most of them, feel that they had been found guilty not because they were guilty but because they were Hutu, and they would wait for the day when they would be able to take revenge. Then they would pay the Tutsi back for the horrendous prison conditions in which they had been held. I told them that the cycle of reprisal and counter-reprisal that had characterised their national history had to be broken, and that the only way to do this was to go beyond retributive justice to restorative justice, to move on to forgiveness, because without it there was no future.

The President of Rwanda responded to my sermon with considerable magnanimity. They were ready to forgive, he said, but even Jesus had declared that the devil could not be forgiven. I do not know where he found the basis for what he said, but he was expressing a view that found some resonance: that there were atrocities that were unforgivable. My own view was different, but I had been given a fair and indeed friendly hearing. Later I addressed the parliamentary and political leadership of that country and I was not shouted down as I repeated my appeal for them to consider choosing forgiveness and reconciliation rather than their opposites.

Why was I not rebuffed? Why did these traumatised people, who had undergone such a terrible experience, listen to an unpopular point of view? They listened to me particularly because something had happened in South Africa that gave them reason to pause and wonder. Was this not a viable way of dealing with conflict? Might those who had been at one another's throats try to live amicably together? The world had expected that the most ghastly bloodbath would overwhelm South Africa. It had not happened. Then the world thought that after a democractically elected government was in place, those who for so long had been denied their rights, whose dignity had been trodden underfoot, callously and without compunction, would go on the rampage, unleashing an orgy of revenge and retribution that would devastate their common motherland. Instead there was this remarkable Commission, where people told their heart-rending stories – victims expressing their willingness to forgive, and perpetrators telling their stories of sordid atrocities while also asking for forgiveness from those they had wronged so grievously.

The world could not quite believe what it was seeing. 'You get new hope for the future,' the former President of the Federal Republic of Germany, Richard von Weizsäcker, told a symposium in Berlin after hearing our country's story in April 1999. South Africans managed an extraordinary, reasonably peaceful transition from the awfulness of repression to the relative stability of democracy. They confounded everyone by their novel manner of dealing with a horrendous past. They had perhaps surprised even themselves at first by how much equanimity they had shown as some of the gory details of that past were rehearsed. It was a phenomenon that the world could not dismiss as insignificant. It was this that enabled me to address my sisters and brothers in Rwanda in a manner that under other circumstances could have been seen as insensitive and presumptuous.

I have had the same experience when visiting other parts of the world where people are seeking to come to terms with their history of conflict and disagreement. In 1998 I went to Dublin and to Belfast. In both these cities audiences warmed to the message that our South African experience showed that hardly any situation could be said to be devoid of hope. Our problem had been one which most had abandoned as ultimately intractable. I said, 'Yes, we have lived through a ghastly nightmare, but it has ended.' The Irish were on the way to an end to their nightmare, for had there not already been the Good Friday Agreement? I said they ought not to grow despondent at the obstacles preventing the implementation of that crucial agreement; our experience had been that quite frequently the enemies of peace would respond to breakthroughs by redoubling their efforts to derail the process. I said the Irish should redouble their own determination and vigilance to ensure that such a priceless gift as the end of their 'Troubles' should not elude them just when it was within their grasp.

I told them that in South Africa it had often felt as if we were on a roller-coaster ride. At one moment we would experience the most wonderful joy, euphoria even, at some new and crucial initiative: we would see the promised land of peace and justice round the corner.

Then, just when we thought we had entered the last lap, something ghastly would happen – a massacre, a deadlock, brinkmanship of some kind, a walkout by one delegation or another – and we would be scraping the rock bottom of despair and despondency. I told them this was normal. The prize at the end is so wonderful that they should not let go of their dream of a new Ireland; of a time when they would be amazed that they had been blind for so long; of a time when they would realise that they had wasted many years and many lives when in fact goodness and peace and tolerance were wonderful and ultimately uncomplicated. I reminded them of how it had seemed so unlikely for us to have got where we now were in South Africa. Just as our nightmare had ended, so too would theirs end, as sure as day follows night.

They heard this message as if in a sense it had been uttered by an oracle. What gave a heightened credibility to what I said was the fact that we had had a relatively peaceful transition and had found this novel way of dealing with the legacy of our past. I want to believe that it helped them a little when I exhorted them not to despair because of a deadlock over the decommissioning of weapons. In Belfast I was deeply impressed with the many dedicated individuals working away in strife-torn communities, building bridges between alienated and traumatised people, being extraordinary agents of peace and reconciliation. I said to them that nothing is ever lost; that their work did not evaporate into the ether and disappear into oblivion, even if it appeared a failure. No, in a way that we could not fathom, their work went to impregnate the atmosphere. We know that happens. We can sense that a home is happy even before anyone tells us because we are able to catch the 'vibes' – it is in the very stones. We know when a church is redolent of sanctity, of holiness; when it has been prayed in. We can almost smell the holiness, sense the energy and reverence of those many who have gone before. A prayed-in church is qualitatively different from one that has the atmosphere of a concert hall. So I told those dedicated workers for peace and reconciliation that they should not be tempted to give up on their crucial work because of the frustrations of seemingly not making any significant progress, that in our experience nothing was wasted, for when the time was right it would all come together and, looking back, people would realise what a critical contribution they had made. They were part of the cosmic movement towards unity, towards reconciliation, that has existed from the beginning of time.

It is and has always been God's intention that we should live in friendship and harmony. That was the point of the story of the Garden of Eden, where there was no bloodshed, not even for religious sacrifice. The lion and the lamb played together and all were vegetarian. Then the primordial harmony that was God's intention for all God's creation was shattered and a fundamental brokenness infected the entire creation. Human beings came to be at loggerheads, blaming one another and being at one another's throats. They were alienated from their Maker. Now they sought to hide from the God who used to stroll with them in the garden. Creation was now 'red in tooth and claw'. Where there had been friendship, now we experienced enmity. Humans would crush the serpent's head before it bruised their heels. This story is the Bible's way of telling a profound existential truth in the form of highly imaginative poetry.

Prosaic, literal-minded spirits who cannot soar in the realms of the muse will be dismissive of this highly imaginative story-telling. And yet even if we doubt that there has ever been such harmony in a mythical Garden of Eden, none but the most obtuse can doubt that we are experiencing a radical brokenness in all of existence. Times are out of joint. Alienation and disharmony, conflict and turmoil, enmity and hatred characterise so much of life. Ours has been the bloodiest century known to human history. There would be no call for ecological campaigning had nature not been exploited and abused. We experience the ground now bringing forth thistles as soil erosion devastates formerly arable land and deserts overtake fertile farms. Rivers and the atmosphere are polluted thoughtlessly and we are fearful of the consequences of a depleted ozone layer and the devastation of the greenhouse effect. We are not quite at home in our world, and everywhere there is a nostalgia for a paradise that has been lost.

Believers say that we might describe most of human history as a quest for that harmony, friendship and peace for which we appear to have been created. The Bible depicts it all as a God-directed campaign to recover that primordial harmony when the lion will again lie with the lamb and they will learn war no more because swords will have been beaten into ploughshares and spears into pruning hooks. Somewhere deep inside us we seem to know that we are destined for something better. Now and again we catch a glimpse of the better thing for which we are meant – for example when we work together to counter the effects of natural disasters and the world is galvanised by a spirit of compassion and an amazing outpouring of generosity; when for a little while we are bound together by our caring humanity, a universal sense of *ubuntu*. When victorious powers set up a Marshall Plan to help in the reconstruction of their devastated former adversaries, for example; when we establish a United Nations Organisation where the peoples of the earth can parley as they endeavour to avoid war; when we sign charters on the rights of children and of women; when we seek to ban the use of antipersonnel landmines; when we agree as one to outlaw torture and racism. Then we experience fleetingly that we are made for togetherness, for friendship, for community, for family; that we are created to live in a delicate network of interdependence.

There is a movement, not easily discernible, at the heart of things to reverse the awful centrifugal force of alienation, brokenness, division, hostility and disharmony. God has set in motion a centripetal process, a moving towards the Centre, towards unity, harmony, goodness, peace and justice; one that removes barriers. Jesus says, 'And when I am lifted up from the earth I shall draw everyone to myself,'[1] as he hangs from His cross with out-flung arms, thrown out to clasp all, everyone and everything, in a cosmic embrace, so that all, everyone, everything, belongs. None is an outsider, all are insiders, all belong. There are no aliens, all belong in the one family, God's family, the human family. There is no longer Jew or Greek, male or female, slave or free – instead of separation and division, all distinctions make for a rich diversity to be celebrated for the sake of the unity that underlies them. We are different so that we can know our need of one another, for no one is ultimately self-sufficient. A completely self-sufficient person would be sub-human.

It was God's intention to bring all things in heaven and on earth to a unity in Christ, and each of us participates in this grand movement. Thus Teilhard de Chardin, the paleontologist, in a passage from *Le Milieu Divin* declares:

We are sometimes inclined to think that the same things are monotonously repeated over and over again in the history of creation. That is because the season is too long by comparison with the brevity of our individual lives, and the transformation too vast and too inward by comparison with our superficial and restricted outlook, for us to see the progress of what is tirelessly taking place in and through all matter and spirit. Let us believe in revelation, once again our faithful support in our most human forebodings. Under the commonplace envelope of things and of all our purified and salvaged efforts, a new earth is being slowly engendered.

One day, the Gospel tells us, the tension gradually accumulating between humanity and God will touch the limits prescribed by the possibilities of the world. And then will come the end. The presence of Christ, which has been silently accruing in things, will suddenly be revealed – like a flash of light from pole to pole. Breaking through all the barriers within which the veil of matter and the water-tightness of souls have seemingly kept it confined, it will invade the face of the earth . . . Like lightning, like a conflagration, like a flood, the attraction exerted by the Son of Man will lay hold of all the whirling elements in the universe so as to reunite them or subject them to his body . . . As the Gospel warns us, it would be in vain to speculate as to the hour and the modalities of this formidable event. But we have to expect it . . . that is perhaps the supreme Christian function and the most distinctive characteristic of our religion . . . The Lord Jesus will only come soon if we ardently expect him . . . Successors to Israel, we Christians have been charged with keeping the flame of desire ever alive in the world. Only twenty centuries have passed since the Ascension. What have we made of our expectancy?

A rather childish haste, combined with the error in perspective which led the first generation of Christians to believe in the immediate return of Christ, has unfortunately left us disillusioned and suspicious. Our faith in the Kingdom of God has been disconcerted by the resistance of the world to good. A certain pessimism has encouraged us . . . to regard the world as decidedly and incorrigibly wicked. And so we have allowed the flame to die down in our sleeping hearts . . . in reality we should have to admit, if we were sincere, that we no longer expect anything.'[2]

And so I was able to say to those remarkable people in Belfast that nothing is lost. What they were doing advanced the course of reconciliation. What each of us does can retard or promote, can hinder or advance, the process at the heart of the universe. Christians would say the outcome is not in question. The death and resurrection of Jesus Christ puts the issue beyond doubt: ultimately goodness and laughter and peace and compassion and gentleness and forgiveness and reconciliation will have the last word. The victory over apartheid was proof positive of the truth of this seemingly utopian dream.

May the time come when men (and women) having been awakened to the close bond linking all the movements of this world in the single all-embracing work of the Incarnation, shall be unable to give themselves to any one of their tasks without illuminating it with the clear vision that their work, however elementary it may be, is received and put to good use by a Centre of the Universe.[3]

I had visited the Holy Land over Christmas 1989 and had the privilege, during that visit, of going to Yad Vashem, the Holocaust museum in Jerusalem. When the media asked me for my impressions, I told them it was a shattering experience. I added that the Lord whom I served, who was Himself a Jew, would have asked, 'But what about forgiveness?' That remark set the cat among the pigeons. I was roundly condemned. I had also expressed my dismay at the treatment meted out to the Palestinians, which was in my view quite at variance with what the Jewish prophets taught and what the Jewish rabbi that we Christians followed demanded from His followers. I was charged with being anti-Semitic and graffiti appeared on the walls of St George's Anglican Cathedral in Jerusalem, in whose close I was staying. It read, 'Tutu is a black Nazi pig.'

I was thus somewhat apprehensive about going there again in January 1999, when I was to visit the West Bank, preach at an Anglican church, and attend a meeting of the Peres Peace Centre, on whose board of directors I serve. But I need not have worried. Our hosts at the meeting in Jerusalem had to turn people away. It was clear everywhere we went that what had occurred in South Africa fascinated people greatly. Shimon Peres, the former prime minister, foreign minister, and Nobel Peace laureate, hailed our reconciliation process as something unique in history.

In the Jerusalem meeting, which was packed, there really was a deep interest among Israelis in the process of the Truth and Reconciliation Commission and in the concept of forgiveness and reconciliation. I was able to point out that we had learned in South Africa that true security would never be won through the barrel of a gun. True security would come when all the inhabitants of the Middle East, that region so revered by so many, believed that their human rights and dignity were respected and upheld, when true justice prevailed. I had not changed my own points of view: I still felt there was a need for forgiveness and that there ought to be both security for the State of Israel and justice and equity for the Palestinians. But somehow in Israel I was seen in a new light.

It was clear in all of these countries – Rwanda, Ireland, Israel and Palestine – that the process in which South Africa had been engaged lent a credibility to whatever I might say that had previously been absent. People could listen to perhaps difficult things without accusing me of being presumptuous and insensitive. More than anything else, it did seem as if many who listened to me were people who derived hope from what we had attempted to do in South Africa. We happened to have been blessed with leaders who were ready to take risks – when you embark on the business of asking for and giving forgiveness, you are taking a risk.

If you ask another person for forgiveness you may be spurned; the one you have injured may refuse to forgive you. The risk is even greater if you are the injured party, wanting to offer forgiveness. The culprit may be arrogant, obdurate or blind; not ready or willing to apologise or to ask for forgiveness in their turn. He or she thus cannot receive the forgiveness they are offered. Such rejection can jeopardise the whole enterprise. Our leaders were ready in South Africa to say they were willing to walk the path of confession, forgiveness and reconciliation with all the hazards that lay along the way. And it seems their gamble might be paying off since our land has not been overwhelmed by the catastrophe that had seemed so inevitable.

It is crucial when a relationship has been damaged or when a potential relationship has been made impossible, that the perpetrator should acknowledge the truth and be ready and willing to apologise. It helps the process of forgiveness and reconciliation immensely. It is never easy. We all know just how difficult it is for most of us to admit that we have been wrong. It is perhaps the most difficult thing in the world – in almost every language the most difficult words are 'I am sorry'. Thus it is not at all surprising that those accused of horrendous deeds and the communities they come from, for whom they believed they were committing these atrocities, almost always try to find ways out of even admitting that they were indeed capable of such deeds. They adopt the denial mode, asserting that such-and-such has not happened. When the evidence is incontrovertible, then they take refuge in feigned ignorance. The Germans claimed they had not known what the Nazis were up to. White South Africans have also tried to find refuge in claims of ignorance. Leon Wessels, the former apartheid cabinet minister, was closer to the mark when he said that they had not wanted to know, for there were those who tried to alert them. For those with eyes to see there were accounts of people dying mysteriously in detention. For those with ears to hear there was much that was disquieting and even chilling. But, like the three monkeys, they chose neither to hear, nor see, nor speak of evil. When some did own up, they passed the blame to others – 'We were carrying out orders' – refusing to acknowledge that as morally responsible individuals, each person has to take responsibility for carrying out unconscionable orders.

None of us tends to rush to expose our vulnerability and our sinfulness. But if the process of forgiveness and healing is to happen and to succeed, ultimately acknowledgment by the culprit is almost indispensable. Acknowledgment of the truth, and of having wronged someone, is important in getting to the root of the breach. If a husband and wife have quarrelled without the wrongdoer acknowledging his or her fault by confessing, so the cause of the rift is clear, and then the husband comes home with a bunch of flowers and the couple pretend all is in order, they are liable to be in for a rude shock. They have not dealt with their immediate past adequately. They have glossed over their differences, for they have failed to stare truth in the face for fear of a possible bruising confrontation. They will have done what the prophet Jeremiah calls 'healing the hurt lightly' and cried, 'Peace, peace where there is no peace.'[4] They will have only papered over the cracks and not worked out why they fell out in the first place. All that will happen is that despite the beautiful flowers the hurt will fester. One day there will be an awful eruption and they will realise that they had tried to obtain reconciliation on the cheap. True reconciliation is not cheap. It cost God the death of His only begotten Son.

Forgiving and being reconciled are not about pretending that things are other than they are. It is not patting one another on the back and turning a blind eye to the wrong. True reconciliation exposes the awfulness, the abuse, the pain, the degradation, the truth. It could even sometimes make things worse. It is a risky undertaking, but in the end it is worthwhile, because in the end there will be real healing from having dealt with the real situation. Spurious reconciliation can bring only spurious healing.

If the wrongdoer has come to the point of realising his wrong, then one hopes there will be remorse, or at least some contrition or sorrow for that wrong. This should lead him to confessing the wrong he has done and asking for forgiveness. This obviously requires a fair measure of humility, especially when the victim is someone in a group that one's community had despised, as was often the case in South Africa when the perpetrators were government agents.

The victim, we hope, would be moved to respond to an apology by forgiving the culprit. As I have already tried to show, we were constantly amazed in the Truth and Reconciliation Commission at the extraordinary magnanimity that so many of the victims exhibited. Of course there were those who said they would not forgive. That demonstrated for me the important point that forgiveness could not be taken for granted; it was neither cheap nor easy. As it happens, these were the exceptions. Far more frequently what we encountered was deeply moving and humbling.

In forgiving, people are not being asked to forget. On the contrary, it is *important* to remember, so that we should not let such atrocities happen again. Forgiveness does not mean condoning what has been done. It means taking what has happened seriously and not minimising it; drawing out the sting in the memory that threatens to poison our entire existence. It involves trying to understand the perpetrators and so have empathy, to try to stand in their shoes, and to appreciate the sort of pressures and influences that might have brought them to do what they did.

Forgiveness is not being sentimental. The study of forgiveness has become a growth industry. Whereas previously it was something often dismissed pejoratively as spiritual and religious, now because of developments such as the Truth and Reconciliation Commission in South Africa, it is gaining attention as an academic discipline studied by psychologists, philosophers, physicians and theologians. In the United States, there is an International Forgiveness Institute attached to the University of Wisconsin, and the John Templeton Foundation, with others, has started a multi-million dollar Campaign for Forgiveness Research. Forgiving has even been found to be good for your health.

Forgiving means abandoning your right to pay back the perpetrator in his own coin, but it is a loss which liberates the victim. At the Commission we heard people speak of a sense of relief after forgiving. A recent issue of the journal *Spirituality and Health*[5] had on its front cover a picture of three US ex-servicemen standing in front of the Vietnam Memorial in Washington DC. One asks, 'Have you forgiven those who held you prisoner of war?' 'I will never forgive them,' replies the other. His mate says: 'Then it seems they still have you in prison, don't they?'

Does the victim depend on the culprit's contrition and confession as the pre-condition for being able to forgive? There is no question that, of course, such a confession is a very great help to the one who wants to forgive, but it is not absolutely indispensable. Jesus did not wait until those who were nailing Him to the cross had asked for forgiveness. He was ready, as they drove in the nails, to pray to His Father to forgive them and He even provided an excuse for what they were doing. If the victim could forgive only when the culprit confessed, then the victim would be locked into the culprit's whim, locked into victimhood, whatever her own attitude or intention. That would be palpably unjust.

I have used the following analogy to try to explain the need for a perpetrator to confess. Imagine you are sitting in a dank, stuffy and dark room. This is because the curtains are drawn and the windows have been shut. Outside the light is shining and a fresh breeze is blowing. If you want the light to stream into that room and the fresh air to flow in, you will have to open the window and draw the curtains apart; then the light which has always been available will come in and air will enter the room to freshen it up. So it is with forgiveness. The victim may be ready to forgive and make the gift of her forgiveness available, but it is up to the wrongdoer to appropriate the gift – to open the window and draw the curtains aside. He does this by acknowledging the wrong he has done, so letting the light and fresh air of forgiveness enter his being.

In the act of forgiveness we are declaring our faith in the future of a relationship and in the capacity of the wrongdoer to make a new beginning on a course that will be different from the one that caused us the wrong. We are saying here is a chance to make a new beginning. It is an act of faith that the wrongdoer can change. According to Jesus we should be ready to do this not just once, not just seven times, but seventy times seven[6] – without limit – provided, it seems Jesus says, your brother or sister who has wronged you is ready to come and confess the wrong they have committed yet again.

That is a challenge, but because we are not infallible, because we will hurt especially the ones we love by some wrong, we will always need a process of forgiveness and reconciliation to deal with those unfortunate yet all too human breaches in relationships. They are an inescapable characteristic of the human condition.

Once the wrongdoer has confessed and the victim has forgiven, it does not mean that is the end of the process. Most frequently, the wrong has affected the victim in tangible, material ways. Apartheid provided whites with enormous benefits and privileges, leaving its victims deprived and exploited. If someone steals my pen and then asks me to forgive him, unless he returns my pen the sincerity of his contrition and confession will be considered to be nil. Confession, forgiveness and reparation, wherever feasible, form part of a continuum.

In South Africa, the whole process of reconciliation has been placed in very considerable jeopardy by the enormous disparities between the rich, mainly the whites, and the poor, mainly the blacks. The huge gap between the haves and the have-nots, which was largely created and maintained by racism and apartheid, poses the greatest threat to reconciliation and stability in our country. The rich provided the class from which the perpetrators and the beneficiaries of apartheid came and the poor produced the bulk of the victims. That is why I have exhorted whites to be keen to see transformation taking place in the lot of blacks. For unless houses replace the hovels and shacks in which most blacks live; unless blacks gain access to clean water, electricity, affordable health care, decent education, good jobs and a safe environment – all things which the vast majority of whites have taken for granted for so long – we can kiss goodbye to reconciliation.

Reconciliation is liable to be a long drawn-out process with ups and downs, not something accomplished overnight and certainly not by a Commission, however effective. The Truth and Reconciliation

Commission has only been able to make a contribution. Reconciliation is going to have to be the concern of every South African. It has to be a national project to which all earnestly strive to make their particular contribution – by learning the language and culture of others; by being ready and willing to make amends; by refusing to deal in stereotypes in making racial or other jokes that ridicule a particular group; by contributing to a culture of respect for human rights, and seeking to enhance tolerance – with zero tolerance for intolerance; by working for a more inclusive society where most, if not all, can feel they belong – that they are insiders and not aliens and strangers on the outside, relegated to the edges of society.

To work for reconciliation is to want to realise God's dream for humanity – when we will know that we are indeed members of one family, bound together in a delicate network of interdependence.

Simon Wiesenthal in the anthology, *The Sunflower*, tells the story of how he was unable to forgive a Nazi soldier who asked to be forgiven. The soldier had been part of a group that rounded up a number of Jews, locked them up in a building and proceeded to set it alight, burning those inside to death. The soldier was now on his deathbed. His troubled conscience sought the relief that might come through unburdening himself, confessing his complicity and getting absolution from a Jew. Simon listened to his terrible story in silence. When the soldier had ended his narration, Simon left without uttering a word, certainly not one of forgiveness. He asks at the end of his account, 'What would you have done?'

The Sunflower is a collection of the responses of various people to Simon Wiesenthal's question. An updated version[7] contains a contribution from me. The dilemma Wiesenthal faced was very real. His own view, which seems to be that of many Jews, is that the living have no right to forgive on behalf of those who were killed, those who suffered in the past and are no longer alive to make the decision for themselves. One can understand their reluctance, since if they were to forgive it might appear they were trivialising the awful experience of the victims; it also might seem the height of presumption to speak on behalf of people who suffered so grievously, especially perhaps if one had not oneself suffered to the same extent. I understand the nature of their dilemma and would not want to seem to minimise it, but I hold a slightly different view.

At the end of 1990 the various South African Churches gathered in the town of Rustenburg in one of the most fully ecumenical and representative Church meetings to have taken place in our country. This meeting was called the Rustenburg Conference. Present were those Churches that had been very vocal in opposing apartheid through their membership of the South African Council of Churches, as well as the major white Dutch Reformed Church (Nederduitse Gereformeerde Kerk; DRC) which had supported apartheid by providing its theological rationale (but which had already retreated significantly from that posture). Then there were the many so-called charismatic or pentecostal Churches that had tried to be apolitical, though they must have been aware that their imagined neutrality in reality supported the unjust status quo. There were representatives too from overseas partner Churches and from the so-called African independent Churches, which had taken varying political stances.

Quite early in the proceedings a leading DRC theologian, Professor Willie Jonker, made an eloquent plea for forgiveness to his black fellow Christians on behalf of Afrikaners, specifically those in the Dutch Reformed Church. It was not clear whether he had a mandate to be a spokesperson for his Church, but as its official delegation subsequently endorsed his statement we can say he was representing that denomination. One could well have asked whether he could claim to speak for past generations of its members, though it would be an oddly atomistic view of the nature of a community not to accept that there is a very real continuity between the past and the present and that the former members would share in the guilt and the shame as in the absolution and the glory of the present. A Church is a living organisation, otherwise history is of no significance and we should concentrate only on those who are our contemporaries – but clearly this is not how human beings normally operate. We boast about the past achievements of those who are no longer with us and point to them with pride even when they are in the dim and distant past. Their influence is as real as when the achievements were first attained, if not more so. It is the same with failures and disgraces: they too are part of who we are, whether we like it or not. When we speak, we speak as those who are aware of the cloud of witnesses surrounding us. No one would doubt that ultimately a confession such as that made by Professor Jonker, if it was not repudiated by those on whose behalf it was purportedly being made, would be accepted as speaking for the living and the dead, for those present and those no longer with us.

I consulted with Frank Chikane, who was at the time General Secretary of the South African Council of Churches, and we agreed that such an impassioned plea, such a heartfelt confession, could not be treated as just another example of rhetoric. Theologically we knew that the Gospel of our Lord and Saviour constrained us to be ready to forgive when someone asked for forgiveness. This was also happening at an important time in the history of our land. Nelson Mandela had been released earlier that year and there was a genuine striving for a negotiated settlement to help the delicate transition from repression to democracy. If the Churches, with their immense potential as agents of reconciliation, could not reconcile with each other it could very well send the wrong message to the politicians and to the people of God. If the Churches, despite their distressing baggage, could reach out to one another in a public act of forgiveness and reconciliation, it could provide a massive shot in the arm for a peaceful transition. And so I got up to say that we accepted the deeply moving and sincere plea for forgiveness.

This could, of course, have been interpreted as a monstrous act of presumption on my part. Who had given me the right to claim to speak on behalf of the millions of contemporary victims of apartheid and even more seriously, for those many millions who were no longer alive? The DRC had introduced apartheid into Church structures, establishing separate Churches for members classified under apartheid as black, Indian and 'Coloured'. Some of the black delegates at the conference, particularly those from these segregated Churches – first called the 'daughter' and later the 'sister' Churches of the DRC – were quite incensed with me because they felt the white Church was being allowed to get away with murder, literally and figuratively. They questioned the seriousness of the confession since they were upset that the DRC was dragging its feet on the question of uniting with the black Churches. They were also distressed because the white denomination was baulking at the prospect of accepting the 'Belhar Confession', which the other Churches in the DRC family had endorsed. This confession, among other things, condemned apartheid as a heresy. However, whilst I was challenged to justify my position, which I did try to do, happily I was not repudiated, and what happened at Rustenburg perhaps did advance the cause of a peaceful transition.

It is a little difficult for me to understand how it is that the Jews should be willing to accept the substantial compensation being paid out as reparation by European governments and institutions for complicity in the Holocaust. For if we accept the argument that they cannot forgive on behalf of those who suffered and died in the past, logic would seem to dictate that those who did not suffer directly as a result of the action for which the reparation is being paid should also be incapable of receiving compensation on behalf of others. Their stance also means that a massive obstacle remains to the resumption of more normal and amicable relationships between the community of the perpetrators and the community of those who were wronged. There will always be this albatross hanging round the neck of the erstwhile perpetrators, whatever they might want to do in acts of reparation and whatever new and better attitudes they may want to bring into the situation. It's a timebomb that could explode at any time, rendering the new relationship vulnerable and unstable.

I hope that philosophers, theologians and thinkers within the Jewish community will reopen this issue and consider whether it is possible to come to a different conclusion for the sake of the world. Their influence on world morality is far too precious to be jeopardised by their current stance. I can just imagine what would happen if Africans were to say that there is nothing that Europeans could do to make amends for the sordidness of the slave trade; that

Africans alive today can never have the temerity to forgive Europeans for the outrage that was slavery, in which at a conservative estimate some forty million people died, apart from all its other pernicious consequences – the families which were destroyed, the women who were abused, and the toll that this scourge took on so many of God's children.

If we are going to move on and build a new kind of world community there must be a way in which we can deal effectively with a sordid past. The most effective way I can think of is for the perpetrators or their descendants to acknowledge the horror of what happened and the descendants of the victims to respond by granting the forgiveness they ask for, providing something can be done, even symbolically, to compensate for the anguish experienced, whose consequences are still being lived through today. It may be, for instance, that race relations in the United States will not improve significantly until Native Americans and African Americans get the opportunity to tell their stories and reveal the pain that is a baneful legacy of dispossession and slavery. We saw in the Truth and Reconciliation Commission how the act of telling one's story has a cathartic, healing effect.

If the present generation could not legitimately speak on behalf of those who are no more, then we could not offer forgiveness for the sins of South Africa's racist past, which pre-dates the advent of apartheid in 1948. The process of healing our land would be subverted because there would always be the risk that some awful atrocity of the past would come to light that would undermine what had been accomplished thus far; or that people would say: 'It is all right so far as it goes in dealing with the contemporary situation, but it is all utterly ineffectual because it has failed to deal with the burden of the past.'

True forgiveness deals with the past, all of the past, to make the future possible. We cannot go on nursing grudges even vicariously for those who cannot speak for themselves any longer. We have to accept that what we do we do for generations past, present and yet to come. That is what makes a community a community or a people a people – for better or for worse.

I have wished desperately that those involved in seeking solutions for what have seemed intractable problems, in places such as Northern Ireland and the Middle East, would not despise the value of seemingly small symbolic acts that have a potency and significance beyond what is apparent. I have been distressed to learn that some of those most intimately connected to the peace process in Northern Ireland have not been seen shaking hands in public, that some have gone to odd lengths not to be photographed together with those on the other side, their current adversaries. It was wonderful that at the funeral of King Hussein of Jordan, President Ezer Weizman of Israel had the courage to shake hands with the leader of a radical Palestinian group. It was a gesture that helped to humanise his adversary, where before much had conspired to demonise him. A small handshake can make the unthinkable, the improbable – peace, friendship, harmony and tolerance – not quite so remote.

I also hope that those who are at this moment enemies around the world might consider using more temperate language when describing those with whom they disagree. Today's 'terrorist' could very well be tomorrow's president. That has happened in South Africa. Most of those who were vilified as terrorists are today our cabinet ministers and others sit in the government benches of our national assembly. If those we disagree with today are possibly going to be our colleagues tomorrow, we might begin by trying to describe them in language that won't be an embarrassment when that time of change does come.

It is crucial too that we keep remembering that negotiations, peace talks, forgiveness and reconciliation happen most frequently not between friends, not between those who like one another. They happen precisely because people are at loggerheads, and detest one another as only enemies can. But enemies are potential allies, friends, colleagues and collaborators. This is not just utopian idealism. The first democratically elected government of South Africa was a Government of National Unity made up of members of political parties that were engaged in a life-and-death struggle. The man who headed it had been incarcerated for twenty-seven years as a dangerous terrorist. If it could happen there, surely it can happen in other places. Perhaps God chose such an unlikely place deliberately, to show the world that it can be done anywhere.

If the protagonists in the world's conflicts began to make symbolic gestures for peace, changed the way they describe their enemies and began talking to them, their actions might change too. For instance, what is it doing for future relationships in the Middle East to go on constructing Jewish settlements in what is accepted to be Palestinian territory when this causes so much bitterness and resentment among the Palestinians, who feel belittled and abused? What legacy does it leave for the children of those who are destined to be neighbours? I have asked similar questions when Arab nations have seemed completely unrealistic in thinking they could destroy Israel. What a wonderful gift to the world, especially as we enter a new millennium, if true peace would come in the land of those who say *salama* or *shalom*, in the land of the Prince of Peace.

Peace *is* possible, especially if today's adversaries were to imagine themselves becoming friends and begin acting in ways that will promote such a friendship developing in reality. It would be wonderful if, as they negotiated, they tried to find ways of accommodating each other's needs. A readiness to make concessions is a sign of strength, not weakness. And it can be worthwhile sometimes to lose a battle in order in the end to win the war. Those who are engaged in negotiations for peace and prosperity are striving after such a splendid, such a priceless goal, that it should be easier to find ways where all are winners than to fight; where negotiators make it a point that no one loses face, that no one emerges empty-handed, with nothing to place before his or her constituency. How one wishes that negotiators would avoid having bottom lines and too many preconditions. In negotiations we are, as in the process of forgiveness, seeking to give all the chance to begin again. The rigid will have a tough time. The flexible, those who are ready to make principled compromises, end up being the victors.

*

I have said ours was a flawed Commission. Despite that I do want to assert as eloquently and as passionately as I can that it was, in an imperfect world, the best possible instrument so far devised to deal with the kind of situation that confronted us after democracy was established in our motherland. With all its imperfections, what we have tried to do in South Africa has attracted the attention of the world. This tired, disillusioned, cynical world hurting so frequently and so grievously has been intrigued by a process that holds out considerable hope in the midst of much that negates hope. People in the different places that I have visited and where I have spoken about the Truth and Reconciliation Commission process see in this flawed attempt a beacon of hope, a possible paradigm for dealing with situations where violence, conflict, turmoil and sectional strife have seemed endemic, conflicts that mostly take place not between warring nations but within the same nation. At the end of their conflicts, the warring groups in Northern Ireland, the Balkans, the Middle East, Sri Lanka, Burma, Afghanistan, Angola, the Sudan, the two Congos and elsewhere are going to have to sit down together to determine just how they will be able to live together amicably, how they might have a shared future devoid of strife, given the bloody past that they have recently lived through. They see more than just a glimmer of hope in what we have attempted in South Africa.

God does have a sense of humour. Who in their right mind could ever have imagined South Africa to be an example of anything but awfulness; of how *not* to order a nation's race relations and its governance? We South Africans were the unlikeliest lot and that is precisely why God has chosen us. We cannot really claim much credit ourselves for what we have achieved. We were destined for perdition and were plucked out of total annihilation. We were a hopeless case if ever there was one. God intends that others might look at us and take courage. God wants to point to us as a possible beacon of hope, a possible paradigm, and to say, 'Look at South Africa. They had a nightmare called apartheid. It has ended. Northern Ireland (or wherever), your nightmare will end too. They had a problem regarded as intractable. They are resolving it. No problem anywhere can ever again be considered to be intractable. There is hope for you too.'

Our experiment is going to succeed because God wants us to succeed, not for our glory and aggrandisement but for the sake of God's world. God wants to show that there is life after conflict and repression – that because of forgiveness, there is a future.

Postscript

Sister Margaret Magdalen of the Community of St Mary the Virgin, an Anglican nun who now lives in South Africa, used telling imagery when she described how Jesus coped with all the pain and anguish He encountered in His ministry. She described it in terms of the difference between a vacuum cleaner and a dishwasher. The vacuum cleaner sucks up all the dirt and keeps it in the bag; whereas the dishwasher cleans up the dirty dishes and immediately spews forth all the filth into the drains. She contended that Jesus acted more like a dishwasher than a vacuum cleaner. He absorbed all that came to Him and then, as it were, passed it out; passed it on to the Father.

At the beginning of our work in the Commission our mental health worker on the staff gave us a briefing about coping with what was to be a gruelling and demanding task. We were advised to make sure that we had a soul mate or some such friend or counsellor to whom we could go to unburden ourselves. We were urged to maintain a well-disciplined existence, otherwise we would be shocked by how easy it was to disintegrate, to become stressed and even to suffer ourselves from post-traumatic stress disorder as we experienced by proxy the anguish and agony of those who came to testify before the Commission. It was emphasised that we should have quality time with our spouses and families, to be sure to take recreational breaks and regular exercise and, if possible, to have a regular spiritual routine as well. We thought we had been reasonably well prepared for the traumatic experience.

Despite all this we were shattered at what we heard and we did frequently break down or were on the verge of it. I tried to follow the advice I had received from our mental health worker but we may never know just how much what we went through has affected us; the cost of it to us and to our families. One Commissioner's marriage broke down. (Wonderfully she has found love in the Commission, and she and her partner, a former Human Rights Violations Committee member, have been blessed with a baby boy – so it has not all been negative!) Many reported disturbed sleep patterns; some were deeply concerned that they were more short tempered, quarrelled far too easily with their spouses, or were drinking far more than they should. The journalists who reported on the Commission regularly were also affected. Some had nervous breakdowns, or cried far more easily than they had known themselves to do previously.

It was particularly rough for our interpreters, because they had to speak in the first person, at one time being the victim and at another being a perpetrator. 'They undressed me; they opened a drawer and then they stuffed my breast in the drawer which they slammed repeatedly on my nipple until a white stuff oozed.' 'We abducted him and gave him drugged coffee and then I shot him in the head. We then burned his body and whilst this was happening, we were enjoying a barbecue on the side.' It could be rough as they switched identities in that fashion. Even those physically distant from the hearings were affected by the deeply moving stories: the person heading our transcriptions service told me one day how, as she was typing transcripts of our hearings, she did not know she was crying until she felt and saw the tears on her arms.

During the sittings of the Commission, in January 1997, I learned that I had prostate cancer. It probably would have happened whatever I had been doing. But it just seemed to demonstrate that we were engaging in something that was costly. Forgiveness and reconciliation were not something to be entered into lightly, facilely. My own illness seemed to dramatise the fact that it is a costly business to try to heal a wounded and traumatised people and that those engaging in that crucial task will perhaps bear the brunt themselves. It may be that we have been a great deal more like vacuum cleaners than dishwashers, and have taken into ourselves far more than we can say of the pain and devastation of those whose stories we have heard.

My cancer helped me to be a little more laid-back, as they say, because I realised more sharply that there was literally not enough time to be nasty. I used my illness sometimes to twist my colleagues' arms: when they were somewhat obstreperous I said with mock earnestness, 'Oh, be nice to me. Remember I am a sick old man!' It sometimes served to defuse tense situations.

Suffering from a life-threatening disease also helped me to have a different attitude and perspective. It has given a new intensity to life, for I realise that there is much that I used to take very much for granted – the love and devotion of my wife Leah, the laughter and playfulness of my grandchildren, the glory of a splendid sunset, the dedication of colleagues, the beauty of a dew-covered rose. I responded to the disease not morbidly but with a greater appreciation of that which I might not see and experience again. It helped me to acknowledge my own mortality, with deep thanksgiving for the extraordinary things that have happened in my life, not least in recent times. What a spectacular vindication it has been for my involvement in the struggle against apartheid, to have lived to see freedom come and to have been involved in our Truth and Reconciliation Commission.

Yes, I have been greatly privileged to engage in the work of helping to heal our nation. But it has been a costly privilege for those of us in the Commission and I have come to realise that perhaps we were effective only to the extent that we were, in Henri Nouwen's celebrated phrase, 'wounded healers'.

Notes

2 Nuremberg or national amnesia? A third way

1 *Illustrated History of South Africa: The Real Story*, Reader's Digest, Cape Town, 1988.

2 Translates as 'Spear of the Nation'.

3 Marvin Frankel and Ellen Saideman, Delacorte Press, New York, 1989.

4 Constitutional Court of South Africa, Case No. CCT 117/96 (25 July 1996), *Azanian Peoples Organization (AZAPO) and others vs President of the Republic of South Africa and others*.

5 *op. cit.*

6 *op. cit.*

7 *The Healing of a Nation?* edited by Alex Boraine and Janet Levy, Justice in Transition, 1995.

3 In the fullness of time

1 Galatians 4:4.

4 What about justice?

1 Constitutional Court of South Africa, *op. cit.*

5 Up and running

1 *The Mind of South Africa*, Ballantine Books, New York, 1991.

7 'We do want to forgive but we don't know whom to forgive'

1 Genesis 6:5.

2 Poem by Geoffrey Studdert Kennedy, quoted in *Corrymeela News*, Journal of the Corrymeela Community, Northern Ireland, Autumn/Winter 1998.

3 A popular hymn, sung as an anthem by supporters of the liberation movements and now incorporated into the South African national anthem.

4 *Exploring Forgiveness*, edited by Robert D. Enright and Joanna North, The University of Wisconsin Press, 1998.

5 Medio Media / Arthur James, London and Berkhamsted, 1997.

8 'It feels like I've got my sight back'

1 Dr Asvat was a Soweto doctor who was killed in his surgery a few weeks after Stompie's death. It was alleged that he was murdered after treating the injured boy.

9 Why am I doing this thankless job?

1 Genesis 2:18.

10 'We did not know'

1 *Human Development Report*, United Nations Development Programme (UNDP), Oxford University Press, 1997.

2 *Apartheid Terrorism: The Destabilisation Report*, by Phyllis Johnson and David Martin, Commonwealth Secretariat in association with James Currey and Indiana University Press.

3 General Magnus Malan, Minister of Defence, in a parliamentary speech on 4 February 1986.

11 Without forgiveness there really is no future
1 John 12:32.
2 Quoted by Mary McAleese in *Reconciled Being: Love in Chaos*, p. 99.
3 Teilhard de Chardin, *op. cit.*, again quoted by Mary McAleese.
4 Jeremiah, 6:14 and 8:11.
5 Vol. 2 No. 1, Spirituality & Health Publishing, Trinity Church, Wall Street, New York.
6 Matthew 18:22.
7 *The Sunflower: On the Possibilities and Limits of Forgiveness*, by Simon Wiesenthal, edited by Harry James Cargas and Bonny V. Fetterman, Schocken Books, 1998.

Index